Twayne's United States Authors Series

Sylvia E. Bowman, *Editor*

INDIANA UNIVERSITY

Henry James

HENRY JAMES

By BRUCE R. McELDERRY, Jr.
University of Southern California

 79

Twayne Publishers, Inc.   ::   New York

FOR FRANCES

Preface

ANOTHER BOOK on Henry James? Yes, for I do not know a previous book that provides precisely what I have attempted to give in this one: a description in brief space of James's whole career, his whole achievement. It was a long career, fifty years of transition from the mid-nineteenth century to World War I, and all the cultural changes linked with the early twentieth century. James's achievement was enormous in quantity, and, at its best, superlative in quality. Even when working below his best level, James worked intelligently, vigorously. The most minor writings are deliberate rather than haphazard. A rapid writer, James nevertheless revised tirelessly. He was unwilling to republish even a travel essay without looking once more at the text, tightening and rethinking the style.

Since James's novels, stories, plays, criticism, reviews and letters all came from the same mind, it is true—as Professor Zabel remarked—that James "must be read, and read in his entirety" (*Portable James*, 18). The sheer bulk of the work makes this impossible for most readers: there are nearly five million words of fiction alone, the equivalent of forty or fifty novels. For this reason there should be a book which describes the body of James's work without trying to use it to support some theory of special interpretation. Such a book I have tried to write. All of the novels, stories, and plays are individually treated, though space has permitted only incidental notice of the travel books, the criticism, the autobiography, and the letters. For stories about which there is wide disagreement, I have given what seems to me a central or basic interpretation, and have provided in my notes references to other views.

To certain students of James I should like to express gratitude for bringing the kind of light which seems to me most useful. First I shall mention Lyon N. Richardson, whose *Representative Selections* (1941) shows how much an anthology can contribute to the serious study of an important author. Professor Zabel's *Portable Henry James* (1951) also brightened and deepened the image of James. F. O. Matthiessen's *The Major Phase* (1944) and *The James Family* (1947) were so well done that they are still basic. Oscar Cargill's *The Novels of Henry James*, bringing together a long series of distinguished special studies, has been of more help to me than my text and notes directly show, since my treatment of individual novels is necessarily brief. Finally, all Jamesians, myself included, owe more than can be set down to the many books and articles by Leon Edel. I regret that the fourth and final volume of his biography of James, and the promised edition of the letters, were not at my disposal. Since his pioneer studies of the dramatic years and of the prefaces (1931), Professor Edel has had the rewarding experience of watching James grow vigorously in general reputation.

Many other students of James might be mentioned for their useful and sometimes brilliant contributions to the understanding of James. Two types of study, however, I have emphasized very little, and would willingly pass over: the psychological and the symbolical. Sometimes such studies are suggestive. Generally, however, they seem to be practiced by persons constitutionally inclined to substitute "must" for "may." Such a disposition, I am persuaded, is unlikely to come close to the finest values of James: to "felt life," and to the truly liberal, permissive spirit he embodied. To psychological and symbolical critics, James's stories are but means to an end: the Message. Though I believe that James's stories are richly impregnated with ideas, I think James used ideas as tools. The end he tried to serve was Art, and his exacting standard was life.

It is a pleasure to acknowledge assistance from the research and publication fund of the University of Southern California for photocopies and for preparation of the Index by Mrs. Helen Shuman.

B. R. McELDERRY, JR.

University of Southern California
July, 1964

Contents

Chronology

1843   Henry James, Jr., born at 2 Washington Place, New York City, April 15. Second of five children born to Henry James, Sr., and Mary Robertson James.

1843- First trip to Europe.
1845

1845- Lived in New York City, chiefly at 58 West Fourteenth
1855   Street.

1855- Travel and study in Geneva, Switzerland; London; Paris;
1858   and Boulogne-sur-Mer.

1858   Settled at Newport, R.I., in the summer. Friendship with Thomas Sergeant Perry and John La Farge.

1859   Return to Geneva, Switzerland, in the autumn.

1860   Summer in Bonn, Germany. Return to Newport in the autumn.

1861   Civil War began with firing on Fort Sumter, April 12. James received "an obscure hurt" in helping volunteer firemen (October).

1862- Henry attended Harvard Law School. Also heard lectures
1863   by J. R. Lowell.

1864   James family moved to Boston. Henry published, unsigned, his first story, "A Tragedy of Error," in February *Continental Monthly*. Published first review in October *North American Review;* made acquaintance of Charles Eliot Norton, the editor.

1865   Published "The Story of a Year," his first signed story, in March *Atlantic Monthly;* and a review in the first issue of the New York *Nation* (July 6).

1866   James family moved to Quincy Street, Cambridge. James met Howells, newly appointed assistant editor of *Atlantic Monthly.*

1869- Traveled alone to England, France, Switzerland, Italy, from
1870   February, 1869, to April, 1870. Received news of Minny Temple's death in March, 1870.

1871   Published *Watch and Ward,* his first short novel, in the *Atlantic Monthly.* Trip to Canada and Niagara (summer) to write travel articles for the *Nation.*

1872   Spent summer abroad with his sister Alice and Aunt Katherine Walsh (his mother's sister). Visited England, France, Switzerland.

1872- Remained abroad alone until autumn, 1874. Spent winter of
1874   1872-73 in Rome; summer, 1873, in Switzerland and Germany; winter, 1873-74, in Florence and Rome, part of the time accompanied by brother William; summer, 1874, in Germany.

1875   Spent first six months in New York. Arranged to write European letters for the New York *Tribune.* Settled in Paris (November). Called on Turgenev, who later introduced him to Flaubert, Zola, Daudet, Maupassant. Published: *A Passionate Pilgrim,* a collection of six stories (January); *Transatlantic Sketches,* travel pieces (April); *Roderick Hudson* (November).

1876   Trip to Rouen (July); to Biarritz and Bayonne (August). Settled in Bolton Street, off Piccadilly, December.

1877   Visited Paris and Rome. Published *The American,* Boston (May); pirated edition published in England.

1878   Published *French Poets and Novelists* (February); *Watch and Ward,* book form of short novel (May); *The Europeans,* short novel (September); "Daisy Miller" in *Cornhill Magazine* (June), and in book form in New York (November).

1879   Entertained Turgenev in London, early summer; visited Paris. Published *The Madonna of the Future and Other Tales,* six in all (October); *Confidence,* short novel (December); *Hawthorne,* critical biography (December).

1880   Visited Florence and Rome in the spring. Met Constance Fenimore Woolson, American novelist. Visited by William in June. Published *Washington Square* (December).

1881   Visited Venice, Milan, and Rome in the spring; Switzerland in the summer; Scotland in the autumn. Returned to Boston (October). Published English edition of *Washington Square,* with two other tales (January); *The Portrait of a Lady* (November).

1882   December, 1881, and January, 1882, in New York and in Washington, D.C. Mother died late January, before James could reach Cambridge. Visited Ireland. Returned to London (May). Made "little tour of France" (October). Called home by illness of Henry James, Sr., who died December 20, just before Henry, Jr., reached home.

1883　Trip to Milwaukee on family business early in the year. Henry sailed for England (August). Published: *The Siege of London*, three tales (February); Collective Edition of 1883, 14 vols. (November); *Portraits of Places* (December).

1884　Visited Paris, February, and again met Daudet, Zola, Edmond de Goncourt. "The Art of Fiction," in September *Longman's Magazine*, led to intimacy with R. L. Stevenson. Published: *A Little Tour in France* (September); *Tales of Three Cities*, three stories (October).

1885　Vacationed with several artists, including Sargent and Abbey, at Broadway, Worcestershire, early autumn. Published: *The Author of Beltraffio*, five stories (February); *Stories Revived*, 3 vols., fourteen stories (May).

1886　Moved to De Vere Mansions. Published: *The Bostonians* (February); *The Princess Casamassima* (October).

1887　Visited Venice (February). Returned to London (July).

1888　Visited Constance Woolson in Switzerland (October). Returned to London (December). Published: *Partial Portraits*, critical essays (May); *The Reverberator*, short novel (June); *The Aspern Papers*, with two other tales (September).

1889　Translated Daudet's *Port Tarascon*. Published *A London Life*, four tales (April).

1890　Visited Italy and Oberammergau, summer. Published *The Tragic Muse* (June).

1891　Visited Ireland, summer. To Dresden, Germany, for funeral of Wolcott Balestier (December). Stage production of *The American*, January 3; London opening, September 26.

1892　Visited Italy, June. Returned to London (August). Published *The Lesson of the Master*, six stories (February).

1893　Visited William in Lausanne (May). Published: *The Real Thing and Other Tales*, five stories (March); *The Private Life*, six stories (June); *Essays in London and Elsewhere* (June); *The Wheel of Time*, three stories (September).

1894　Constance Woolson died in Venice, January 24. Visited Miss Woolson's grave in Rome. To Torquay and Cornwall

(August). Published: *Theatricals*, 2 vols., four plays (June and December).

1895   First production of *Guy Domville* (January 5); closed after forty performances. To Torquay, summer. Published: *Terminations*, four stories (May).

1896   Summer in Playden, Sussex, near Rye; discovered Lamb House. Published: *Embarrassments*, four stories (June); *The Other House*, fictional version of play (October).

1897   Summer at Bournemouth and Dunwich. Leased Lamb House, later purchased it. Published: *The Spoils of Poynton* (February); *What Maisie Knew* (September).

1898   Published: *In the Cage* (August); *The Two Magics,* "The Turn of the Screw" and "Covering End," a fictional version of the one-act play *Summersoft* (October).

1899   Visited Italy, summer. Published *The Awkward Age* (April).

1900   Published: *The Soft Side*, twelve stories (August).

1901   Published: *The Sacred Fount,* short novel (February).

1902   William delivered lectures in Edinburgh. Published: *The Wings of the Dove* (August).

1903   Published: *The Better Sort*, eleven stories (February); *The Ambassadors* (September), composed prior to *The Wings of the Dove; William Wetmore Story and His Friends,* 2 vols. (September-October).

1904   Returned to America after twenty-one years, August. Spent autumn in New England. Published: *The Golden Bowl* (November).

1905   Visited New York; Philadelphia; Washington, D.C.; Charleston, S.C.; and Florida (January and February); Chicago (March); California (April). Returned to Lamb House (August). Published: *The Question of Our Speech, The Lesson of Balzac: Two Lectures* (October); *English Hours* (October).

1907   Motor trip in France with the Whartons, summer. Published: *The American Scene,* travel essays and social criticism (January); The New York Edition: *The Novels and Tales of Henry James,* 24 vols. (December, 1907, to July, 1909). Two posthumous volumes added, 1917.

1908   *The High Bid,* three-act version of *Summersoft,* produced in Edinburgh by Forbes-Robertson (March); in London (February, 1909).

1909 Long illness late in the year. Published: *Italian Hours* (October).

1910 Henry accompanied the William Jameses to Chocorua, New Hampshire, William's summer home. William died, August 26. Henry remained in Cambridge until August, 1911. Published: *The Finer Grain,* five stories (October).

1911 *The Saloon,* one-act dramatization of "Owen Wingrave," produced in London, January 17. Honorary degree conferred by Harvard. Published: *The Outcry,* fictionalized version of play of 1910 (October).

1912 Honorary degree conferred by Oxford.

1913 Seventieth birthday honored by friends with an arrangement for portrait by Sargent. Published: *A Small Boy and Others* (March).

1914 Published: *Notes of a Son and Brother* (March); *Notes on Novelists* (October).

1915 James became a naturalized British subject, July 26. Published: *England at War: An Essay. The Question of the Mind* (July); Uniform Edition of *The Tales of Henry James,* 14 vols., 1915-20.

1916 Order of Merit conferred, January. Died, February 28.

1917 Published: *The Ivory Tower* (September); *The Sense of the Past* (September); *The Middle Years,* autobiography (October). All three volumes incomplete.

1919 Published: *Within the Rim and Other Essays,* five wartime essays (March).

CHAPTER *1*

Introduction: 1843-1876

HENRY JAMES, born in New York City in 1843, died in London in 1916, a resident in England since 1876, and a naturalized British subject since the summer of 1915. The external pattern of his long life—a congenial, appreciative family; his youthful experience of Europe; and the career of authorship begun in 1864— was simple and satisfying. James never married; he never achieved great popular success; but his intelligence, wit, and affectionate nature brought him friendship with dozens of the most notable people of three generations.

As a small boy, he was accustomed to seeing Ralph Waldo Emerson as a family guest, and on one occasion was brought into the family circle to meet Thackeray. As a young man, James knew such contemporaries as Henry Adams, Henry Cabot Lodge, young Oliver Wendell Holmes, John La Farge, and Thomas Sergeant Perry. When, after the Civil War, William Dean Howells settled in Boston as assistant editor of the *Atlantic Monthly,* James was one of his closest friends, and the young men talked much about the methods and objectives of the new realism.

Before James settled in England he had two extended trips to Europe. Then a year's residence in Paris, 1875-76, enabled him to become well acquainted with Turgenev, who was living in France; through Turgenev he met Flaubert, Zola, and other literary men. In England, James knew George Eliot, Matthew Arnold, and Ruskin. He became intimately acquainted with James Russell Lowell when Lowell served as ambassador. Later he was on friendly terms with younger writers such as Robert Louis Stevenson, Joseph Conrad, H. G. Wells, J. M. Barrie, G. B. Shaw, and the Americans Stephen Crane and Edith Wharton. One of James's last literary acts was to write a tribute to Rupert Brooke, whose death in 1915 typified for James the savage waste of World War I.

Henry James grew up happily in a formal society now all but vanished. Because his stories deal so largely with that society, with its conventions, its circumspection, and its circumlocutions, there is for many readers a tea-party atmosphere that seems trivial and archaic. On first acquaintance, James may seem like a dilettante, out of touch with the "real life" of the twentieth century. The quality of his insight into real life—as attested, for example, in the father-daughter conflict in *Washington Square*—is a major concern of this book. It is important to see at the beginning, however, that no writer deserves less to be called a dilettante. From the beginning, he was professional in his unceasing production, his studious planning, his tireless analysis. That he could at the same time maintain a demanding social life and a voluminous correspondence is evidence of extraordinary energy and resilience. Indeed, as one studies the photographs and portraits of James in his last years it is not far-fetched to see in him a Churchillian vigor.[1] The head is large, the brow broad, the lips firm. The shoulders are heavy, the figure stocky. The whole bearing suggests strength and competence.

The sheer mass of James's production in a working life of fifty years bears out this impression, especially when it is recognized that hardly any of his writings escaped haphazardly into print. There are ten long novels, ten short ones, and two left incomplete but far enough advanced to be published the year after his death. Besides the novels, James published between 1864 and 1910 one hundred and twelve tales, many of them of forty or fifty thousand words. There are nine full-length plays and several short dramatic pieces. Beyond fiction and plays, he published some four hundred and fifty articles, chiefly literary criticism and travel pieces, and introductions to a variety of volumes.

From time to time James collected such pieces and published the following volumes: *French Poets and Novelists* (1878); *Hawthorne* (1879); *Portraits of Places* (1883); *A Little Tour in France* (1884); *Partial Portraits* (1888); *Essays in London and Elsewhere* (1893); *William Wetmore Story and His Friends* (1903—the biography of the American sculptor); *English Hours* (1905); *The American Scene* (1907); and the autobiographical volumes, *A Small Boy and Others* (1913), *Notes of a Son and Brother* (1914). For the selective edition of his works published 1907-09 (the New York Edition) James wrote elaborate prefaces which constituted an analysis of his theory and practice of fiction; the prefaces have been supplemented by publication of his *Notebooks* (1947). Since 1916 some thirty volumes have been issued which are in whole or in part "first" book publication of some of his writings.

In 1920 James's friend, Percy Lubbock, edited in two volumes about four hundred of his letters. Twice that number have since appeared in a bewildering variety of reminiscences and special studies. Perhaps ten thousand more remain unpublished. James's peculiar gift of expression seemingly made it impossible for him to send even a telegram without some individuality. There is the memorable one announcing his impending visit to the artist Edwin Abbey: "Will alight precipitately at 5:38 from the deliberate 1:50."[2] The twirl of adverb and adjective is characteristic.

In mass and variety, these writings offer literally endless opportunity for study and interpretive comment. The "periods" of his career: is there truth or distortion in Philip Guedalla's witticism about James the first, James the second, and James the Old Pretender? The stories: is it true that James was best in the novelette of thirty to sixty thousand words? The plays: despite James's failure in the theater of the 1890's, does the dramatic work throw light upon the important changes in James's later fictional method? The criticism: what of James's judgments of his contemporaries, and how, particularly, does his criticism of other fiction reveal his own developing concept of fiction as the art form with the greatest future? The *Notebooks*: what is to be made of the highly self-conscious methods of composition there illustrated? Add to such questions the natural curiosity about James's relations with dozens of notable figures in England and America, and the bibliographical problem of accounting for his numerous publications, collections, and revisions. The flow of books, articles, and academic dissertations on James in recent years is a natural response to such questions and such opportunities. There is little sign of lessening interest. Reviewers profess to be tired of James, but more and more people are discovering him, especially younger people. It is natural that they should wish to write about their discovery, even if they are not the first to travel the James country.

James himself had once whimsically predicted (1888): "Very likely, too, some day, all my buried prose will kick off its various tombstones at once."[3] When James died on February 28, 1916, however, the exhuming of his prose seemed quite unlikely. England had been preoccupied by war for eighteen months, and the stalemate of the trenches was to last for two more years. In a letter of August 10, 1914, James had sadly recognized the war as a ruthless exposure of the world he had critically examined but fondly enjoyed: "Black and hideous to me is the tragedy that gathers, and I'm sick beyond cure to have lived on to see it. . . . It seems to me to *undo* everything, everything that was ours, in the most horrible retroactive way."[4] When at last peace came, the new writers—particularly such Americans as Sherwood Anderson, Theodore Dreiser, Sinclair Lewis, and Eugene O'Neill—were dedicated to rebellion against the pre-war world and all it stood for. James would not have been surprised that majority opinion doubted the validity of his achievement.

There was, however, a minority opinion. While the war still went on in 1918, T. S. Eliot was remarking that James "had a mind so fine that no idea could violate it."[5] In 1913 Ford Madox Hueffer (later Ford Madox Ford) had published an admiring critical study of James, and in 1918 Joseph Warren Beach's *The Method of Henry James* laid the basis for later analysis of James's artistic achievement. Ezra Pound published in 1920 a long essay full of shrewd insights to be developed by others years later. Van Wyck Brooks in *The Pilgrimage of Henry James* (1925) saw in the career of James an illustration of the then popular idea that America had always been inhospitable to her artists. As literary discussion entered the 1930's, there were two general alternatives. One was to move in the direction of social protest, with a heavy emphasis of Marxism. The other was to go in the direction of significant literary form, with a heavy emphasis on psychological interpretation.

For writers and for critics taking the second direction, the work of Henry James proved surprisingly relevant. Republication of the prefaces to the New York Edition, with a distinguished introduction by R. P. Blackmur (*The Art of the Novel*, 1934), provided a solid center for the endless and sometimes trivial discussion of the novel as an "art." In the same year, in a special issue of *Hound and Horn*, an influential little magazine, Edmund Wilson, Edna Kenton, and others made high claims for James. More specialized studies just prior to 1934 included Morris Roberts' *Henry James's Criticism* (1929) and Cornelia Pulsifer Kelley's *The Early Development of Henry James* (1930). Leon Edel had begun his distinguished career as a James scholar by publishing in Paris (1931) his *Henry James: Les années dramatique* and *The Prefaces of Henry James*. The publication of a revised edition of Le Roy Phillips' *A Bibliography of the Writings of Henry James* (1930: first ed. 1906) was both a straw in the wind and a stimulus to further study. It can thus be said that on the scholarly and critical levels the "Henry James boom" was well started by 1934. From that time on, James stories began to receive more emphasis in anthologies for general readers and for college classes. James's essay, "The Art of Fiction," which for fifty years after its publication in *Longman's Magazine* had been neglected, now began to be regularly reprinted in "survey" anthologies of American Literature.

One of the strangest aspects of the James Revival was the successful dramatization of his stories for stage, movies, radio, and eventually television. James's own failure in the commercial theater of his time had been so nearly complete that few even of his admirers had troubled themselves to read or collect the surviving texts. Not until Leon Edel's edition of *The Complete Plays of Henry James* (1949) was it possible to see clearly what James had tried to do, and what he had learned despite failure. Most readers had so strongly associated James's elaborate, parenthetical style with his writings that they could scarcely conceive that dramatizing his stories could be anything but a vulgarization of them. Without question, something is lost, even in relatively successful versions like *The Heiress* (based on *Washington Square* in 1947) or *The Aspern Papers* (1959). Yet the very number of attempts and the occasional effective moments even in the weaker scripts illustrate the solid interest of Jamesian fiction for twentieth-century audiences. The very remoteness of the society he presents has at last become an advantage. Without being quaint—as the characters of Dickens, or even Hardy, are likely to seem—James's people have an esthetic distance that allows an emphasis of the central human problems. Without any of the psychological jargons or mechanisms, the insight into motive—usually into realistically mixed motives—is incisive. Without vulgarity, James is searching; without sentimentality, he is tender and humane.

I   Life: 1843-69

Henry James was born near Washington Square, then a fashionable neighborhood of New York City. Even today the north side of the Square suggests the elegance of the mid-nineteenth century. Henry James, Sr., was thirty-two, and for ten years had enjoyed a lifetime inheritance of ten thousand dollars a year. One of the few rich men of the period not particularly anxious to become richer, the elder James gave his time to philosophical study, becoming a close friend of Emerson and other intellectuals. Later, when his sons, embarrassed by their father's lack of occupation, asked what they should tell their friends, he replied, "Just say I'm a student."[6] In 1869 the elder James published a book entitled *The Secret of Swedenborg*. Howells' witty verdict, "He kept it," has been over-quoted. The philosophical writings were an intelligent attempt to add a satisfactory theory of evil to Emersonian idealism.

It is notable that both Henry, Jr., and his older brother William had considerable respect for their father's ideas. At the very least, the sons took over their father's serious attitude toward moral questions, as well as his flexibility and wit in dealing with them. The elder James had grown up in a stern Calvinistic household. His youthful rebellion had alienated him from his own father. In consequence, he brought his own family up with a religious permissiveness unusual for that time. His education—he had graduated from Union College and had attended Princeton Theological Seminary—bred in him a distrust of American education and led to a pattern of travel and residence abroad in the attempt to find the best tutors and schools for his children. A kindly and indulgent father, Henry, Sr., kept the affection and respect of his children, even when they differed with him.

When Henry, Jr., was born on April 15, 1843, William was but fifteen months old. Nevertheless, father and mother and the two babies sailed for England in September, remaining abroad until early in 1845. In New York that summer a third son, Garth Wilkinson, was born; in 1846 Robertson, the fourth son; and in 1847, Alice, the only daughter. In 1847 the family settled in a house at 58 West Fourteenth Street, where it resided from the time Henry was four until he was twelve, the time of the European trip of 1855. There were occasional interludes in Albany, where the paternal grandmother and various cousins lived. It was a rich boyhood. William, "the Ideal Elder Brother," as Henry was to call him, tended to dominate the younger children. On one occasion he declined young Henry's company because, "*I* play with boys who curse and swear!" They shared much, however.

Both attended a school presided over by Richard Pulling Jenks, "a civilizer—whacks and all," whom they remembered well enough to call on years later. Surprisingly, the school had a great many Cuban and Mexican boys, and such companionship supplemented the talk at home of foreign places. The elder James's lack of business or professional pursuits was reflected in frequent conversation about Europe, especially England. American politics seemed far away—despite the Mexican War, *Uncle Tom's Cabin*, and the actual escape of two slaves in the neighborhood, who had accompanied their Kentucky master to New York. As a boy, young Henry saw many of the exotic and melodramatic plays of the time. Nothing, it later seemed to him, mattered at all, "but that I should become personally and incredibly acquainted with Piccadilly and Richmond Park and Ham Common." Though Emerson's visits were frequent reminders of New England, Thackeray, when he called, was London. The spell of Dickens, too, was overwhelming in the 1850's. Even the conformity of dancing lessons—"Don't look at *me*, little boy—look at my feet"—could not make proper New Yorkers of the James children.[7]

Henry James's mother was a quiet woman, but one of great strength. She was born Mary Robertson Walsh, of an upstate New York family that was Irish in origin, like the Jameses, and stoutly Presbyterian. Once married, she seems to have accepted her husband's free-thinking ideas sufficiently for family harmony. Her younger sister, "Aunt Kate," lived much in the James household. When Mary James died in 1882, her novelist son wrote of her: "She was our life, she was the house, she was the keystone of the arch. She held us all together, and without her we are scattered reeds. She was patience, she was wisdom, she was exquisite maternity. Her sweetness, her mildness, her great natural beneficence were unspeakable, and it is infinitely touching to me to write about her here as one that *was*."⁸ Henry, Sr., on the death of his wife, lost the will to live, and died before the year was out.

In the forty years following the birth of William, her first child, Mary James had need of unusual strength. Four more children came in rapid succession. After the eight settled years in New York, the family moved incessantly from 1855 to 1864. The two older boys were for health reasons not available for military service in the Civil War, but Wilky and Robertson both volunteered and saw active service. Wilky was brought home wounded in 1863; Robertson came out of the War a captain at nineteen. The subsequent lives of both younger brothers were unhappy. Business ventures in the South failed, and their early promise was never fulfilled. Wilky died in 1883, and Robertson in 1910. Alice, the one daughter, developed an obscure nervous disorder as a young girl, and she sometimes discussed suicide with her father. After his death, care of Alice devolved upon Henry. A succession of apartments, companions, and physicians marked her life in England, until she died in 1892. Her *Journal* testifies to the wit and intelligence of her spirit. That Mary James held the affection of so varied, vigorous, and talented a brood goes far to support Henry, Jr.'s eloquent tribute to her.

In July, 1855, the James family sailed for England. After brief stops in London and Paris, they journeyed in two carriages to Switzerland, railroads not yet being available for this route. Schools at Geneva initially pleased the elder James, but by October he had decided to move back to London and to rely on tutors. In the summer of 1856 the family went to Paris, living there and at Boulogne-sur-Mer until they returned to America in the summer of 1858. After fifteen months in Newport, Rhode Island, in two different houses, they went back to Geneva, where the four boys were distributed in three different schools. The summer of 1860 was spent in Germany, and in September the family was in Newport once more. In 1864, while the two younger boys were in the army, the elder James moved to Boston and a little later to Quincy Street in Cambridge.

Henry James, Jr., was twelve in 1855, when the family went abroad, seventeen on the return to Newport in 1860. It is hard to estimate the full effect on him of these rootless years. In his reminiscences he does not dwell on these years as unhappy. It is evident that for him reading was a great resource, as it was for

William. The English and French stage gave great pleasure. Eventually, after making little progress in mathematics, Henry was given the freedom of the Academy in Geneva, and he turned naturally enough to lectures in literature and philosophy. In the interest of science, however, he did once witness a dissection at the Medical School. The final summer in Germany gave him a lasting dislike for Germans. The last months abroad were brightened by copies of the new *Cornhill,* including a serialized Trollope novel, and by issues of *Once a Week,* with Meredith, Charles Reade, and du Maurier as contributors.

There was an occasional echo of home. In 1856 the boy saw Senator Charles Sumner recovering in Paris from the beating given him by an angry South Carolinian. In Geneva, Henry heard about the Harper's Ferry raid of December, 1859. Residence in Newport in 1858 and again in 1860 was not a very full reintroduction to American life, for Newport was then a quiet, isolated town. For William and Henry the chief attractions were Thomas Sergeant Perry, later a distinguished literary critic, and John La Farge, the painter, then in his early twenties. One of the reasons for the family's return in 1860 was William's desire to study art under W. M. Hunt, another Newport painter. William made some progress before turning to science, and Henry himself did some sketching. During the Newport period, young Edward Emerson left an amusing description of the household at dinner. The boys argued violently, gesticulating wildly with knives and forks in hand while Henry, Sr., looked on as an ineffective moderator. Perry gives the impression of more serious quarrels when the parents were away. Whatever the boys had lost through their years of wandering and desultory education, they had not been smothered by pedantry or over-discipline.[9]

The coming of the War in April, 1861, was, of course, the great event of Henry's youth. The family had strong Union sympathy, and Henry, Sr., was asked to give the Fourth of July oration in Newport that year. Since Wilky and Robertson volunteered, the natural question is, why did not William and Henry serve? Letters from Henry James, Sr., indicate that they wished to and that he dissuaded them. This is not convincing, however, for both were strong-minded boys. In his *Notes of a Son and Brother,* Henry throws little light on the matter, though he takes much satisfaction in recounting the military exploits of his younger brothers. The "obscure hurt" received when helping out at a fire was apparently an incident of October, 1861. Many critics have speculated that this "hurt" was a sexual one, but Professor Edel, the most thorough biographer, thinks it was a back injury.[10] In later years Henry makes frequent allusions to trouble with his back. Whatever the circumstances of his own case were, it is strange that Henry makes no clear comment on William's situation. William's biographer merely says that "physical frailty precluded the possibility of his enlistment."[11] In September, 1861, William gave up art to enroll in the Lawrence Scientific School at Harvard, and the following spring Henry entered the Law School.

Henry remained a "singularly alien member" of the Law School for a year. Law was not for him; Lowell's literary lectures were of greater interest.[12] Part of 1863 must have been given to writing "A Tragedy of Error," his first story, published anonymously in *The Continental Monthly* for February, 1864. Later that year he ventured to submit a review of a work on fiction to the *North American Review*. Charles Eliot Norton, the editor, paid James twelve dollars, and in 1865 published seven additional reviews by James. In July, 1865, E. L. Godkin started the *Nation* in New York, and to it James contributed eight reviews in 1865. Meanwhile he had published his first signed story in the *Atlantic Monthly*. Thus the end of the war found James making quiet progress. When Howells joined the staff of the *Atlantic* in 1866, James soon met him, and the two young men found much in common. Howells was eager to publish James and did so. Their close friendship was unbroken, as their extensive and lively correspondence shows, until James died.

Through the late 1860's James maintained a steady flow of stories and reviews, finding a new outlet in the *Galaxy*, a New York magazine, in 1868. In these years he was virtually self-supporting, though he continued to live in the family home now on Quincy Street, Cambridge. James was not altogether happy, however. There was a certain degree of rivalry between himself and William. William, like his father, was somewhat condescending toward a "mere" literary career. When William was away—once on a scientific expedition, once for study in Germany—Henry seemed healthier and more productive. But in Cambridge there was not enough of the kind of companionship he wanted. Old friends were scattered and busy. New friends were hard to find. Howells was one resource. Norton, of the *North American Review*, was another, but he was considerably older. Minny Temple, the cousin he so greatly admired, was unwell, and he did not see her often.

II *Early Stories*

"A Tragedy of Error," James's first story (1864), is set in a French seaport town. In this conventional melodrama, a wife hires a rough boatman to murder her husband, since the husband's return threatens to break up her affair with a lover. Going to meet the husband, the lover is mistaken for him and killed by the boatman. As the story ends, the horror-stricken wife is confronted by her husband, happily oblivious of the love triangle and the plot to kill him. "A Tragedy of Error" is superficial and mechanical, but for a young man of twenty-one the author seems at ease with the foreign setting and the "literary" situation. The wife, the lover, and the assassin are not sentimentalized, but seen with detachment and touches of irony that partially redeem the contrivance of the plot.[13]

In "The Story of a Year" (1865) James showed much more convincingly the peculiar kind of intelligence that distinguishes his fiction. A tale of the Civil War, "The Story of a Year" deals only indirectly with battle. Lieutenant Ford, before going South with his regiment in 1863, becomes engaged to Elizabeth Crewe, the ward of his mother. Mrs. Ford does not favor the match, considering Elizabeth too shallow a girl. Months later, Ford is brought home seriously wounded. When he realizes that he is dying, he urges Elizabeth to ignore the tawdry sentiment of being "constant to his memory," and to live her own life. Elizabeth, already attracted to another man, is shocked to realize that indeed she cannot be constant to Ford's memory. Without the least vindictiveness, James has exposed Elizabeth as the woman of shallow feeling Ford's mother knew her to be. This story, with its "felt life" and its complete absence of sentimentality, is an astonishing performance for a young man of twenty-two, and its publication in the *Atlantic Monthly* (March, 1865) while the war was still raging, is even more surprising. James never reprinted this tale, and he left no clue as to how he found his theme.

Two other stories with a Civil War background are less impressive. In "Poor Richard" (1867) the rather dissolute title character competes for the affections of an heiress against the attractions of two army officers, and at the end goes off to war himself. In "A Most Extraordinary Case" (1868) an invalided young officer dies after Caroline Hoffman prefers the young doctor.[14]

In fourteen other early stories James experimented with American situations, but he achieved little of substantial interest. "A Day of Days" (1866), for example, seems deliberately contrived to disappoint the sentimental expectations of readers who scent a developing romance between the young couple who meet by chance and enjoy each other's company. The title character of "My Friend Bingham" (1867) accidentally shoots a little boy while hunting. Bingham does what he can for the boy's mother, discovers she is a widow, and eventually marries her. "Osborne's Revenge" (1868) deals with Henrietta, a young woman over whom Osborne's friend has committed suicide. Determined to teach Henrietta a lesson, Osborne courts her with the idea of later jilting her. He discovers, however, that Henrietta had never been in love with his friend and had repeatedly discouraged his attentions. In the end, Osborne himself marries Henrietta. "Guest's Confession" (1872) turns upon the signed confession of Guest's fraud, which for a time blocks the narrator's marriage to Guest's sister. Guest refuses to be blackmailed, but, when the narrator burns the confession, Guest assents to the marriage. "Professor Fargo" (1874) deals with mesmerism; Fargo uses his powers to get the deaf-and-dumb daughter of his associate to leave her father for him. "Crawford's Consistency" (1876) tells of a bachelor who, when jilted, marries a coarse girl socially much beneath him. She takes to drink and leads him a bad life. After her death, the narrator comments: "I cannot say that this event restored his equanimity, for the excellent reason that in the eyes of the world—and my most searching ones—he had never lost it."

Several of these stories with American settings are less notable for inherently American situations than for their use of themes that were to interest James in later years: artists, the supernatural, and the "international" or traveled American. In "A Landscape Painter" (1866) the wealthy artist lives for a time with a retired sea captain, carefully concealing the fact that he is wealthy. When the artist marries the captain's daughter, he discovers that she has known of his wealth all along and that she has deliberately, though with good will, married him for his money. In "The Story of a Masterpiece" (1868) an artist paints the true character of a vain young woman for the man she is to marry.

James's concern with the supernatural looks back to Hawthorne, but at this stage in his development James is far from the subtlety of such a ghostly tale as "The Turn of the Screw." In "The Romance of Certain Old Clothes" (1868) two sisters successively marry the same man. When the younger sister begs for her dead sister's fine clothes, she herself is found dead with "marks of ten hideous wounds from two vengeful ghostly hands." In "A Problem" (1868) an Indian fortuneteller's prophecy causes jealousy and separation of a couple. Later the death of their daughter causes a reconciliation, bearing out the prophecies that each would be "twice married." Most fanciful is "The Ghostly Rental" (1876), in which the rental of a deserted house is presumably paid by the ghost of a daughter "killed" by Captain Diamond. The narrator—a Cambridge divinity student—unmasks the actual daughter of the Captain. The Captain dies, and during the night the house mysteriously burns.

James is clearly more at home in the stories of Americans who represent the perspective of foreign travel. "De Grey: A Romance" (1868) deals with a wealthy young man sent abroad to help him break off an engagement unwelcome to his mother. On his return he falls in love with his mother's companion, a young girl named Margaret. Family friends warn Margaret against young De Grey. When De Grey dies, Margaret goes insane. "A Light Man" (1869) is a story of rivalry between two friends for an old man's inheritance; both lose it. and in so doing are relieved of the pretenses they had been forced into. "Master Eustace" (1871) perhaps owes least to its American setting. Eustace, who has been abroad, comes home shortly after his widowed mother has remarried. Eustace's refusal to accept his stepfather kills his mother. The stepfather forgives Eustace, but Eustace does not forgive his stepfather.

In all of these early stories there are touches of descriptive skill and Jamesian insight, yet they seem artificial. Meetings, jiltings, marriages, revelations, family jealousies—there is an air of contrivance and literary inspiration about them all. Seldom does James seem to have caught the air of reality, the "felt life" that permeates "The Story of a Year," with its common-sense revulsion at sentimentality and its unmalicious exposure of a shallow woman. That James recognized the weakness of these stories is evident from his failure to reprint most of them. Twentieth-century anthologists as well have avoided them, but they are worth review: they testify to James's diligent attempt to find native material suitable for fiction. Whatever the reasons, ten years of effort brought him little success.

III *Abroad and at Home: 1869-75*

In February, 1869,. James departed for Europe, remaining until the end of April, 1870. He traveled in England, and through acquaintance with Leslie Stephen, an English critic who had visited Boston, and American friends then in London, James met a number of literary figures, including Aubrey de Vere, William Morris, and John Ruskin. James then went to France and Switzerland, and finally, in September, to Italy. From the first, Italy enchanted him; but, when he reached Rome, he rhapsodized: "At last—for the first time—I live! It beats everything: it leaves the Rome of your fancy—your education—nowhere. It makes Venice—Florence—Oxford—London—seem like cities of pasteboard. I went reeling and moaning through the streets, in a fever of enjoyment." It is reassuring to find, a few weeks later, some qualifying footnotes to this ecstasy. He is "sick unto death of priests and churches." He loathed Naples, and "felt for a moment as if I should like to devote my life to laying railroads, and erecting blocks of stores on romantic sites."[15] The revulsion was momentary, as his fifteen subsequent visits to Italy, the last in 1907, were to show.

In March, 1870, James received news of Minny Temple's death of a lung ailment. He had gone to see her before departing for Europe, and her occasional letters were events in his rather lonely life abroad. There was even some suggestion that she herself might come to Europe. Though Minny's health had been bad for years, James was not prepared for news of her death. In a long letter to William he tried to compose his feelings. Writing at one point as if to Minny herself, James said: "Don't fancy that your task is done. Twenty years hence we shall be living with your love and longing with your eagerness and suffering with your patience." It is generally thought that the charm of Isabel Archer in *The Portrait of a Lady* and of Milly Theale in *The Wings of the Dove* derives largely from Minny. Was James in love with her, in the romantic sense, and with the intention to marry? Professor Edel thinks not.[16] Nor does he think that Minny was in love with James. Love is a flexible word. The surviving records do not define it in this case.

Back in Cambridge, James quickened the pace of his writing. He did a series of American travel articles about Saratoga, Quebec, and Niagara for the *Nation*. He talked with Emerson, who had been impressed with the family letters shown him by Henry's father. James became art reviewer for the *Atlantic*, in which he published *Watch and Ward*, his first short novel, late in 1871. Cambridge seemed arid, however, and he was glad of the chance to go abroad once more in May, 1872. His sister Alice had long suffered a nervous disorder, and it was thought that a trip abroad might be good for her. Mrs. James's sister, "Aunt Kate," and Henry accompanied her. That summer followed a familiar pattern: Liverpool, Chester, Oxford, London, Paris, and Geneva. Alice was unwell in Switzerland, and in the autumn Aunt Kate took her back to Cambridge. James stayed on in Europe for two years, returning in September, 1874.

Most of this period James spent in Italy. He worked steadily, turning out travel articles and a number of short stories with Italian settings. In the spring of 1874 he wrote much of *Roderick Hudson* in Florence. But many social contacts were also available to him. In the fall of 1872 he met in Paris both Lowell and Emerson. In Rome that winter there were a number of American expatriates and travelers, including William Wetmore Story and Thomas Crawford, the sculptors. In November, 1873, William joined Henry in Florence, and the two brothers were together for several months. William was not well, and their tastes were now sufficiently divergent so that the companionship was not always harmonious. In March, 1874,

William started for home. In September, Henry, too, was back in Cambridge.

After spending the autumn at home, James went to New York for the first six months of the new year. In January, *Roderick Hudson* began to appear in the *Atlantic*. James received a hundred dollars for each monthly installment, and was also earning a similar sum through reviews and travel articles. In 1875 alone he published seventy magazine pieces besides his novel. Early in 1875 his first book appeared, *A Passionate Pilgrim,* which included six early stories. In June, *Transatlantic Sketches,* a collection of travel articles, followed. New York, however, proved not very much more attractive than Boston and Cambridge. He wished for some kind of arrangement to do regular newspaper articles from abroad. Through a friend, the New York *Tribune* engaged him. In October, James left America for Paris, this time with the announced intention to stay. He did not return until 1881.

There has been much discussion of James's decision to live abroad. A sentence in a letter to Charles Eliot Norton early in 1871 gives essential light: "To write well and worthily of American things one need more than elsewhere to be a *master*. But unfortunately one is less!" An entry in James's *Notebook* in 1881 on his return to Boston further clarifies this idea: "My choice is the old world—my choice, my need, my life. . . . One can't do both—one must choose. No European writer is called upon to assume that terrible burden, and it seems hard that I should be. The burden is necessarily greater for an American—for he *must* deal, more or less, even if only by implication, with Europe; whereas no European is obliged to deal in the least with America." In this passage James goes on to suggest that a hundred years later things may be different, but he must deal with the world of his own time. That the choice was not a wholly satisfactory one is illustrated by a casual remark in a travel sketch of 1877: "To be a cosmopolite is not, I think, an ideal; the ideal should be to be a concentrated patriot."[17]

James's early years abroad, the lack of regular progress through American schools, and, above all, his failure to be directly involved in the Civil War contrived to alienate him from the young men of his own generation. Independent in spirit, James remained at least outwardly dependent on his parents far beyond the usual pattern. In 1875, when he went abroad to stay, he was thirty-two. Save for three previous years abroad between 1869 and 1874, he had always lived at home. Though he was self-supporting soon after the Civil War, he accepted while abroad an arrangement whereby publisher's payments were made to his father and forwarded to James.

This led to some petty bickering over his expenses which might have been avoided. The active and impulsive William tended to overshadow his younger brother, and Henry's failure to marry increased the passiveness of his role in the family. It was, in short, high time that he strike out for himself. He had looked about, he had had time to consider his future. Europe was simply more congenial than America, and, as will be seen, he was more at ease with fictional settings there than in America. But though James deliberately became an expatriate, and in 1915 because of wartime circumstances became a British subject, he retained a strong feeling of devotion to his native country. His letters, his journals, his autobiographical volumes are proof of that. The fiction itself shows awareness of American virtues as well as American vulgarities. Moreover, Europe and Europeans are seldom idealized.

IV *European Stories: 1869-75*

Aside from James's first story "A Tragedy of Error," the early attempts at fiction with European setting all date from 1869 on. "Gabrielle de Bergerac" (1869) is James's one experiment in historical fiction. He wrote it before he went abroad that year, attracted to the romance surrounding the French Revolution. The narrator has acquired from the last representative of the De Bergerac family a beautiful portrait of Gabrielle, who with her husband was guillotined as a Girondist. Gabrielle, an aristocrat, fell in love with Coquelin, a tutor for her nephew, who passes on their adventure to the narrator. Gabrielle rejected an aristocratic suitor, who then tried to kill her. She escaped from her suitor with Coquelin, and until the Revolution they lived happily in Paris. This tale is fluent and agreeable in a conventional way, but it gave James no opportunity to develop what was to be his peculiar quality. It is probably the least Jamesian of his fiction, and James himself never reprinted it.

The visits to Italy in 1869 and 1872 resulted in four stories. In "Traveling Companions" (1870) the slender action begins with the narrator's casual meeting with an American girl. A missed train appears to compromise the young lady in the eyes of her father. When the young man honorably proposes marriage, the young woman as honorably refuses. After the death of her father, however, the two young people marry. This trivial action is merely the thread on which James strings his own responses to Europe and to traveling Americans. In another story, "At Isella" (1871), the American narrator identifies himself with romantic Europe by helping a beautiful Italian lady escape to Switzerland to join her lover, a

friend of her dead brother. The American gives her money for a
carriage and receives a smile as she departs. The next day the
pursuing husband is turned back by the sly deceit of the sympathetic
innkeeper. As in "Traveling Companions," description partly makes
up for a thin plot.

Two stories center upon Italian characters. "Adina" (1874) is the
story of a young English girl engaged to a crass young man. Finding an Italian boy with a beautiful carved topaz, the foreigner
buys it for a small price, as a gift for Adina, the English girl. Later
the Italian, having discovered the great value of the topaz, seeks
revenge. He talks with Adina, and attracts her. Some time later,
Adina runs away with the Italian. In disgust, the jilted lover throws
the topaz away. "The Last of the Valerii" (1874) is about an
Italian count who marries the goddaughter of an American artist
in Rome. When the count's old villa is cleaned up, the American
wife becomes interested in the possibility of finding antiquities on
the estate. After some search, carried on against the count's wish, a
beautiful statue of Juno is dug up. When the count reverts to pagan
worship of the goddess, his wife has the statue reburied and re-
gains her husband. This odd tale is a rather external treatment of
American suspicion. The artist-godfather of the wife cries out: "I
was a thousand times right . . . an Italian count may be mighty
fine, but he won't *wear!* Give us some wholesome young fellow of
our own blood, who will play us none of these dusky old-world
tricks" (*Complete Tales*, III, 106). Artist though he is, the god-
father has much in common with Mr. Evans, the representative
American in "Traveling Companions."

"A Passionate Pilgrim" (1874) became the title story of James's
first collection the following year. The familiar pattern of the
American claimant to an English inheritance is a frame for appreciative descriptions of a typical London hotel, Hampton Court,
the Malvern Hills, and an old country house stocked with pictures
and old furnishings. The narrator accompanies Clement Searle, the
claimant, to the family estate. From the English Searle who lives
there, the American experiences first hospitality, then resentment.
He then goes on to Oxford, and so completely identifies with his
English surroundings that he thinks of himself as an Englishman.
Just before he dies, the American Searle gives what few valuables
he has to a poor Englishman who desperately wishes to seek his
fortune in America.

This early story was much praised, and thirty years later James
included it in the New York Edition. Read today, it seems cluttered
and indecisive. The suggestion of a love affair between the American Searle and the sister of his English kinsman is implausible

and remains incidental. The young Englishman who wants to migrate to America has too slight a place in the structure of the story to create the intended balance for the American's infatuation with England. The narrator's purpose in telling his friend's story is ill-defined. The descriptions, however, have great charm, and for them the story may still be read with pleasure.

"Eugene Pickering" (1874) is one of the few fictional uses of Germany in James's stories. The narrator recognizes young Eugene, a former schoolmate, at the Homburg gambling casino. Eugene confides that the death of his father has liberated him from the sheltered, overdisciplined life which the narrator remembers. Eugene is discovering "life," particularly in the person of a beautiful German woman, but before long she jilts him. Eugene also confides to the narrator that he had made a deathbed promise to his father than he would marry the daughter of a business associate in Smyrna, but he has just received word that the girl in Smyrna has absolutely refused to marry a man she has never seen. At the end of the story, Eugene takes the narrator's advice and goes to Smyrna. Later, the narrator receives word that the girl reconsidered; she and Eugene are now happily married. This overcomplicated narrative, with its emphasis of Eugene's discovery of "life," is a very pale anticipation of Strether's plight in *The Ambassadors;* Eugene's remark that "life is learning to know one's self" is a faint note on the same key as Strether's advice to Little Bilham: "Live all you can."

Three European stories turn on the nature of art. "The Madonna of the Future" (1873) tells of an American artist in Florence who has found the ideal model for a Madonna and for years has worked on what is to be his masterpiece. The narrator, a New Yorker who meets the artist by chance, learns of his dedication to this great work. Later, on inquiry, the narrator discovers that other Americans in Florence regard the artist as a fake. Meeting the artist again, the narrator is on his guard. When he goes to the artist's rooms he finds that his model is a coarse old woman, and that the painting to which years have supposedly been devoted has not even been begun. Trying to encourage the artist, the narrator urges him to get to work, and even offers to buy the finished painting. The artist, humiliated by his exposure, soon dies.

This tale of artistic incompetence includes some interesting comments, which must be interpreted in the light of the character who makes them. The artist speaks of Americans: "We are the disinherited of Art! We are condemned to be superficial! We're excluded from the magic circle! The soil of American perception is a poor little barren artificial deposit." This idea, however, is good-naturedly rejected by the narrator. The artist's last speech is an impetuous

defense of the artist who fails: "I suppose we're a genus by our-
selves in the providential scheme,—we talents that can't act, that
can't do nor dare! We take it out in talk, in plans and promises, in
study, in visions! But our visions, let me tell you . . . have a way of
being brilliant, and a man has not lived in vain who has seen the
things I have!" There is tacit approval of this idea in the
narrator's refusal to show the artist's vacant canvas to a critical
friend. "You'd not understand her," he says. There is also a note of
sympathy for the dreamer in the ugly representation of commercial
success that echoes through the story. The successful artist is the
one who has made popular his hideous little caricatures of human
beings in the form of monkeys and cats. His cry is, "Cats and
monkeys, monkeys and cats—all human life is there!" (*Complete
Tales,* III, 15, 47-48, 50, 52).

"The Sweetheart of M. Briseux" (1873) is a slight story, the
confession of how a lady, being painted by one artist, is won away
from him by M. Briseux, who finishes the portrait. M. Briseux goes
on to fame. After his death, the subject of the portrait, now his
widow, comes frequently to the gallery to see it, and there she
attracts the narrator's eye. This emphasis of the vitality of art is
loosely related to "Benvolio" (1875), which contrasts in allegorical
fashion the attractions of poetry and scholarship. Poetry is represented by a countess, who inspires Benvolio to write witty
comedies; Scolastica, the daughter of a philosopher, represents the
studious life which Henry James might have fancied himself as
enjoying if he had followed his father's footsteps. The story ends
equivocally. Benvolio does not really choose. It is the very contrast of the creative and the intellectual that Benvolio relishes.

V "*Madame de Mauves*" (1874)

Far the most impressive story James wrote prior to 1877, both in
theme and in structure, is "Madame de Mauves." Originally published in the *Galaxy* for February and March, 1874, it was included
by James in four later collections; but in a letter of 1905 he referred to it as "a very early and meagre performance"[18] which he
preferred not to have translated into French. In the preface to the
New York Edition, James is unable to recall the origin of a story
that runs to thirty thousand words and must have occupied him for
several weeks. Euphemia Cleve, the heroine who becomes Madame
de Mauves, James does refer to as "experimentally international,"
thus recognizing the importance of the story as an early treatment
of the international theme. Euphemia, a virtuous American girl, is
married to a profligate Frenchman. By chance, young Longmore, an

American traveling in Europe, sees in a Paris park his shipboard acquaintance, Mrs. Draper, in the company of Madame de Mauves. Longmore is not formally introduced to the lady, but later Mrs. Draper promises to send him a letter of introduction. When it comes, the letter includes this significant remark: "I hope you appreciate the compliment I pay you when I recommend you to go and console an unhappy wife. I have never given a man such a proof of esteem, and if you were to disappoint me I should renounce the world. Prove to Madame de Mauves that an American friend may mingle admiration and respect better than a French husband" (*Complete Tales*, III, 128).

Dropping in the second part of the story the restricted point of view of Longmore, James explains how Euphemia, educated at a convent school in Europe, visited one of her schoolmates and fell romantically in love with the handsome but irresponsible elder brother, Baron de Mauves. The grandmother of the household, a *grande dame* ruthless in her worldly wisdom, has two interviews with the young American girl. At the first of these interviews she gives this advice:

> If you expect to live in France, and you want to be happy, don't listen too hard to that little voice I just spoke of,—the voice that is neither the curé's nor the world's. . . . I was brought up to think that a woman's first duty was to please, and the happiest women I've known have been the ones who performed this duty faithfully. As you're not a Catholic, I suppose you can't be a dévote; and if you don't take life as a fifty years' mass, the only way to take it is as a game of skill. Listen: not to lose, you must—I don't say cheat; but don't be too sure your neighbor won't, and don't be shocked out of your self-possession if he does (III, 133).

A few days later, having watched Euphemia and talked with her grandson the Baron, the old lady calls the girl to her once more: "There never was a man in the world—among the saints themselves—as good as you believe the Baron. But he's a *galant homme* and a gentleman, and I've been talking to him tonight. To you I want to say this,—that you're to forget the worldly rubbish I talked the other day about frivolous women being happy. It's not the kind of happiness that would suit you. Whatever befalls you, promise me this: to be yourself" (III, 140).

Thus in the first two parts of the story, the faithless European husband, the naturally virtuous American wife, and the trustworthy American friend are clearly introduced. Moreover, from a worldly old French noblewoman comes the Emersonian advice which is to be tested as the story develops. The next five parts of the narrative show the acquaintance of Euphemia and Longmore growing into friendship, and for him into love. The degree of Euphemia's affection is never quite certain. The Baron's widowed sister, who at first herself angles for Longmore, becomes the woman scorned and the go-between. When Longmore returns to Madame de Mauves, after having seen her husband dining with another woman at a fine restaurant, it is Madame Clairin (the sister) who passes on the story of the Baron's quarrel with his wife, and repeats his taunting: "Console yourself!" A little later, when Longmore is on the verge of offering to take Euphemia away from a hateful marriage, Euphemia checks him: *"Don't disappoint me.* If you don't understand me now, you will tomorrow, or very soon. . . . if I were to find you selfish where I thought you generous, narrow where I thought you large . . . vulgar where I thought you rare,—I should think worse of human nature. . . . If you wish to please me forever, there's a way" (III, 194-95).

The way is clearly to withdraw, not to urge, not even to seem to desire a course which Madame de Mauves could not accept. The concluding section of the story is technically awkward, but James secures through a twist of plot an unconventional emphasis of idea latent in preceding events. The Baron, discovering with astonishment that Longmore has gone back to America instead of "consoling" his wife, cancels an evening engagement, thus signifying a renewed interest in this unusual woman. Two years later, Longmore hears from his friend Mrs. Draper (who had introduced him to Madame de Mauves) that the Baron has committed suicide: Euphemia had refused the forgiveness the Baron had begged. And so the way is clear for a happy ending, with Longmore returning to Europe to marry the beautiful widow. But James rejects such an ending for this quiet concluding paragraph: "Longmore was strongly moved, and his first impulse after he had recovered his composure was to return immediately to Europe. But several years have passed, and he still lingers at home. The truth is, that in the midst of all the ardent tenderness of his memory of Madame de Mauves, he has become conscious of a singular feeling,—a feeling for which awe would be hardly too strong a name" (III, 209).

The chief objection felt by modern readers of this story is simple disbelief in the reality of the love affair. After nearly a century of relaxed conventions and increasingly realistic fictional standards, such reticence, such restraint, such absence of even the mildest caress weaken the appeal of the story. Yet it is easy to show that James reflects the manners and the fictional standards of his time.[19] Most readers of "Madame de Mauves" succeed in pushing past the surface strangeness to the sharply intelligent insight which the story offers. James does not make his tale didactic. He explores the implications of the given situation, the *donnée*. Longmore and Euphemia are not introduced as "average" persons, but as unusual ones. Their virtue, as it turns out, is a trap: they cannot engage in an adulterous affair, no matter how open the opportunity. If they did, they would not be the people they are. Yet the purpose of the story is not to praise them unreservedly for this virtue. At the end, it is awe, rather than love, which Longmore feels for Euphemia. The reader is bound to sense that Euphemia's rigidity, justifiable as it may seem, is somehow less admirable than a more generous spirit—toward either Longmore or the Baron—would have been. In such a situation, it is evident that James has found his true subject: the intellectual treatment of a moral dilemma, the private problem of well-defined individuals who are not so much concerned to revolt against social custom as to see their way within it. So much at home is James with his story that he achieves his characteristic irony without strain.

Of special importance is James's firm grasp of the theme of renunciation, so central in his later work. In terms of this story, whatever Longmore and Madame de Mauves did would involve renunciation. They could renounce their impulse for happiness together, as they did; or, following that impulse, they could renounce themselves. And James's awareness of the intellectual aspect of renunciation gives his treatment of this theme strength, for many of his contemporaries were content to present it in simply emotional terms.

There is, to be sure, melodrama in the Baron's suicide, but it is briefly reported and made to seem incidental rather than essential. Like the dream in part seven it is a clumsy device, but James did what he could to minimize it. A conspicuous technical success in the story is the use of the restricted point of view. Instead of the "narrator" so characteristic of James's early stories, Longmore himself supplies the "intelligence" through which the reader experiences the story. The second part, giving Euphemia's early history, and the final ninth part, developing the conclusion, are awkward departures from the restricted point of view, and they probably account for James's dissatisfaction when he looked at the story years later. The major part of "Madame de Mauves," like the nearly contemporaneous *Roderick Hudson*, is evidence that intellectually and technically Henry James had come of age. In his European stories, moreover, he had tapped an emotional response far richer than that achieved in the earlier stories set in America.

VI *France: 1875-76*

Henry James arrived in Paris in November, 1875, already familiar with the city from visits in 1855, 1858, 1869, and 1873. He found rooms not far from the Rue de Rivoli in the center of Paris, and he set to work on the letters he was to furnish for the New York *Tribune*. By the following August, he had written twenty of these, at twenty dollars each; but he and the *Tribune* editor had discovered that, however agreeably James could write for the magazines, he had no talent for newspaper writing. He was unwilling to exploit his personal acquaintances. He even objected to subheads in the printing of his column-long letters. He commented in general terms on French politics, art, music, literature, and the stage. Readers of the *Tribune* showed little interest, and eventually James wrote the editor that he could not learn how to provide satisfactory material: "If my letters have been 'too good,' I am honestly afraid that they are the poorest I can do, especially for the money!"[20] The connection was ended in a friendly spirit, and James was invited to submit letters from time to time on topics that might interest him. He did not do so, perhaps partly because he soon moved to London, where the *Tribune* had a particularly able correspondent.

James's major concern in Paris at this time was the writing of *The American,* which began to appear serially in the *Atlantic* in June, 1876. He continued to review books for the *Nation,* and he wrote two belated stories with American settings (already discussed). Aside from his writing, the most important feature of this period was James's meeting with Turgenev in November, 1875—and, through Turgenev, the French writers Flaubert, Zola, Maupassant, Daudet, and Edmond de Goncourt. In 1874 James had published a laudatory review of a German version of Turgenev's *A Lear of the Steppes.* He therefore wrote Turgenev, asking to call, and was charmed by the Russian's cordial manner. Turgenev, a large, vigorous man, exuded confidence and breadth of experience. James found congenial Turgenev's concentration on character and his low opinion of "plot." Turgenev was to remain one of James's great enthusiasms.

For the French writers to whom Turgenev introduced him, James felt less personal warmth. Flaubert's Sunday salons he frequently attended. James admired *Madame Bovary,* but thought Flaubert himself a limited person. Zola he respected for the courage and largeness of his attempt, but his numerous allusions to Zola reflect distaste for the unrelieved ugliness of his Naturalism. The group around Flaubert and Zola he thought narrow. They had little respect for the *Revue de deux mondes,* and little knowledge of English literature. Outside this small circle of literary people, James had little contact with French life; and, despite his excellent command of the language, he saw little future for himself in France. In July, 1876, he wrote William regarding the French: "I have done with 'em forever, and am turning English all over." From Italy he had written his mother in an earlier letter that the English "glow with the light of the great fact, that after all they love a bath-tub and they hate a lie."[21] At thirty-three, and after many travels, James settled in London in December, 1876, There he was at home for forty years.

CHAPTER 2

Early Novels: 1871-1880

WHEN JAMES SETTLED in London late in 1876, he had written three novels, all serialized in the *Atlantic Monthly*. The last installment of *The American* was in the December issue of that magazine, and *Roderick Hudson* was already in book form in America, though not in England. Aside from personal liking for the English, it was clear that James must look to England, as well as America, for a public. There was encouragement as well as annoyance in the appearance of a pirated English edition of *The American* in 1877. Authorized editions of this novel and of the earlier *Roderick Hudson* were published in 1879.

I Watch and Ward (*1871*)

James's early novel of New York, a story of about sixty-five thousand words, was his most extended attempt at fiction with an American setting before *The Bostonians* (1885-86). Though *Watch and Ward* achieves a more solid reality than most of the early short stories of American setting, it is handicapped by the forced movement of the plot. James revised the novel minutely before publishing it in book form in 1878, but he never included it in any collection of his works. He customarily referred to *Roderick Hudson* as his "first" novel.

Watch and Ward has as a central figure Roger Lawrence, a wealthy young man who has just been refused by Miss Morton, the young lady he had hoped to marry. In his disappointment, Roger meets at his hotel another young man in a desperate situation, who appeals to him for help. Roger refuses the help because his acquaintance will not specify his difficulties. During the night, the desperate young man shoots himself, leaving alone in the world his little daughter Nora. Feeling some responsibility for the little girl's situation, Roger adopts Nora and writes Miss Morton that he intends to bring the girl up in the hope that she will some day become his wife. Roger's friends, his housekeeper, and his clergyman-cousin are duly skeptical, especially as little Nora is not a very attractive child. Devoting his whole time to Nora, Roger does help her to develop into a pleasing young woman, congenial in her tastes, and in all ways a credit to his guidance.

Full of implausible and melodramatic elements, *Watch and Ward* is still recognizably Jamesian; for there is considerable emphasis on problems rather than merely on sensational events. Assume, says James, that a wealthy bachelor adopts a young girl and devotes himself to bringing her up. How will the girl's personality and character reflect this special situation? How will the project affect the wealthy young bachelor who undertakes it? How will the differences between the methodical bachelor and his brilliant cousin be sharpened by their eventual conflicting interest in the young girl? There is a fine irony in the fact that Roger's very generosity raises a barrier to his ward's acceptance of him. He has so encouraged delicacy of feeling in her that gratitude to him prevents the free response of affection he most desires. James's solution of this dilemma may seem preposterous, but the problem is one worthy of high talent. In Roger's calculating approach to marriage there is a faint suggestion of *The American*, and in Nora there are occasional gleams of the charm of Isabel Archer in *The Portrait of a Lady*. The problem of guardianship foreshadows the peculiar relationship between Roderick Hudson and his benefactor.

Though Professor Edel sees this novel as "a harbinger of greatness,"[1] many readers will be more impressed with the thinness of incident and the dependence on melodrama so characteristic of James's shorter American stories of this early period. The novel, like the stories, raises the question: Why, in the period from 1864 to 1867, do so many of James's stories seem "literary" and abstract? Why is "The Story of a Year" the one substantial fiction related to the Civil War? Though James himself was not directly involved in the war, two of his brothers and many of his friends—Oliver Wendell Holmes, Jr., for example—were. The readjustments of such young men to civilian life and the plight of women who lost sweethearts, young husbands, or sons would seem to be themes appropriate to James's talents. The rise of New York City, the decline of Boston, the impact of Western development surely presented fictional material. Yet literature does not necessarily result from taking inventories of available subjects. In the direct and obvious sense, James refused to become a social historian.

II Roderick Hudson (*1875*)

The title character of *Roderick Hudson* is a young New Englander with an unusual talent for sculpture. Roderick's only brother having died in the Civil War, his mother is both emotionally dependent on him and at the same time unable to comprehend his artistic ambitions. Into the village of Northampton, Roderick's home, comes a somewhat older man to visit a cousin Cecilia, a friend of the Hudsons. This gentleman, Rowland Mallet, is quickly impressed with Roderick's promise and offers to take him to Rome so that he may have the fullest opportunity to develop his talent. The misgivings of Mrs. Hudson, and of the village lawyer in whose office Roderick has been trying to read law, are amusingly rendered. The genuine concern of Mary Garland, a cousin to whom Roderick later becomes engaged, strikes a note of foreboding: how will Roderick's magnificent opportunity affect him as a man?

Chapter Three finds Roderick and his benefactor in Rome on a warm autumn day. Roderick's talent has proved so genuine that in a season he has won the admiration of Gloriani, a successful American sculptor of European extraction and training. Roderick's joy in creation is great, and the artistic world comes to praise his "Adam" and his "Eve." The following summer, however, Roderick is restless. Going off by himself, he gambles his money away at Baden-Baden, and is forced to appeal to Mallet. Back in Rome, he takes a new tack, modeling "a woman leaning lazily back in her chair, with her head drooping as if she were listening, a vague smile on her lips, and a pair of remarkably beautiful arms in her lap."[2] Gloriani is pleased, but somewhat puzzled by Roderick's changed mood. Roderick himself turns querulous and uncertain of his aims. At this point the great beauty, Christina Light, is brought by her mother to Roderick's studio. Mrs. Light wants to arrange for a portrait bust of her daughter, capitalizing on Roderick's current fame. Roderick agrees, but Mallet is apprehensive; he knows that Mrs. Light, widow of an American consul, has made a career of displaying her marriageable daughter. Christina herself shows complete awareness of her mother's designs and no affectionate gratitude whatever.

The bust of Christina is a success, but Roderick's professional satisfaction is overshadowed by his infatuation with Christina. At a ball, the mysterious Cavaliere, an old gentleman who accompanies Christina and her mother, discourages Roderick's attachment. At the same ball, Christina talks at length with Mallet about Roderick. In the course of the conversation, Mallet mentions that Roderick is engaged to Mary Garland, the Northampton girl. Later, when he mentions this conversation to Roderick, the young sculptor takes offense. Meanwhile, Christina's mother has attracted Prince Casamassima as an appropriate suitor for her daughter, and Christina duly accepts him. Roderick is sufficiently upset to cancel a lucrative commission from a wealthy American. Mallet then urges Roderick to send for his mother and Miss Garland, now the mother's constant companion. On their arrival, Roderick is happy. He basks in their admiration of his work, and he conceives the idea of doing a bust of his mother. At length, however, Roderick confides to Mallet that his mother and Mary Garland simply bore him. Though Roderick does not break off his engagement to Mary, he maintains a lively interest in Christina. Mary, meeting Christina by chance, instinctively dislikes her. News then comes that Christina has broken her engagement to the Prince.

Christina's mother, believing that the girl's interest in Roderick is mere infatuation, sends for Mallet to reason with her. Mallet, who fails to influence her, sees that Christina's interest in Roderick is deep and sincere. The next day Mallet learns that Christina has suddenly married the Prince after all. Mallet theorizes that Mrs. Light finally threatened to reveal that Christina is the natural daughter of the mysterious Cavaliere. Mallet returns to find Roderick in a temper, disillusioned with Christina, angry with himself, callous toward his mother and Mary, and ready, at last, to leave Rome. Roderick, his mother, Mary, and Mallet go to Florence for a few weeks; but Roderick's mood is not improved. They then go on to a Swiss village near Lucerne. An accidental meeting with the Prince and Princess leads Roderick to go alone the next day to see Christina. He tells Mallet that "she is still incomparably beautiful, and . . . she has waked me up amazingly" (456). Despite Mallet's protests, Roderick sets off once more to see Christina, and when he does not return that night, a search party is sent out the next morning. Roderick's body is found at the foot of a cliff. When the body is brought back, it is not Mrs. Hudson's tottering grief for her son but Mary Garland's "loud tremendous cry" that sinks into Mallet's memory. A concluding paragraph informs us that Mallet only occasionally visits Northampton, where Mary lives with Mrs. Hudson. Accused of being a restless man, Mallet replies: "No, I assure you I'm the most patient!" His devotion to Mary, long apparent to the reader, continues; but no hope is implied.

The four introductory chapters devoted to Northampton are similar in tone to James's many stories touching New England life from "The Story of a Year" to *The Ambassadors*. There is a respectful reference to Rowland Mallet's father, "a chip of the primal Puritan block . . . a man with an icy smile and a stony frown" (9). The maternal grandfather, a sea captain, had married a Dutch wife. Rowland Mallet grew up with a strong sense of duty, which led him to perform honorable service in the Civil War. But he has also an enjoyment of pictures which leads him to a life of cultivated leisure. The treatment of New England life in terms of such characters as Striker, the village lawyer, Mrs. Hudson, the young sculptor's mother, and Mary Garland, his sweetheart, is appreciative, but critical. The solid virtues are genuine, but New England life is limited. Mary Garland remarks that Mallet is the first unoccupied man she ever saw. To Mallet, as to James, it is the margin of leisure that is essential for the cultivation and enjoyment of the arts.

James's Impressionistic method is clearly evident in his treatment of Roderick as a sculptor. There is no attempt to use technical jargon or circumstantial detail, but the "feel" of the studio is so successfully created that Roderick's rather preposterously rapid success seems natural. James's acquaintance in Rome with the two American sculptors, W. W. Story and Thomas Crawford, and with their artist friends helped James to make the novel convincing. The joy of Mallet and Roderick in the beauties of Rome—the streets, the churches, the countryside—was a simple transference of James's own delight in his visits there. It is likely that the fictional character of Christina Light owes something to Elena Lowe, the Boston beauty of mysterious charm whom James met in Rome.[3] The plan of the novel gave James an opportunity to incorporate the discussion of art perennial in such circles as he was a part of in the early 1870's. Roderick Hudson, the talented young American, is a counterpart of James himself, expressive of the passions and frustrations of an artistic career. Rowland Mallet is the counterpart of James the critic, as in the passage where he comments to his cousin: "I believe that a man of genius owes as much deference to his passions as any other man, but not a particle more, and I confess I have a strong conviction that the artist is better for leading a quiet life."[4]

Writing to a friend twenty years later, James gently rebuked his praise of *Roderick Hudson*: "It isn't very, very good—and it might have been. However, it is what it is—and let me not blaspheme against the ingenuity of my youth. Very faint and far and feeble it seems." Still later, in the New York Edition, he was more specific. A chief fault in the novel, he thought, was the rapidity of Roderick's disintegration. In Christina Light, however, he felt he had produced "even more life than the subject required," and hence he was glad to take up Christina again in *The Princess Casamassima* (1885-86).[5]

III *The American (1876-77)*

Though in some ways a weaker novel than *Roderick Hudson*, the appeal of *The American* is broader, and it is generally regarded as James's first major novel. Christopher Newman, the title character, has come to Paris in 1868 at the age of forty to seek "culture" and a "first-class" wife.[6] Newman is described as a Western man who has rapidly become rich after serving in the army with distinction. In the unfamiliar world of Paris, Newman is willing to take a good deal of advice, but he forms his own impressions. He appears first in the Louvre, admiring masterpieces and arranging to buy copies of them made by a young girl who later tells him how unskillful she is. Through American friends, Newman later meets Mme. Claire de Cintre, a widow and the young daughter of the aristocratic Marquise de Bellegarde.

Between Newman and Claire's younger brother Valentin a mutual attraction springs up, and Newman learns through Valentin of Claire's unhappy first marriage. Little more than a month after his first meeting with Claire, Newman confides to Valentin his desire to marry her. Good-naturedly but bluntly, Valentin points out the obstacles to such a marriage: " 'Why, you are not noble, for instance,' he said" (143). Nevertheless, Valentin agrees to do what he can to help Newman's cause. He advises Newman, "Don't try to be anyone else; be simply yourself, out and out" (148). This advice is precisely that given Euphemia by old Madame de Mauves in James's story of 1874.

Shortly after, in a page-long speech as unimpassioned as it is impetuous, Newman proposes to Claire. She politely refuses, but she agrees that he may speak again in six months. When he does, Claire accepts him with little outward show of passion on either side. A few weeks later, without giving any reason, Claire tells Newman she has given him up. Newman soon learns that her family wishes Claire to marry Lord Deepmere, a distant English relative. Instead, however, she decides to enter a Carmelite convent. Meanwhile Valentin Bellegarde has become attached to Noémie Nioche, Newman's little copyist at the Louvre. Valentin's sense of honor leads him into a duel with another of Noémie's admirers; and in Geneva, Valentin, fatally wounded, sends for Newman. When Valentin learns that his family has made Claire break off with Newman, Valentin confides that something terrible happened to his father and that Mrs. Bread, Claire's servant, knows the details. Mrs. Bread, concerned for Claire's future, gives Newman a paper written by the dying Bellegarde, stating that his wife had killed him by refusing him medicine, in order to clear the way for Claire's first marriage. Armed with a copy of this paper, Newman confronts Madame Bellegarde and her oldest son, the present Marquise. Though somewhat shaken, the Bellegardes are not intimidated. Newman considers the situation, makes a brief trip to England and America, and returns to Paris. Finally, in the home of the American friends who had first introduced him to Claire, Newman burns the incriminating paper. Mrs. Tristram makes the final comment: " 'My impression would be that since, as you say, they defied you, it was because they believed that, after all, you would never really come to the point. Their confidence, after counsel taken of each other, was not in their innocence, nor in their talent for bluffing things off; it was in your remarkable good nature! You see they were right' " (473).

In some ways, *The American* is unsatisfying. Newman is far from a convincing "Western" man. His military and his business past are too vaguely alluded to, his sudden interest in European culture hardly accounted for. He is capable of occasional gaucheries: he telegraphs friends in America of his engagement before the family has a chance to make a formal announcement; he proposes to give a ball, not realizing that Claire's family should do so first. Moreover, Newman's English has hardly a touch of the vernacular, and he says "My dear lady" with the accent of James himself. Toward arranged marriages and duels, Newman shows a proper American indignation, yet even the indignation is deadly serious, untouched by the humorous condescension so elaborately displayed by Twain's *Innocents Abroad* in 1869. The bickering Tristrams, Newman's friends, seem much more American than Newman himself; but the story allows them little space.

The presentation of French life has been objected to. James himself, in the 1907 preface, says that the Bellegardes "would positively have jumped . . . at my rich and easy American." All that can be said is that, despite the lack of adequate motive, the Bellegardes are vivid in their haughty rejection of Newman's claims to Claire, and later of his threats of exposure. Objections to the manners of the Bellegardes—for example, Valentin's offer to show Newman the house on his first call—as not appropriate to their breeding, rest on a too rigid concept of human behavior. Valentin is from the first presented as an odd character, "crazy" is his own word. Noémie Nioche and her father are diverting in their mixture of deceit and frankness. Yet the French characters are seen from the outside, and they doubtless depend heavily on the French novels and plays which James knew. Newman is, as James intended him to be, "the lighted figure."[7]

The plot of *The American* is resolved by melodrama. Valentin's duel, weakly motivated, leads to his deathbed revelation. The revelation, in turn, leads to the discovery of the deathbed charge by his father that he had been murdered by his wife. Claire, forced to break with Newman and faced with the prospect of a second unhappy marriage, takes refuge in a convent—one of the most hackneyed plot devices in nineteenth-century fictional romance. Yet the story is not remembered in terms of its melodrama. It is a novel of character, of idea. Newman, the intelligent, honest man, is trapped by his own virtue; he cannot avail himself of revenge, since it is foreign to his nature: "He was ashamed of having wanted to hurt them." Had he been capable of revenge, however, he would never have attracted Claire. In a similar way, his phlegmatic emotional nature, which ruled out passionate lovemaking, made him seem interesting and sincere to a woman whose first marriage had been a cruel disillusionment.

It is evident that the young man of thirty-three who published *The American,* whatever the gaps of his experience in life, had learned something of value about the heart. That is why this early novel is still valuable.

IV   *London: 1876-80*

When James came to London late in 1876, he found rooms near Piccadilly, and was soon glad he "had wasted no more time in Paris." He met G. W. Smalley, the New York *Tribune* correspondent in London, and several young Englishmen. In February, 1877, the American historian John Lothrop Motley arranged for James to make temporary use of the Athenaeum Club, and a little over a year later he was made a member of the nearby Reform Club. Lord Houghton, the biographer of Keats, invited James to come to one of his famous breakfasts for distinguished literary and political people, and soon James was attending dinners noted for their impressive guest lists. He could write home about meeting Gladstone, Tennyson, and other notables. From the first, James was a social success.

And literary notice was not long delayed. In February, 1878, Macmillan published a collection of his literary essays, *French Poets and Novelists.* In September the same publishers brought out *The Europeans,* already serialized in the *Atlantic.* In June and July, *Cornhill* published "Daisy Miller," and in December, "An International Episode." Some thirty other stories and articles appeared in 1878. With playful exaggeration, but with obvious confidence, James prophesied to Macmillan that his collection of essays "will be a beginning of my appearance before the British Public as *the* novelist of the future, destined to extract from the B.P. eventually a colossal fortune."

Literary recognition resulted in more invitations. James confided to Grace Norton in Cambridge that he had dined out one hundred and seven times in the season of 1878-79. He met Arnold and Meredith, T. H. Huxley (whom he liked very much), Bryce, and Justin McCarthy. And he came to know well three older women in the center of London society: Mrs. Anne Benson Proctor, whose acquaintance with notable people went back to Byron's day; Mrs. Duncan Stewart, a friend of Disraeli; and Fanny Kemble, the former actress.[8]

If James's actual earnings at this time were barely enough for a comfortable living, a larger success seemed within his grasp.

V *"Daisy Miller"* (1878)

Though it is a story of only twenty thousand words, "Daisy Miller" has many times appeared as a small book, and it has probably been the most widely read of James's fiction. Many readers think of it as a short novel. In the beginning, "Daisy Miller" created a controversy, since it seemed to some readers in the United States a satiric attack on the heroine as a representative ill-mannered American girl. In recent years the story has become a period piece, an easy introduction to the manner of a society for which there is hardly a contemporary counterpart. Moreover, slight as it is, "Daisy Miller" is an excellent example of James's most important technical device: the restricted point of view. Throughout, the reader sees events through the eyes of Winterbourne, a young American living abroad with no clearly defined purpose.

While visiting his aunt at her hotel in Vevey, Switzerland, Winterbourne meets Daisy Miller without formal introduction. Her friendly frankness pleases but also puzzles him. Winterbourne's aunt is shocked when he tells her that Daisy has agreed to visit the Castle of Chillon with him. "What a dreadful girl," she comments. A convenient headache enables the aunt to escape a meeting with Daisy. Some months later, Winterbourne again encounters Daisy, this time in Rome; and his aunt is there as well to continue her social disapproval of Daisy. The aunt is reinforced by a Mrs. Walker, who kindly tries to impress upon Daisy that she must not go about alone with young Italian men who have no social standing. When Daisy insists on bringing an admirer, Mr. Giovanelli, to Mrs. Walker's party, the hostess refuses to speak to her. Undaunted, Daisy continues to go about with Giovanelli, and it is rumored that they are engaged. Some time later, Winterbourne meets them one evening in the Colosseum. Winterbourne rebukes Giovanelli for bringing the girl there and exposing her to Roman fever, but learns that it was Daisy herself who insisted on coming. When Daisy does fall seriously ill, she sends a message to Winterbourne, denying that she was ever engaged to Giovanelli. Daisy dies, and at her funeral, Giovanelli comments to Winterbourne: "She was the most beautiful young lady I ever saw, and the most amiable. . . . Also—naturally!—the most innocent. . . . If she had lived, I should have got nothing. She would never have married me." Gossip based on conventions unfamiliar to Daisy proved to be wrong. Winterbourne's natural, spontaneous appreciation of Daisy was right, his caution wrong. At the end of the story he says to his aunt: "You were right in that remark you made last summer. I was booked to make a mistake. I have lived too long in foreign parts."[9]

Daisy's quality is delicately evoked in the story. "You won't back out," she says to Winterbourne as they talk about going to Chillon (20). She complains that there is no society in Vevey: "I'm very fond of society, and I have always had plenty of it" (16). When Winterbourne takes her arm, she declares, "I like a gentleman to be formal" (36). In Rome, when Mrs. Walker warns Daisy that she is being "talked about," Daisy first asks what she means and then says: "I don't think I want to know what you mean. . . . I don't think I should like it" (62). A little later, when Winterbourne explains that flirting is improper he adds, "They don't understand that sort of thing here." To this, Daisy replies with spirit: "I thought they understood nothing else." Flirting, she thinks, is "much more proper in young unmarried women than in old married ones" (71). Daisy's own temperament is a believable and attractive contrast to that of her insufferable little brother, her self-effacing mother, and her absent father, a wealthy man in Schenectady, New York.

In the New York Edition preface, James tells the commonplace anecdote which gave him the idea for the story. Though flatness was the essence of it, he thought that with Daisy "a sufficiently brooding tenderness might eventually extract a shy incongruous charm." A more circumstantial comment James made in a letter, about 1880, to an English lady, a friend of James involved in a bitter quarrel over the interpretation of Daisy's conduct. She had written to ask if he meant his readers to understand that Daisy "went on in her mad way with Giovanelli just in defiance of public opinion . . . or because she was simply too innocent . . . ?" To this James replied:

> The keynote of her *character* is her innocence—that of her *conduct* is, of course, that she has a little sentiment about Winterbourne, that she believes to be quite unreciprocated—conscious as she was only of his protesting attitude. But, even here, I did not mean to suggest that she was playing off Giovanelli against Winterbourne— for she was too innocent even for that. She didn't try to provoke and stimulate W. by flirting overtly with Giovanelli. She never believed that Winterbourne was provokable.[10]

VI The Europeans: A Sketch (*1878*)

The Europeans reverses the international theme by bringing two Europeans to visit cousins who live near Boston. The Europeans are Felix Young and his sister, Baroness Munster, the morganatic wife of a German prince, who now wishes to dissolve the marriage. Felix and the Baroness are the children of an American girl, the half-sister of Mr. Wentworth, whose marriage in Europe alienated her from her family.

This short novel, hardly half as long as *The American,* is an agreeable but distinctly minor work of James. Republished in 1879 and in 1883, it was not included in the New York Edition. William James thought it thin and empty, and in his reply (*Letters,* I, 65) Henry justified it as "an artistic experiment." In *The Europeans,* as in "Daisy Miller," there is greater dependence on dialogue than in *Roderick Hudson* and *The American,* and the reader's attention is focused on the concrete situation. There is often a light, pleasing effect in the juxtaposition of Europeans and Americans. Felix describes Mr. Wentworth to the Baroness: "My uncle, Mr. Wentworth, is a tremendously high-toned old fellow; he looks as if he were undergoing martyrdom, not by fire, but by freezing." There is in this comment a good-humored exaggeration, but in the rigidity of the Baroness's manners there is an unconscious, and on her part unintended, humor. She was, James says, "no friend to the primitive custom of 'dropping in.'" The juxtaposition of manners, however, remains superficial and limited. The Europeans learn little of America; the Americans, little of Europe.[11]

VII Confidence (*1879-80*)

A short novel about Americans abroad, *Confidence* is another narrative shallow in characterization, and one also overdependent on contrived reversals of situation. Bernard Longueville, a young American of some fortune, is traveling in Italy. One day in Siena he sketches a scene outside a church, including in the foreground a very attractive young lady who happens to be waiting for her mother. When the young lady starts to leave, she is annoyed at Bernard's request to give him a few more minutes to finish his sketch of her. She grants the request, but his good-natured compliments and his gift of the sketch to her mother do not mollify the young lady. Two months later, Bernard arrives in Baden-Baden, summoned there by his friend Gordon Wright, an even wealthier young American, who contemplates marriage and wants Bernard's advice. The object of Gordon's affection, of course, turns out to be

Angela Vivian, whom Bernard had sketched in Siena. She makes no sign of having previously met him, and she later tells Bernard not to allude to the incident. While Gordon is away on a brief trip, Bernard derives the impression that Angela and her mother are more interested in Gordon's money than in Gordon, and, when Gordon returns, Bernard tells him so. Gordon departs abruptly the next morning, leaving Bernard to wonder whether he has not perhaps misjudged Angela and thus done her a serious injury.

The latter part of the novel includes the marriage of Gordon to Blanche Evers, Angela's chatterbox companion in Baden-Baden; a temporary disaffection between Blanche and Gordon because of Gordon's preoccupation with science; a third accidental meeting between Bernard and Angela; their engagement, after a quarrel between Gordon and Bernard, since Gordon now thinks his friend and Angela have betrayed him; a general reconciliation of all concerned; and the marriage of Bernard and Angela.

All of this does very little to enrich the reader's comprehension of the title-word "Confidence." When Gordon writes Bernard that he has married Blanche, he says that her tender affection has given him "confidence," but subsequent events show that his confidence had a very shallow basis. Indeed Blanche seems more suited to the adoring Captain Lovelock, a British admirer she met in Baden-Baden. As for Angela, it is not she but her mother who expresses "confidence" in Bernard.[12] Weak as the novel is in idea and in its central characters, there is in it a sort of professional competence. Any lesser novelist might well take pride in having written Captain Lovelock's account of his visit to America:

> You know the Americans are so deucedly thin-skinned—they always bristle up if you say anything against their institutions. The English don't care a rap what you say—they've got a different sort of temper, you know. With the Americans I'm deuced careful—I never breathe a word about anything. While I was over there I went in for being complimentary. I laid it on thick, and I found they would take all I could give them. I didn't see much of their institutions, after all; I went in for seeing the people. Some of the people were charming—upon my soul, I was surprised at some of the people (200).

VIII   Washington Square *(1880)*

With *Washington Square* James achieved the dignity of simultaneous serial publication in England and America, and virtually simultaneous book publication at the end of 1880. At the time, James was rather condescending toward this novel,[13] partly because he was already deep in the larger project of *The Portrait of a Lady;*

later, he excluded *Washington Square* from the New York Edition. Nevertheless, this short novel—about two-thirds the length of *The American*—remains one of the best of James's works to read first. It is told in a straightforward manner by an omniscient narrator. The story moves quietly and deliberately, with keen analysis of the relationship between a dominating father and a proud girl imprisoned by the social customs of her day and her class. The easy opportunities for sentimental appeal and melodramatic solution are firmly resisted.

Catherine Sloper is the dull daughter of a clever father, who has never forgiven her for not attaining the brilliance and beauty of her mother, who died at her birth. Sloper is a successful doctor, who lives with his only daughter in a fine house on Washington Square. Dr. Sloper's sister, the widowed Mrs. Penniman, resides with them. Another sister, a Mrs. Almond, has a large family, and Catherine's social experience is chiefly limited to her family connections. Despite a modest fortune, ten thousand a year as a legacy from her mother, and even greater expectations from her father, Catherine has attracted no suitors. At last, through Mrs. Almond a young man named Morris Townsend meets Catherine. She responds to this first suitor discreetly, but with pathetic eagerness. Dr. Sloper distrusts Morris, and eventually verifies from Morris' sister that the young man is an idler. When Dr. Sloper refuses to consent to the marriage, Catherine remains faithful to Morris; but Morris temporizes in the hope that the father can be won over and will not disinherit her, as he has threatened. Since Morris counsels delay, Catherine agrees to spend six months in Europe with her father. Her continued quiet allegiance to Morris during the trip merely further exasperates Dr. Sloper. On her return, Catherine is ready to go away with Morris, but again he temporizes, and eventually leaves town without informing her. Catherine is humiliated to discover his departure by calling at his rooms and being told that he has left town.

Years pass by and eventually Dr. Sloper dies, leaving a will that reduces Catherine's share in his estate, since "she is amply provided for from her mother's side." Aunt Penniman continues to live in the Washington Square house with Catherine, having always sympathized with the girl and having encouraged the affair with Morris. Twenty years after he had left New York, Morris returns. Mrs. Penniman sees him and, without consulting Catherine, encourages him to call. When Mrs. Penniman does inform Catherine that Morris is again in town and wants to see her, Catherine is resentful: "There can be no reason . . . no good reason." Morris is nevertheless ushered in, almost unrecognizable in his beard and middle-aged figure; Catherine is coldly polite. Trying to make the best of it, Morris says: "We have only waited, and now we are free." To this Catherine responds: "You treated me badly." When he inquires why she has never married—she has had opportunities—she says merely: "I didn't wish to marry." Morris departs, exasperated with Mrs. Penniman for encouraging him to hope for a reconciliation. Catherine, remaining behind in the parlor, picks up her fancy work; then she "seated herself with it again—for life, as it were."[14]

Washington Square is a distinguished story. The subject is real and of perennial interest. The treatment is intelligently analytical without being mannered or unsympathetic. It would have been easy, for instance, to make Dr. Sloper a mere conventional tyrant. He is a tyrant, but not a conventional one. He is a very clever man, and he is right about Morris Townsend. Catherine could easily have been made a sentimental, weeping victim. She is not brilliant, but she is too intelligent for that. The strength of her resistance to her father is exactly the strength that is proof against Morris' belated offer. Morris, instead of being a villainous deceiver, is merely a weak man, destined to fail in business as in romance. It may be objected that Morris, with Catherine's ten thousand dollars a year as a certain prospect, would never have passed it by. Yet it may be argued that this is but one more evidence of Morris' weakness. He was unable to accept a competence when the hope of grandeur beckoned.

IX   Hawthorne (*1879*)

James's *Hawthorne* is an important insight into his view of literature at this period. Invited to undertake the volume because his *French Poets and Novelists* (1878) had been so well received, James added to the well-known facts of Hawthorne's career his own impressions of the man and his books. Hawthorne's preface to *The Marble Faun* furnished a cue for James's statement of the difficulties of a young writer in a country without a literary tradition:

> No sovereign, no court, no personal loyalty, no aristocracy, no church, no clergy, no army, no diplomatic service, no country gentlemen, no palaces, no castles, nor manors, nor old country-houses, nor parsonages, nor thatched cottages nor ivied ruins; no cathedrals, nor abbeys, nor little Norman churches; no great universities nor public schools—no Oxford, nor Eton, nor Harrow; no literature, no novels, no museums, no pictures, no political society, no sporting class—no Epsom nor Ascot! (43).

Despite the chilling effect of this famous passage, which must have been in part ironic, the discussion of Hawthorne during the past thirty years has largely been an elaboration of James's view that thinness of subjects and occasional deficiencies in form did not prevent Hawthorne from combining "in a singular degree the spontaneity of the imagination with a haunting care for moral problems" (183).

In 1880 James was thirty-seven. He could look back ten years with a feeling of accomplishment: two full-length novels, four short ones, some twenty short stories, and over two hundred reviews and articles. He could look back with satisfaction, too, at his decision in 1875 to live abroad. Aside from the mediocre *Watch and Ward*, almost all the work of this decade was inspired by European experience. He had made a place for himself in London, but he had kept the interest of American editors. Looking back, however, was always incidental to James. Looking forward was much more to his liking. In October, 1880, the first installment of *The Portrait of a Lady* appeared.

CHAPTER 3

The Middle Years: 1880-1890

FOR HENRY JAMES the dominant pattern of the 1880's was steady production. In rapid succession there were three long novels: *The Portrait of a Lady* (1880-81); *The Bostonians* (1885-86); and *The Princess Casamassima* (1885-86). In addition James wrote the short novel, *The Reverberator* (1888); eighteen tales, including such extended works as "The Siege of London" (1883), "The Aspern Papers" (1888), and "A London Life" (1888); and some forty reviews and travel sketches. At the end of the decade came another long novel, *The Tragic Muse,* to be discussed in the next chapter because of its close connection with James's interest in the drama.

Complicating this larger pattern of ceaseless writing were several smaller patterns of James's activity. There were his travels, his family responsibilities, and his numerous friendships, now traceable in considerable detail through the survival of thousands of his letters.

James liked to travel and he traveled a great deal. A change of scene stimulated him. As a bachelor, he found it easy to come and go as he pleased. Friends in England invited him to country homes, even to Scotland. When James traveled on the Continent, as he did nearly every year between 1880 and 1890, there were always friends to visit. In Italy, his favorite haunt, many Americans lived for months at a time or, like the Storys in Rome, permanently. Italy, which he had first seen in 1869, never failed to charm him. His delight in Florence and Rome found expression in *The Portrait of a Lady.* Venice is the scene of "The Aspern Papers." In 1882 James toured France in order to produce a series of articles, published as *A Little Tour in France* (1884). Frequently he stopped in Paris to attend the theater and to renew acquaintance with French writers he had met in 1875. Occasionally he visited Switzerland, but he had only a moderate liking for mountain scenery.

In October of 1881 James went home to Cambridge, his first visit since he had left in 1875. His mother, now past seventy, looked worn, but there was no special apprehension. In order to be free to write, James stayed at a Boston hotel, often dining with his parents in Quincy Street, Cambridge. In January, 1882, he saw in New York his old friend E. L. Godkin of the *Nation* and Whitelaw Reid, editor of the *Tribune.* He went on to Washington, where he saw the Henry Adamses and met President Chester Arthur, who had known members of the James family in Albany.

Late in January, James was called back to Cambridge by his mother's serious illness; she died before he reached home. James's eloquent tribute to his mother has already been quoted (Chapter 1). That she was "the keystone of the arch" seems to have been felt by the rest of the family. William, Wilky, and Robertson were now all married. The home in Quincy Street was given up, and the elder Henry James and Alice established a new home in Boston. In May, Henry, Jr., was back in London, and in the autumn he was joined by William. In December, their father became seriously ill, and it was agreed that Henry should return, leaving William to pursue his studies in England. The father's funeral was held the very day that Henry landed in New York, and soon after came a farewell letter from William to his father. On December 31, Henry went alone to the cemetery, and beside his father's grave read aloud William's letter. It closed with this sentence: "It is so much like the act of bidding an ordinary good-night. Good-night, my sacred old Father. If I don't see you again—Farewell! a blessed farewell!" Henry described the scene in a letter to William, adding: "I am sure he heard somewhere out of the depths of the still bright winter air."[1] Two years later, William collected his father's scattered essays in *The Literary Remains of the Late Henry James.* When the *Nation* gave the work scant notice, Henry wrote from London a vigorous protest to his friend E. L. Godkin.[2]

Henry remained in America until August, 1883. His father's estate of about $80,000 was left to the five children in equal shares. Henry immediately made over his share to his sister Alice, whose health was a continuing problem. Alice was now thirty-four. She had been well enough to go abroad in 1872 and again in 1878, Henry having some responsibility for her on each trip. In November, 1884, it was decided that she should go to England permanently, to be generally looked after by Henry. A friend of Alice's, Katherine Loring, came with her and stayed on as a companion. A variety of living arrangements were tried, and Alice's health fluctuated. For a time she was well enough to have a good many friends as visitors. Her wit, as evidenced by her letters and her posthumously published *Journal,* was a sufficient attraction. Her illness was diagnosed as neurasthenia, and later cancer developed. Alice died in 1892.

Thus for several years after the death of his parents, Henry had the chief responsibility for an ailing sister whom he loved devotedly. In her *Journal*, Alice referred to him as "Henry the Patient," and left this tribute: "I have given him endless care and anxiety, but notwithstanding this and the fantastic nature of my troubles, I have never seen an impatient look upon his face or heard an unsympathetic or misunderstanding sound cross his lips."[3] It was Henry's fortune to outlive all his family. Wilky died in 1883; Robertson, a few weeks before William in 1910.

A friendship close to family feeling was Henry's attachment to Grace Norton, sister of Charles Eliot Norton, the Boston art critic. Usually separated by the Atlantic Ocean, James and Miss Norton carried on an extended correspondence for forty years. It was to her that James wrote the often-quoted consolation which represents the wisdom he had gained from his own family griefs:

> I am determined not to speak to you except with the voice of stoicism. I don't know *why* we live—the gift of life comes from I don't know what source or for what purpose; but I believe we can go on living for the reason that (always of course up to a certain point) life is the most valuable thing we know anything about, and it is therefore presumptively a great mistake to surrender it while there is any yet left in the cup. . . . remember that every life is a special problem which is not yours but another's, and content yourself with the terrible algebra of your own. Don't melt too much into the universe, but be as solid and dense and fixed as you can. We all live together, and those of us who love and know, live so most (*Letters*, I, 100-1).

Another friendship rooted in Boston was with the wealthy widower Francis Boott and his daughter Lizzie—"the easy-fitting Bootts" as James called them. Lizzie had known Minny Temple and others of James's youth. Because the Bootts were greatly interested in the arts, they lived for many years in Florence, where James saw them frequently. When Lizzie was forty, she married a German-American artist named Duveneck. The bond between Lizzie and her father had for years been so close that the situation gave James some of the insight used in the late novel *The Golden Bowl* (1904). The Bootts and Duveneck lived together quite happily until 1888 when, some time after the birth of her son, Lizzie suddenly died. Her death was a severe shock to James. Both Francis Boott and Duveneck returned to America, thus diminishing James's circle of friends in Italy.

Another friend of this period was Constance Fenimore Woolson, grandniece of James Fenimore Cooper and herself a minor novelist.

"Fenimore," as James came to call her, was closely associated with James and such mutual friends as the Bootts, from 1880 until Miss Woolson's death in Venice in 1894 from a fall that may have been suicidal. A few months later, James came to Venice to assist relatives in disposing of her effects. At this time he seems to have destroyed a large number of letters he had written her.[4] It is probable that Miss Woolson was in love with James for several years, and possible that he considered marrying her. A year after he met Miss Woolson, however, he had told Grace Norton, his Cambridge friend, that he was unlikely to marry, and it is clear that all his life the art of writing was his real mistress. Yet, as Professor Edel suggests, such stories as "The Beast in the Jungle" and "The Altar of the Dead" may indirectly reveal in James a sense of something missed and regretted.[5]

Friendships of a different sort James found in John Singer Sargent and in Edwin A. Abbey, American artists living in England. There was a pleasant interlude in 1885 at the village of Broadway, where these two artists, Edmund Gosse, and others spent a vacation. The previous year, through friendly argument over the art of fiction in *Longman's Magazine,* James had become intimate with Robert Louis Stevenson. James was a frequent visitor until Stevenson left England in 1888. From then until Stevenson's death in 1894 the two corresponded. Sargent was a link, since he painted portraits of both writers.

The early 1890's were marked by several deaths that touched James. Though he had known neither Browning or Tennyson well, their deaths in 1889 and 1892 were emphasized for him by his attendance at the ceremonies for them in the Abbey. In 1891 Lowell died, an older man whom James had learned to know and love through association in Paris, Italy, and London. In 1892, young Wolcott Balestier, an American publisher much interested in James, died sudenly in Dresden. The closeness of the tie is indicated by the fact that James went to Germany for the funeral. In 1893 Mrs. Kemble, who had given James ideas for many fine stories, died suddenly at a great age. Meanwhile, younger persons sought James out; among them were Henry Harland of the *Yellow Book,* and Logan Pearsall Smith, a wealthy Philadelphian.

I The Portrait of a Lady (1880-81)

James's longest novel, *The Portrait of a Lady,* is also one of his best, and probably still the most widely popular of his works. When James revised it for the New York Edition twenty-five years after its first publication, he considered it "the most proportioned of my

works after *The Ambassadors*." Proportion is certainly one of the
novel's virtues, for one reads the fifty-five substantial chapters with
a sense of almost effortless progress from event to event. There is
little reliance on "big scenes"; situations quietly engage the reader's
attention and hold it without strain. Characters come and go. It is
their relationship to the Lady—Isabel Archer—that counts. When the
novel ends, her portrait is complete, though James leaves the reader
to guess about some subsequent events.

The first twelve chapters introduce the young American girl to
the English household of her uncle, Mr. Touchett. Touchett, who
has for many years conducted a profitable banking business in England, is now retired and in very ill health. His only son Ralph,
sensitive, and educated both at Harvard and Oxford, lives at ease
with his father, prevented by health and inclination from following
any occupation. Mrs. Touchett, a cold and managerial woman,
travels a great deal and prefers to live in Italy. As the novel opens,
Touchett and his son are chatting pleasantly on the lawn with
Lord Warburton, a neighbor. Into this quiet country house of
Gardencourt comes Isabel. Her father has just died, her sisters are
married, and she has a little money. Mrs. Touchett, paying one of
her rare visits to America, liked Isabel's independent spirit, and
decided she should be brought to Europe for a time. Isabel's natural
manner at once charms Touchett and his son, and she attracts the
attention of Lord Warburton as well. By the end of the twelfth
chapter, Lord Warburton has proposed marriage, and—to everyone's
surprise—been refused: "She could not marry Lord Warburton; the
idea failed to correspond to any vision of happiness that she had
hitherto entertained, or was now capable of entertaining."[6] In other
words, Isabel was not ready to give up her freedom, even to a handsome English lord, with properties, position, and an obviously
sincere regard for her.

In Chapter Sixteen, Isabel refuses another suitor: Caspar Goodwood, an energetic young American who has against her wishes
followed her to England. A third possible suitor, who because of
his ill health does not speak to Isabel, is her cousin Ralph. Ralph's
father urges him to offer marriage, but instead of proposing, Ralph
persuades his father to provide handsomely for Isabel in his will.
At the end of Chapter Twenty, the elder Touchett dies, and Isabel
finds herself with a fortune of seventy thousand pounds. That Ralph
is responsible for this munificent bequest she does not learn for a
long time.

Isabel now accepts Mrs. Touchett as a companion and advisor.
After brief stops in Paris and in San Remo, where Ralph has gone
for the winter sunshine, Isabel finds herself at home in Florence,

Mrs. Touchett's settled abode. They are often in the company of Madame Merle, a talented and rather mysterious American widow. Through Madame Merle, Isabel meets Gilbert Osmond, an American with too little talent for artistic success and too little money to be happy as a man of leisure. Madame Merle persuades Osmond to propose to Isabel, though why Madame should concern herself is not evident at the time. Isabel is pleased with Osmond's knowledge and taste, and she is much drawn to Pansy, his little convent-educated daughter. Despite the opposition of Mrs. Touchett, Ralph, and even Osmond's sister, Countess Gemini, Isabel accepts Osmond. The marriage takes place just after Chapter Thirty-five, though it is not directly narrated.

The first years of Isabel's marriage are passed over. Madame Merle informs an acquaintance that "two years ago" the Osmonds lost a boy six months old. Living now in Rome, the Osmonds launch Pansy into society. Her principal suitor is a man formerly known to Isabel, an expatriate American named Edward Rosier. Gilbert Osmond is anxious to make a good marriage for Pansy, and considers that Rosier has not enough money. A casual meeting with Lord Warburton leads to the hope that he may marry Pansy, though of course he is much older than she. He does not (Chapter Forty-six), and Gilbert Osmond most unfairly charges Isabel with opposing the marriage. Actually, Pansy's greater interest in Edward Rosier has led her to be merely polite to Lord Warburton. Quarrels over Lord Warburton reveal to the reader how far Isabel's marriage is from the ideal so gifted and fortunate a young woman might have hoped for. During this period Ralph Touchett has spent much time in Rome, and to Ralph, Isabel confesses her plight. Later, Ralph returns to England, certain that he is near death. When Isabel is sent for, Osmond objects to her going (Chapter Fifty-one). Explaining her difficulty to Osmond's sister, Countess Gemini, the Countess decides it is time Isabel knew the truth: that Madame Merle was formerly Osmond's mistress, and that Pansy is their child. Thus it is revealed that Madame Merle schemed the marriage of Osmond to Isabel in order to provide for her own daughter. Isabel's vague suspicions are thus given a horrible confirmation. She decides to go to England without Osmond's consent. There Ralph is able to talk a little with her before he dies. He reaffirms his own love for Isabel: ". . . if you have been hated you have also been loved" (507). But it is as to a brother that Isabel returns his affection.

The last chapter includes the provisions of Ralph's will, an account of his funeral, a friendly call from Lord Warburton, and finally an impassioned plea from Caspar Goodwood, Isabel's persistent American suitor. Caspar argues desperately that Isabel should give up Osmond: "You must save what you can of your life; you mustn't lose it all simply because you have lost a part. . . . The world is all before us—and the world is very large." To this Isabel's reply is: "Do me the greatest kindness of all. . . . I beseech you to go away!" Two days later, Caspar learns in London that Isabel has already left for Florence. The sympathetic girl who tells him this, also tells him: " 'just you wait!' On which he looked up at her." Thus, in 1881, the novel ended. The New York Edition added these lines: "—but only to guess, from her face, with a revulsion, that she simply meant he was young. She stood shining at him with that cheap comfort, and it added, on the spot, thirty years to his life. She walked him away with her, however, as if she had given him now the key to patience." The intent of the revision is not to change but to make more definite the implication of the original passage. The mutual friend is an incorrigible optimist. Caspar himself feels a finality in Isabel's return to Italy.[7]

Why did Isabel return to her husband? The question is more insistent now than it was in 1881, for the alternative urged by Caspar is now more widely accepted. Isabel saw marriage as a serious and binding relationship. To her close friend she confides: "One must accept one's deeds. I married him before all the world; I was perfectly free; it was impossible to do anything more deliberate." Oddly enough, Osmond echoes this idea, hypocritically, when he reminds Isabel that their marriage is indissoluble: "I think we should accept the consequences of our actions, and what I value most in life is the honor of a thing."[8] James characteristically leaves it uncertain whether a seemingly sound principle applies in all circumstances, but for Isabel, the principle holds. Moreover, she has a genuine concern for Pansy. With Pansy safely married, perhaps after all to Edward Rosier, Isabel might reconsider her own marriage. Yet even if she should find life with Osmond impossible, it is doubtful that she would turn to Caspar, whom she respects but clearly does not love—or does not wish to love. Whatever Isabel may do, she will be a Lady, too intelligent and too proud to act on selfish whim.

The objection that the story is left incomplete was anticipated by James as he planned the novel: "The *whole* of anything is never told; you can only take what groups together. What I have done has that unity—it groups together. It is complete in itself—and the rest may be taken up or not, later."[9] What "groups together" is the portrait. To readers who may feel that Isabel is unduly idealized, James had in another connection made a pertinent comment. In an essay on Flaubert in 1876 he said with regard to Madame Bovary:

"M. Flaubert gives his readers the impression of having known few kinds of women, but he has evidently known intimately this particular kind."[10] As James wrote this sentence, he must have reflected that whatever the limitations of his own experience, he had at least known Minny Temple. It was Minny who later enabled him to achieve the reality of Isabel Archer.

The synopsis just given omits an important secondary character, Henrietta Stackpole, a mannish American newspaperwoman who is Isabel's close friend. Henrietta first enters the story in the tenth chapter by coming down to visit Isabel at Gardencourt. She is in England to "do" a series of articles on English life. Her approach is suggested by her comment to Lord Warburton on first acquaintance: "I don't approve of lords, as an institution. I think the world has got beyond that—far beyond." To this, Lord Warburton good-naturedly replies, "Oh, so do I. I don't approve of myself in the least."[11] Thus Henrietta is a comic foil to Isabel's generally sympathetic approach to European life. Henrietta's engagement to Mr. Bantling, formerly a Guards officer, is an amusing irony. Besides representing another American point of view, Henrietta serves as go-between for Caspar Goodwood and Isabel. Henrietta believes Isabel should marry Caspar, and she distrusts all possibilities of European marriage—until her own engagement. It is Henrietta who in the thirteenth chapter persuades Ralph to invite Caspar to Gardencourt, though Caspar has the good sense not to come. It is Henrietta, too, who tries to comfort Caspar at the very end of the novel.

Technically, *The Portrait of a Lady* is an old-fashioned novel. Telling the story from the omniscient point of view, James is free to move from character to character, to analyze and interpret as he goes. Characters frequently turn up with no particular motive except to be useful to the author. Caspar Goodwood, Isabel's rejected American suitor, is said to be manager of a large cotton mill in America, yet for four or five years he pursues Isabel with little evidence that there are other demands on his time. Henrietta's journalistic assignments, indefinite as they are, fit extraordinarily well the convenience of the novelist, and Warburton's visits to Rome (Chapters Twenty-seven and Thirty-nine) seem fortuitous. Yet these transparent devices are not seriously objectionable. Once these characters appear, they always add interest. Caspar seems to represent the possible, even when Isabel rejects him in the last chapter. The very violence of her response to his kiss suggests that she may have more feeling for him than she will admit even to herself. Lord Warburton, after his rejection in Chapter Twelve, is a reminder of what might have been; the contrast between him and

Osmond glaringly emphasizes the tragic misjudgment in Isabel's marriage. Henrietta, in her garish Americanism, is the shadow of Isabel's well-bred independence. In their various ways, these, and lesser characters, help to balance and to deepen the portrait of Isabel. In her the new woman is set forth with a psychological insight that looks toward the twentieth century.

II   The Bostonians (*1885-86*)

Twice the length of the New York novel *Watch and Ward* (1871), *The Bostonians* is a far more thoughtful treatment of the American scene. James had high hopes for its success and was much depressed by its relative failure. In recent years the attempt to emphasize it as a conservative or anti-reform novel has not removed some obstacles to its wide acceptance. There is no sympathetic character with whom the reader can identify, as he can with Christopher Newman or Isabel Archer. The descriptions of New England life, though observant and witty, are often static. Chapters unbroken by dialogue are frequent, and interpretive paragraphs of a thousand words are not uncommon. For the patient reader, however, *The Bostonians* is a rewarding novel.

The chief Bostonian is Olive Chancellor, "a spinster as Shelley was a lyric poet, or as the month of August is sultry." Under the inspiration of the venerable Miss Birdseye, the noted Abolitionist, Olive has taken up the new cause of women's rights. Lacking herself in platform eloquence, Olive is enchanted by the inspired utterance of young Verena Tarrant, whose father's talent for mesmerism originally propelled her into public notice. Taken up by Olive and her associates, Verena proves a willing parrot for the cause. Into this situation comes Basil Ransom, a Confederate veteran from Mississippi and a cousin of Olive Chancellor. Ransom, like everyone else, is enchanted by Verena, but by temperament and conviction he is hostile to her doctrine, and eventually he is hostile to Olive as Verena's virtual tyrant and captor. Verena, feeling an obligation to Olive, with whom she lives and travels, struggles hard to remain loyal. At the end, Verena is virtually abducted by Ransom, just before she is to make a triumphal speech. James, lest he be accused of contriving a happy ending, adds this comment on Verena's tears as she goes away with Ransom: "It is to be feared that with the union, so far from brilliant, into which she was about to enter, these were not the last she was destined to shed."[12]

Olive Chancellor is presented as a well-to-do woman of good intentions. She gave Ransom "an uneasy feeling—the sense that you could never be safe with a person who took things so hard." Though her features suggested good breeding, the tint of her eyes made one think "of the glitter of green ice." She was "a woman without laughter." From the beginning, her attachment to Verena is possessive. She begs Verena to promise not to marry, and she feels betrayed when Verena even ventures to consider Ransom's proposal. The intensity of her resentment when Verena fails to mention a conversation with Ransom reveals a woman emotionally unbalanced, and her agony at the final parting is beyond the normal range of behavior. Whether it justifies the term Lesbianism, recently applied, is a matter of opinion.[13]

Verena herself seems incapable of independence. She accepts easily the arrangement by which she leaves her rather seedy parents and goes to live in the luxury of Olive's Beacon Street home. Her eloquence, as the reader experiences it through Basil Ransom's response, is juvenile: "It was full of schoolgirl phrases, of patches of remembered eloquence, of childish lapses of logic, of flights of fancy which might indeed have had success at Topeka. . . ." As Basil tells her later, he listens only to her voice. If, as James says, Olive's taking up of Verena is "only a kind of elderly, ridiculous doll-dressing," then Verena is the doll. When she spends a day with Ransom in New York, she does show a gleam of intellectual vigor. She is pleased to hear that he has been writing articles, though they argue against her views. As Ransom parts from Verena, he asks if she has given up the hope of converting him to women's rights; she replies, "I want you to remain as you are!" The following summer, when Ransom follows Verena and Olive to Cape Cod, Verena is highly emotional; but in the melodramatic conclusion, when Ransom takes her away from the Boston Music Hall, Verena seems almost a bystander. The argument against her "career" is pressed by Ransom against Verena's parents, Olive, and a harried promoter of the program. Verena finally tells her mother, "it's all for the best, I can't help it, I love you just the same; let me go, let me go!"[14]

Ransom himself, through whose eyes the reader follows much of the story, is independent enough, but confused. His departure from his native Mississippi is explained only in the general terms of family ill-fortune. New York City seems a strange destination for him, and even at the end of the novel, after three years in the North, his prospects are poor. He is supposed to be shrewd enough to see through the self-deception of the reformers, yet he has been cheated by an absconding partner. His conception of woman's place as being in the home seems a cliché that never takes into account economic pressures to loveless marriage and the very real legal inequities of the old arrangements. Ransom reads de Toqueville, and is "an immense admirer of the late Thomas Carlyle." Yet this lofty intellectual at least considers the possibility of marrying for money, Olive Chancellor's fashionable sister, Mrs. Luna. To that lady he could talk about "the state of the South, its social peculiarities, the ruin wrought by the war, the dilapidated gentry, the queer types of superannuated fire-eaters, ragged and unreconciled, all the pathos and all the comedy of it. . . ." He is also capable of appropriate sentiments when Verena takes him to visit Memorial Hall at Harvard, "a kind of temple to youth, manhood, generosity." His view of human nature is low, however. He tells Verena that the spread of education was "a gigantic farce—people stuffing their heads with a lot of empty catchwords that prevented them from doing their work quietly and honestly. You had a right to an education only if you had intelligence . . . the attribute of one person in a hundred."[15]

No doubt the one entitled to an education would be male, for Ransom seemed to think that women in general, and Verena in particular, were made "for love." In this age of danger, Ransom goes on to say, the true occupation of women is "in making society agreeable." Ransom's pursuit of Verena hardly creates confidence in his crusade against women, and it seems doubtful if Verena is the ideal person to make society agreeable for Ransom himself more than a short time.

That James intended this inference to be drawn is evident from the last sentence of the novel, already quoted. Ransom, like Verena herself, is an ironic character. She shows the ridiculous pretensions of the feminist movement; Ransom, the ridiculous side of the opposition. Each position included some truth, though James does seem to make the opposition more substantial. Both Verena and Ransom, however, remain fictional characters. The folly and the wisdom in their respective ideas and conduct must be sorted out by the reader. The middle ground of common sense is left to be inferred.

In the character of Miss Birdseye, James's own attitudes are more clearly represented, for she is a background character, not directly involved in the action. A kind of presiding genius over the reform movement, she is past eighty and so venerable that even Ransom must respect her. James treats her most often in his own person, as "historian" of events. The treatment is, to say the least, varied. It is to Miss Birdseye's salon that Olive Chancellor takes her cousin Ransom in the second chapter of the novel. Miss Birdseye is, explains Olive, "the woman in the world, I suppose, who has labored most for every wise reform."

> She was a little old lady, with an enormous head; that was the first
> thing Ransom noticed—the vast, protuberant, candid, ungarnished
> brow, surmounting a pair of weak, kind, tired-looking eyes, and
> ineffectually balanced in the rear by a cap which had the air of
> falling backward, and which Miss Birdseye suddenly felt for while
> she talked, with unsuccessful, irrelevant movements. . . . She
> always dressed in the same way: she wore a loose black jacket,
> with deep pockets, which were stuffed with papers, memoranda
> of a voluminous correspondence; and from beneath her jacket
> depended a short stuff dress.[16]

Such a description is not prepossessing, but it hardly prepares the
reader for the denunciation which follows. Miss Birdseye's manifold
activities, it is said, "did not prevent her being a confused, entangled,
inconsequent, discursive old woman, whose charity began at home
and ended nowhere, whose credulity kept pace with it, and who
knew less about her fellow-creatures, if possible, after fifty years of
humanitary zeal, than on the day she had gone in the field to testify
against the iniquity of most arrangements." Miss Birdseye, says
James, gives to Ransom "a delicate, dirty, democratic little hand."
Then comes an explanation of her appearance of poverty: "No one
had an idea how she lived; whenever money was given her she
gave it away to a negro or a refugee. No woman could be less
invidious, but on the whole she preferred these two classes of the
human race." It is then suggested that she may actually regret that
the Civil War is over, since its end deprived her of the opportunity
to aid the slaves. Not only was Miss Birdseye an "essentially form-
less old woman, who had no more outline than a bundle of hay";
her bare rooms "told that she had never had any needs but moral
needs, and that all her history had been that of her sympathies."[17]

Now the most interesting thing about this attack on Miss Birdseye is not the supposed use of Elizabeth Peabody (Hawthorne's
sister-in-law) as a model. Of much greater importance is James's
gradual conversion of it to a tender tribute when Miss Birdseye dies
toward the end of the book. In the twentieth chapter, for example,
Verena's impression of Miss Birdseye is given. Though she is a
prejudiced witness, Verena's impressions are phrased in a factual
and modest way that implies concurrence by the narrator:

> She had had escapes, in the early days of abolitionism, which it was
> a marvel she could tell with so little implication that she had shown
> courage. She had roamed through certain parts of the South, carry-
> ing a Bible to the slave; and more than one of her companions, in
> the course of these expeditions, had been tarred and feathered.
> She herself, at one season, had spent a month in a Georgian jail.
> She had preached temperance in Irish circles where the doctrine was

received with missiles; she had interfered between wives and husbands mad with drink; she had taken filthy children, picked up in
the street, to her own poor rooms, and had removed their pestilent
rags and washed their sore bodies with slippery little hands. In her
own person she appeared to Olive and Verena a representative of
suffering humanity; the pity they felt for her was part of their
pity for all who were weakest and most hardly used; and it struck
Miss Chancellor (more especially) that this frumpy little missionary
was the last link in a tradition, and that when she should be called
away the heroic age of New England life—the age of plain living
and high thinking, of pure ideals and earnest effort, of moral
passion and noble experiment—would effectually be closed. It was
the perennial freshness of Miss Birdseye's faith that had had such
a contagion for these modern maidens, the unquenched flame of her
transcendentalism, the simplicity of her vision, the way in which,
in spite of mistakes, deceptions, the changing fashions of reform,
which make the remedies of a previous generation look as ridiculous
as their bonnets, the only thing that was still actual for her was the
elevation of the species by the reading of Emerson and the fre-
quentation of Tremont Temple (552).

There are in this passage some overtones of irony, but they are far
more restrained than in the earlier chapter. There is no irony about
the courage; the courage was real, and it commanded James's
respect.

Through Ransom, too, James softens the reader's impression of
Miss Birdseye. Meeting her on a visit to Boston (in Chapter Twenty-
three) he approaches the old lady politely and recalls to her their
previous meeting. After a moment she says: "I remember you now,
and Olive bringing you! You're a Southern gentleman—she told me
about you afterwards. You don't approve of our great struggle—you
want us to be kept down." James adds: "she spoke with perfect
mildness, as if she had long ago done with passion and resentment."
Then she continues, mildly: "Well, I presume we can't have the
sympathy of all." Such a passage retains nothing of the irony of the
reader's first introduction to Miss Birdseye. As Ransom walks along
with Miss Birdseye, she explains that, instead of carrying Bibles to
slaves as she once did, she now wants to carry statute-books to
women. Ransom's reply seems more than an empty compliment:
"Wherever you go, madam, it will matter little what you carry.
You will always carry your goodness." On Cape Cod, when Ransom
meets Miss Birdseye for the last time, he shows the same respect.
His thoughts of her, just before her death, are her eulogy:

Her head was thrown back against the top of the chair, the ribbon
which confined her ancient hat hung loose, and the late afternoon

light covered her octogenarian face and gave it a kind of fairness, a double placidity. There was, to Ransom, something almost august in the trustful renunciation of her countenance; something in it seemed to say that she had been ready long before, but as the time was not ripe she had waited, with her usual faith that all was for the best. . . .[18]

From so appreciative a leave-taking of the old lady, one turns back with a shock to the initial characterization of "a confused, entangled, inconsequent, discursive old woman." Why did James use these acid words? They are not really necessary to the logic of the novel; and, if they were, they might come with better grace from one of the characters than from the historian. Perhaps this is the way James would like to have regarded Miss Birdseye and all other reformers. One thinks of Eliot's often-quoted remark: "He had a mind so fine that no idea could violate it." Reformers must always be violated by the reforms they serve. Thus reformers as a class were to James suspect. Yet character, commitment, renunciation are great human values. As the novel progresses, James emphasizes these values in Miss Birdseye. Courage Miss Birdseye had, unmarred by pretension or self-pity. With age, she came to an inner peace which overshadows the bustling activity of other characters. After all, she was a link with Emerson, whom James characterized in 1907 as "the first, and the one really rare, American spirit in letters."[19] As an artist, James wanted the model to stand still, and he resented the fussy interference of reformers. As a man, he found the appeal of courage too strong to be denied, even in Miss Birdseye.

III   The Princess Casamassima (1885-86)

For many readers the least representative of Jamesian novels is *The Princess Casamassima*. It is a serious treatment of the theme of political revolution, a threat underlined in 1886 by riots in Chicago and in London. James's letters show that his concern with social corruption was deeper than is commonly believed. Moreover, he had his friend Turgenev's *Virgin Soil* (1876) as a model for theme, characters, and situations.[20] James's own earlier novel, *Roderick Hudson,* supplied the title character. Christina Light, forced by her mother to marry an Italian prince rather than the American sculptor, is shown in the later novel as alienated from her husband and as antagonistic to the aristocratic society she now knows so well. The Princess, however, is not the central character in the revolutionary novel, and she does not appear in the first quarter of it.

The story begins with Amanda Pynsent, a spinster seamstress who is bringing up a small boy named Hyacinth Robinson. Amanda's friend tells her that the boy's mother is dying in prison and passionately desires to see her son. The boy is too young to understand that his mother is in prison for killing his father, a nobleman who refused to acknowledge his illegitimate son Hyacinth. After he sees the strange old woman in the disagreeable prison ward, Hyacinth puzzles over the incident and gradually comes to understand it. He continues to live with "Pinnie," and, as he has some taste and cleverness, gets a job in a bookbinder's shop. Into his dull, placid existence comes Millicent Henning,—a girl he had known as a childhood neighbor in "the Plice"—now a shopgirl of bold beauty and pert manner. She is curious about Hyacinth and one day stops at Pinnie's to inquire about him. Pinnie distrusts Millicent, but, when Hyacinth comes in from work, he remembers her kindly and is pleased to renew acquaintance. Millicent irritates Hyacinth by the tawdriness of her taste, the airs of her low-class snobbery (she is shocked that he wears an apron at the bookbinder's), the boldness of her demands for entertainment. Yet there is something dependable in her friendship, some solace in their common recollection of childhood poverty. A full-fledged romance never develops, but, as Millicent comes on the scene from time to time, romance remains a possibility.

Hyacinth has a variety of other friends. Mr. Vetch, a violinist in Lomax Place, is confidant to Pinnie, and helps to get Hyacinth his job at the bookbinder's. There Hyacinth meets Poupin, a fine craftsman and a political exile from France. Through Poupin, Hyacinth meets Paul Muniment, a working-class revolutionary and his invalid sister Rose. The Muniments are befriended by Lady Aurora, the unmarried daughter of a peer and an aristocrat of generous sympathy for the poor. Despite these friendships, Hyacinth is often vaguely unhappy: "In such hours the great roaring indifferent world of London seemed to him a huge organization for mocking at his poverty, at his inanition; and then its vulgarest ornaments, the windows of third-rate jewellers, the young man in a white tie and a crush-hat who dandled by on his way to a dinner-party in a hansom that nearly ran over one—these familiar phenomena became symbolic, insolent, defiant, took on themselves to make him smart with the sense that *he* was above all out of it."[21]

When Hyacinth takes Millicent to the theater one night, he is startled to be invited into the box of Princess Casamassima during an intermission. Captain Sholto, companion of the Princess, has met Hyacinth casually at meetings of political clubs. The Princess, Sholto explains, "has a tremendous desire to meet some one who

looks at the whole business from your standpoint, don't you see?"
The Princess is such a person as Hyacinth has never known before.
Beautiful, accomplished, gay and serious by turns, she has an intimate knowledge of the great world to which Hyacinth's blood
entitles him but from which circumstances have excluded him. He
confides to her his impression of "the movement":

> "It's beyond anything I can say. Nothing of it appears above the
> surface; but there's an immense underworld peopled with a thou-
> sand forms of revolutionary passion and devotion. The manner in
> which it's organized is what astonished me. . . . And on top of
> it all society lives! People go and come, and buy and sell, and
> drink and dance, and make money and make love, and seem to
> know nothing and suspect nothing and think of nothing; and
> iniquities flourish, and the misery of half the world is prated
> about as a 'necessary evil,' and generations rot away and starve in
> the midst of it, and day follows day, and everything is for the best
> in the best of possible worlds. All that's one half of it; the other
> half is that everything's doomed! In silence, in darkness, but under
> the feet of each one of us, the revolution lives and works."[22]

By this time, Hyacinth has volunteered to undertake a dangerous
mission whenever the mysterious Diedrich Hoffendahl gives the
signal, and the last half of the novel proceeds under the shadow of
this ominous mission. When Pinnie dies, Hyacinth uses his small
inheritance for a trip to France and Italy on the advice of Vetch,
Pinnie's old friend. Hyacinth's natural good taste is captivated by
the beauties of art about him. He comes to doubt "the movement."
He writes the Princess:

> The monuments and treasures of art, the great palaces and prop-
> erties, the conquests of learning and taste, the general fabric of
> civilization as we know it, based if you will upon all the despotisms,
> the cruelties, the exclusions, the monopolies, and the rapacities of
> the past, but thanks to which, all the same, the world is less of a
> "bloody sell" and life more of a lark—our friend Hoffendahl seems
> to me to hold them too cheap and to wish to substitute for them
> something in which I can't somehow believe as I do in things
> with which the yearnings and the tears of generations have been
> mixed. . . . He would cut up the ceilings of the Veronese into
> strips, so that everyone might have a little piece. I don't want
> everyone to have a little piece of anything and I've a great horror
> of that kind of invidious jealousy which is at the bottom of the
> idea of redistribution.[23]

In this letter, Hyacinth insists that he is faithful to his vow to
the socialists and is not a traitor. On his return to London, he re-
news his association with the Princess, with Paul Muniment, and

with old Mr. Vetch. Vetch is increasingly apprehensive about Hyacinth's revolutionary activities, and at last he appeals to the Princess to "get the boy out of his muddle." She appeals in turn to Paul Muniment, but without success. When Hyacinth calls on the Poupins one evening, the agent is there with a letter of instructions for him. Hyacinth is to attend a certain party to assassinate a duke. On reaching his own room, Hyacinth finds Vetch waiting for him. In response to direct entreaties, Hyacinth promises: "I shall never do any of their work." Calling later on the Princess, Hyacinth does not tell her of his assignment. The next day he takes a final view of Millicent, without her observing him. When the Princess learns from Paul Muniment of Hyacinth's assignment, she goes to his room to investigate. Hyacinth has turned on himself the pistol intended for the duke.

James's grasp of lower-class London life in this novel is remarkable. In preparation for Hyacinth's visit to his mother just before she dies in prison, James himself went to Millbank Prison. "You see I am quite the Naturalist," he wrote his friend Perry.[24] No visit, however, could supply the details of the puzzled boy's mixture of revulsion and fascination. Pinnie, Mr. Vetch, Millicent, the Poupins, Paul and Rose Muniment, as well as Hyacinth himself, are sympathetic portraits, without sentimentality and without condescension. Hyacinth's letters, to be sure, have too much of James's fluency, but the ideas they express ring true to the young man's given temperament. The Princess is a convincing combination of whim and principle; she is too shrewd to be wholly naïve, but too undisciplined to be an effective revolutionary. The Prince, who comes to London in the vain effort to influence the Princess, and Madame Grandoni, companion to the Princess, are well drawn. Even Captain Sholto, intended to be a type and a convenience to the plot, is a lively figure as he angles for Millicent's interest.

With such a wealth of characters and situations, why did the novel fail? There was, it is true, some favorable opinion when it appeared, and there have been vigorous defenses of it in recent years, but even among Jamesians it is not a popular novel.[25] One reason is the vagueness of the revolutionary action in which Hyacinth is engaged. The duke is never identified. There is never any indication why he is to be assassinated. Hyacinth's suicide comes not from some personal unwillingness to kill this particular duke, but from his disaffection with "the movement" which he expressed in his letter to the Princess. The conflict between this disaffection and his earlier solemn promise remains too abstract, is too indirectly revealed. Hence the suicide seems melodramatic instead of truly dramatic, as intended. Despite James's considerable understanding of revolutionary psychology, he seems not completely at home with this central aspect of his subject. The most enduring memories of the novel are the streets of London and Paris, the visit Hyacinth makes to the great country house occupied for a time by the Princess, and the rooms occupied by Paul and Rose Muniment. Above all there is Lomax Place of the opening chapters, and its inhabitants: Pinnie, Hyacinth, and Mr. Vetch.

IV *Shorter Fiction: 1877-90*

It will be convenient to review James's tales of the late 1870's with those of the following decade. For this period there are twenty-five, besides "Daisy Miller," already discussed. These "tales," as James called them, vary from a brief anecdote like "Rose Agathe," which runs to seventy-five hundred words, to "The Aspern Papers" and "A London Life," which run to fifty thousand words each. A dozen others are over twenty thousand words in length. The short fiction of this period is overshadowed by James's extraordinary achievement in the full-length novel, yet the variety of character and situation in the shorter pieces helps substantially to demonstrate the richness of his observation, the fertility of his invention, and his thoroughly professional application to his chosen profession.

Of all these stories, "Rose Agathe" (published as "Theodolinde," 1878) is not only the shortest but the slightest; it illustrates in the simplest way what James meant by saying that a tale is an anecdote, "something that oddly happens to someone." The narrator of the story, who has invited a Parisian friend to dinner, watches the friend approach and stare in the window of a hairdresser's establishment below. The narrator concludes that his friend is smitten with the hairdresser's pretty wife. Numerous conversations build up this impression, and the speaker is only surprised at the frankness of his friend's expressed intention to take "her" home with him. In the end it is revealed that "she" is a blonde effigy in the hairdresser's window, coveted and finally secured for the friend's collection of *objets d'art*. This amusing tale is devoid of any serious interest, unless the reader gratuitously reflects that such an incident illustrates the power of preconception, the rigidity of our expectations. James himself does not point this heavy moral. Yet he tells the story with the finish of a craftsman.

Comparing the stories of these middle years with the earlier ones of 1864-76, one notices a generally higher level of craftsmanship. Beyond the skill, and perhaps an important cause of it, are the richer and more varied themes. The stories of these middle years may be loosely grouped under four themes: the international story set at least partly in America, dealing with Europeans in America or with Americans returned from Europe; international stories set in Europe; stories of courtship and marriage in which setting is of little importance; and stories dealing with writers.

V *Stories with American Settings*

"Four Meetings" (1877) tells the story of Caroline Spencer, a shy New York village girl much in love with Europe. Meeting the narrator when he visits her village, she is much awed by his account of his travels and his nightly visits to the French theater. The narrator warns her: "You've the great American disease, and you've got it 'bad'—the appetite, morbid and monstrous, for color and form, for the picturesque and the romantic at any price." A few months later, the narrator goes to Havre to meet his sister. There he sees Miss Spencer, who has been met by a cousin, eagerly enjoying the accent of France. Next morning the narrator sees her again and is astonished to learn that she is going home immediately, having loaned her cousin all her money because of his current misfortunes. Five years later the fourth meeting occurs in the New York village. Caroline Spencer has as a permanent guest the supposed widow of her cousin, now dead. "The Countess," as she calls herself, not only takes Caroline's support but treats her like a servant. Caroline's dream of European travel is over. Everything, she confesses, is different now. After talking briefly with the bogus "Countess" the narrator ironically concludes that Caroline will still see "something of that dear old Europe."

"An International Episode" (1878-79) is also critical of Europe but in a lighter vein. Lord Lambeth accompanies an English friend to America on a short business trip. When the two young men present their letter of introduction to Mr. Westgate, a New York businessman, he hospitably helps them with their business and then sends them to his home in Newport. Lord Lambeth is attracted to the unmarried Bessie Alden, sister of his hostess. The following year Bessie goes to London with Mrs. Westgate. Despite her hospitality to Lord Lambeth, Mrs. Westgate is experienced enough to realize that she and her sister may be snubbed in England. By chance, they meet Lord Lambeth, and he is very attentive; but, when he manages to have his mother and sister call on the Americans, the English ladies are very condescending. When Lord Lambeth proposes, Bessie refuses him, very much as Isabel Archer refuses Lord Warburton in *The Portrait of a Lady*.

The simple thread of action in "An International Episode" gives sufficient opportunity to juxtapose the manners of the two countries, very much to the advantage of the Americans. In New York the two young Englishmen are amusingly obtuse, finding the city "a rum-looking place." When Lord Lambeth expresses a wish to see Boston, Mr. Westgate chaffs him: "Oh, Lord Lambeth, wait till the great heat is over! . . . Boston in this weather would be very trying; it's not the temperature for intellectual exertion. At Boston, you know, you have to pass an examination at the city limits; and when you come away they give you a kind of degree." Mrs. Westgate, it is true, welcomes the two Englishmen to Newport with a "miniature torrent" of four uninterrupted pages of comment on her limited acquaintance with England. Bessie, however, dismays Lord Lambeth with her knowledge of English life in fiction. "You mustn't mind what you read," he comments. In London, when he attempts to show Bessie around, she is shocked by his ignorance of history. When she wants to visit Parliament, he thinks she will be bored to death. Bessie decides that he lacks interest in affairs, and she particularly objects to the failure of his class to seek the acquaintance of authors and artists. Bessie, in short, is an intelligent Daisy Miller; like Daisy, Bessie also is frank in manner, genuinely curious and observant, instinctively repelled by lethargy and by artificial customs and manners.[26]

"Lady Barberina" (1884) somewhat parallels "An International Episode" in that two English sisters marry American men. Lady Barb is the daughter of Lord and Lady Canterville. Jackson Lemon, a wealthy American doctor, becomes acquainted with Lady Barb in London and later asks to marry her. Lady Barb is strangely passive—this seems, indeed, part of her charm. Her parents dislike the idea of their daughter's marrying a doctor, and they are annoyed at Lemon's resistance to making financial settlements in the usual European style. The marriage takes place, however, and soon Lady Barb is established in a luxurious Fifth Avenue house. Unfortunately, American life and American people simply do not interest her. Her younger sister, Lady Agatha, visits her, takes at once to American life, and elopes with a Western man. Lady Barb returns to England; and, since she will set no date for going back to America, her husband joins her in London.

There is in "Lady Barberina" a remarkable alertness to a type of British aristocracy; assured and appropriate in its native setting, it is, nevertheless, rigid, unimaginative, and unadaptable. These negative qualities are portrayed without malice, especially since they are balanced by Lady Agatha's lively appreciation of American ways.

She saw that it was great fun to be a woman in America, and that this was the best way to enjoy the New York winter—the wonderful, brilliant New York winter . . . the perpetual liberties and walks, the rushings-out and the droppings-in, the intimacies, the endearments, the comicalities, the sleigh-bells, the cutters, the sunsets on the snow, the ice-parties in the frosty clearness, the bright, hot velvety houses . . . the suppers at restaurants after the play . . . and in all, through all, a kind of suffusion of bright, loud, friendly sound, which was very local, but very human.[27]

In "New England Winter" (1884), Florimond Daintry's impression of life in Boston is less flattering. Florimond has returned home after six years of art study in Paris. He is a supercilious young man, "a little vain, a little affected, a little pretentious, a little good-looking, a little amusing, a little spoiled, and at times a little tiresome." His widowed mother, who hopes that he will marry and settle down in Boston, even arranges that a distant cousin from Brooklyn spend the winter in Boston. Florimond, however, is more attracted to Mrs. Mesh, with whom the Brooklyn cousin is staying. When Florimond's mother learns this, she and Florimond sail for Europe. In this story James seems to have transferred to Florimond some of the impressions gathered during his stay in Boston in the winter of 1881-82. Yet Florimond, like James, discovered that "even amid the simple civilization of New England there was material for the naturalist. . . ."[28]

"Pandora" (1884) draws on James's visit to Washington in 1882. Pandora Day, a young American girl returning home on a German steamer, meets Count Otto Vogelstein, who is assuming a position at the German embassy in Washington. The Count is described as "a stiff conservative, a Junker of Junkers," antagonistic to democracy. The casualness of his meeting with Pandora and her free manner, reminiscent of Daisy Miller, fascinate the Count. Two years later he meets Pandora at a Washington party and later on a boat trip to Mount Vernon. Just as the Count's reserve toward Pandora is breaking down, he learns that she is engaged. He also learns that her fiancé's appointment as Minister to Holland is partly due to Pandora's personal acquaintance with the President. In truth, the Count has observed that strange phenomenon described to him by an American woman as "the self-made girl." An amusing instance of Pandora's manner is her conversation with the President at the Washington party. When she hears the President say that his wife will wonder why he doesn't come home, Pandora "benevolently" inquires: "Why didn't you bring her with you?" The President patiently explains that his wife's sister is visiting her. Pandora extends the conversation until the President casually invites her to call some evening.

VI *Americans Abroad*

"The Pension Beaurepas" (1879) is a good example of how James used the European setting to create a perspective on American traits. The story is an inconclusive juxtaposition of two American families staying in Geneva. Mr. Ruck, traveling for his health and not finding it, is the typical uncultivated but polite American who has lived only for buying and selling; his wife and daughter live only for buying. Mrs. Church, who brings her daughter to the same pension, is the typical demanding, managerial widow who is anxious to protect her daughter from vulgar American influences. On the slenderest evidence, Mrs. Church decides that Sophy Ruck is vulgar and thereupon leaves the pension. The narrator is a tolerant young American, well disposed to both young ladies.

"The Point of View" (1882), through its eight loosely related letters, is a sequel of sorts. Aurora Church, now in New York, writes the first and last of these letters to a friend in Paris; in them she makes clear her lack of success in finding a husband. Aurora's first letter, followed by one from her mother to a friend in Geneva, comments in a helpless way about the incomprehensible changes in American life during her absence of several years. Then follow letters from fellow-passengers who had met the returning Churches on shipboard. There is Mr. Louis Leverett, a cultivated Bostonian in love with "the rich, the deep, the dark Old World" (*Complete Tales,* IV, 503). In contrast is Marcellus Cockerel, who rejoices that a trip abroad has helped him to get "Europe off my back" (512). He rejoices in American trains and democratic manners. "As for manners," he comments, "there are bad manners everywhere, but an aristocracy is bad manners organized" (515). Cockerel had seriously thought of marrying Aurora Church, but gave up the idea: "She has been spoiled by Europe!" (516).

Despite the narrative weakness of these two stories, James was never wittier in his exposure of American faults and of European pretenses. A gratuitous inclusion in "The Point of View" is a letter from Mr. Antrobus, a member of Parliament. As he travels about America with his portable tin bathtub, the bewildered Mr. Antrobus describes in a long letter to his wife the peculiar arrangements of an American sleeping car. Mr. Antrobus is a sufficient refutation of the charge that James was Anglophilic without reservation.[29]

Loosely related to these stories is "A Bundle of Letters" (1879), centering about Miss Miranda Hope, a schoolmistress of Bangor, Maine. Miss Hope, who is traveling alone in Europe, is described in the letters of various people she meets. One is Louis Leverett, the cultured Bostonian who appears in "The Point of View." Of Miranda

Hope, Leverett writes a friend that she is a specimen "of the emancipated young American girl—practical, positive, passionless, subtle, and knowing, as you please, either too much or too little." Miranda expresses in one of her letters little interest in Leverett; he is too Bostonian: "I ought to direct all my efforts to European culture now," she writes her mother, "and keep Boston to finish off with." A New York girl thinks Miranda a specimen of "artless Yankeeism." A French tutor quite misinterprets her frank manner. As for Miranda herself, her frequent slighting reference to a certain William Platt of Bangor conveys to the reader her romantic interest in that young man, and it is evident in her last letter that she looks forward to returning home. A notable feature of these stories told in letters is James's skill in mimicry, for each correspondent writes with amusing self-characterization. Nowhere is the elaborate Jamesian epistolary style in evidence.[30]

"The Modern Warning" (published as "The Two Countries," 1888) strikes a serious note. Against the wishes of her anti-British brother, Agatha Grice marries Sir Rufus Chasemore. Later, the Chasemores visit America, and Sir Rufus travels widely, basing a book on his rather unfavorable observations. When Agatha reads the proofs of *The Modern Warning*, she persuades her husband not to publish it. Then she withdraws her objections, but poisons herself rather than face the displeasure of her brother, who is coming to London to visit her. Sir Rufus and his brother-in-law learn of her death together. The impact of this story is hampered by the fact that, characteristically, James tells the reader too little about the content of *The Modern Warning*.

VII *Stories of Courtship and Marriage*

"Longstaff's Marriage" (1878) concerns two Americans in Europe, but the setting is incidental in developing a situation—a delayed and unsatisfactory marriage—that has no bearing on the nationality of the characters.

"Diary of a Man of Fifty" (1879) recalls a lover's quarrel which prevented marriage to a charming widow years before. The keeper of the diary is reminded of the past by the young man in love with his lady's daughter. When he confides his story, the older man is told by the younger, "Depend upon it you were wrong." That the story is set in Italy permits some nostalgic description, but is otherwise unimportant.

"The Siege of London" (1883) uses a wealthy American widow of damaged reputation to test the London social code. This story is a conscious variation on the French play *Demi-Monde*. In an essay of 1878, James had discussed *Demi-Monde* as representing a French rather than an English attitude. An English audience, he then thought, would have felt: "I say, that's not fair game. Can't you let the poor woman alone?"[31] "Georgina's Reasons" (1884) treats a secret marriage between a young American naval officer and a girl whose parents oppose the match. Later the girl remarries, forcing her husband to keep the secret of the earlier marriage.

Several other stories are more credible treatments of the general theme of jilted lovers. "Mrs. Temperly" (originally "Cousin Maria," 1887) centers in a mother who repeatedly postpones the marriage of her daughter because she has plans for a more ambitious match. In "Louisa Pallant" (1888), the story of a double jilting, the narrator tells how Louisa Pallant jilted him as a young man. Years later, when his nephew is in love with Louisa's daughter, Louisa herself has the generosity to break up the match because she knows her daughter is utterly selfish. "Patagonia" (1888) is titled for the name of the ship on which Grace Mavis sails to meet her American fiancé, who has been studying architecture in Europe for several years. On shipboard, Grace falls in love with the son of her traveling companion. Realizing that he does not love her and that she no longer loves her fiancé, Grace commits suicide by jumping overboard. The narrator has the melancholy task of explaining to Grace's fiancé what has happened. In "The Solution" (1890), the theme of jilting is turned to comic effect. A young American, attached to the embassy in Rome, is tricked by two young diplomats into believing that he has compromised a young girl to whom he is not at all attracted. He immediately proposes, and is accepted. His companions, seeing that their joke has gone too far, seek the aid of an agreeable English widow. She extricates the young American from his engagement and then marries the chivalrous young man herself.

"The Path of Duty" (1884), though not a story of a jilted lover, does involve renunciation of a special kind. Ambrose Tester, heir to a baronetcy, is in love with Lady Vandeleur, the wife of another nobleman. After some struggle with himself, Tester takes the advice of the narrator (a woman friend) and becomes engaged to a young woman named Jocelinde, who is very much in love with him. At this point Lady Vandeleur's husband dies. Tester holds to his engagement and marries Jocelinde, but the marriage is disturbed by her awareness that Lady Vandeleur has great attraction for Tester. The narrator, whose advice Tester has followed, is apprehensive.

In all of these stories there is a strong analytical interest in the logic of the situation and its development, but the characters have little intrinsic interest. All the stories are intelligent in approach and competent in treatment; they often seem contrived. An extreme example of contrivance is "Impressions of a Cousin" (1883). This story of some thirty-five thousand words is a double romance developed through false leads. The cousin records in a diary the relationship of Eunice, a New York heiress, to a Mr. Caliph, executor of the family estate. Mr. Caliph introduces to Eunice his stepbrother Adrian Frank, and at one point it appears that he wants Eunice to marry Adrian in order to cover some mishandling of Eunice's funds. Eunice, however, retains her faith in Caliph and refuses to marry Adrian. Adrian then turns his attention to the diary-keeping cousin. She refuses him; but later, when it appears that Caliph is to marry Eunice, the cousin conditionally accepts Adrian.

Far more impressive is James's achievement in "A London Life" (1888). This fifty-thousand word narrative points toward *What Maisie Knew* (1898) and to *The Awkward Age* (1898-99), for all three are fine blends of analysis and of brooding insight applied to the corruption of marriage. Laura Wing, a young American girl of great innocence, is living with her sister Selina in England. Laura is shocked to discover that Selina and her husband Lionel Berrington now hate each other. They are frequently away from their two small boys, whom they profess to love. Eventually Selina runs off with an admirer, giving Lionel a chance to get the divorce he wants. While Laura witnesses these developments in horror, she has the friendship of Lady Davenant, a worldly, imperious old lady who sees with tenderness Laura's plight. It is Lady Davenant who encourages a romance between Laura and a handsome American who arrives in London with a letter of introduction to the Berringtons. At the end of the story, Laura has failed to persuade Selina to go back to her husband and has herself gone back to America. Wendover has still to persuade Laura to marry him.

The story is not technically strong, but readers who associate James with an unrealistic gentility will find "A London Life" a remarkably candid treatment of domestic discord. Lionel, who is rather fond of Laura, defends to her his own misconduct by saying of his wife: "She'd like to stamp on me and hear me crack like a black beetle, and she never opens her mouth but she insults me." Selina's duplicity, the meanness with which she tries to involve Laura in her final stratagem, and her ready vindictiveness make Selina one of James's most disagreeable women. Laura gains by contrast, but it is evident that her innocence is inadequate to cope with the world in which she finds herself. As for Lady Davenant, she is an appealing result of aristocratic privilege. In her last interview with Wendover, she tries to clear up the misunderstanding between him and Laura: "Don't be afraid to tell me I'm meddling with what doesn't concern me. . . . Of course I know I'm meddling; I sent for you here to meddle. Who wouldn't for that fine creature? She makes one melt."[32]

VIII   *Authors and an Artist*

"The Author of Beltraffio" (1884) is a study in the incompatibility of an author and his wife. A young admirer of novelist Mark Ambient tells of a thirty-six hour visit to the writer's country home. The narrator soon becomes aware that Mrs. Ambient has no interest in her husband's work; in fact, she dislikes and distrusts it. There is an obvious conflict between husband and wife for the affection of their beautiful seven-year-old boy. When the boy becomes ill, the mother shuts him away from his father and even from the doctor. As a result, the boy dies. The narrator feels involved because it is he who persuades Mrs. Ambient to read the proof sheets of her husband's latest and greatest novel. From Ambient's sister comes this explanation of the mother's fear for her son: "The book gave her a horror; she determined to rescue him—to prevent him from ever being touched."

This seemingly implausible action is made surprisingly convincing. Mrs. Ambient has great beauty of the Romney and Gainsborough type, and part of Ambient's charm is his quiet forbearance toward his wife's antagonism. Ambient's sister, too, lends credibility since the strangeness of the situation apparent to the narrator is accepted by the sister as an oddity of the household so established that it is part of the natural order. Notable is the way in which the quality of Ambient's writing is suggested. Nothing is said of its content. On a walk through the fields, "everything was full of expression" for Ambient. Later he says, "I want to give the impression of life itself." He wants not only to make his work firm and bright but to avoid the "horrible sandy stretches." He cares for beauty: "I delight in it, I adore it, I think of it continually, I try to produce it, to reproduce it. My wife holds that we shouldn't cultivate or enjoy it without extraordinary precautions and reserves. She's always afraid of it, always on her guard." Thus the spirit of Ambient's writing is conveyed without any synopsis of *Beltraffio*.[33]

"The Lesson of the Master" (1888) turns also on the marriage of a writer and its effect on his aims. Paul Overt, a young writer, is invited to a weekend party where he meets St. George, the great novelist whom he admires. Mrs. St. George and a young woman, Marian Fancourt, are also there. St. George, noticing that Overt is attracted to Miss Fancourt, warns Overt against marriage as an interference with his career. Overt abruptly leaves England to put temptation out of his reach. Sometime later he hears of Mrs. St. George's death. Overt finally decides to return to England, hoping to marry Miss Fancourt, only to find that St. George has already made her his second wife. St. George admits to Paul that he married the girl partly to "save" Paul; he says further that he has now given up writing. The story closes with Paul's ironic fear that St. George will now, under the inspiration of Marian Fancourt, write his great novel after all and disprove his own theory. So far, St. George has published nothing since his second marriage. In his various talks with Paul, St. George firmly holds to the opinion that marriage is incompatible with writing. His first wife burned the only book he himself valued; the others he has written to earn the money needed to support his expensive family. Paul, he hopes, will remain the true artist, striving for "the concentration, the finish, the independence" demanded by an artistic conscience. The unwary reader may take this story as a rationalization by James for never having married. The ironic ending seems to imply that, though the theory expounded by St. George sounds plausible, one can never be sure.

"The Liar" (1888) is the story of a famous painter, Oliver Lyon, who revenges himself on a woman who once refused him: Lyon paints a portrait of her husband that shows him up as an inveterate liar. The early part of the story throws Lyon in the company of Colonel Capadose and his beautiful wife. The Colonel is notorious as an "abundant" but not "malignant" liar: he would himself laugh when caught in a falsehood, as if the whole thing were a joke. When the portrait is nearly finished, the Capadoses go to Lyon's studio while the painter is away. Horrified at the ugly revelation, they slash the canvas to ribbons. Lyon, coming back unexpectedly, is able to witness the vandalism without being seen himself. Later, the Capadoses make discreet inquiries about the portrait and are properly shocked to learn that it has been destroyed. Speaking to the painter, Mrs. Capadose has the last word: "For you, I am very sorry. But you must remember that I have the original!" In "The Liar" James himself solves a difficult artistic problem of balance. The reader, like Lyon, feels the shock of Mrs. Capadose's being forced to lie to back up her husband. Yet the greater shock comes from Lyon's calculated cruelty toward a woman he once loved. So real is this pattern of mixed motives that the reader is unlikely to deliberate on the fundamental implausibility of a portrait's being so literal an indictment of the liar.

IX The Reverberator (1888)

Though *The Reverberator* hardly deserves the adjective "immortal" conferred on it by William James,[34] it is one of Henry James's short productions which goes far to correct the stereotyped impression that he is too serious, "artistic," and involved to be enjoyed. This short novel takes its title from the gossipy newspaper served by George Flack, its Paris reporter. Flack is a friend of Francie Dosson, an American girl who becomes engaged to Gaston Probert, American by birth but French by upbringing and family connections. The two young people meet in the studio of an American artist who is painting Francie's portrait. Gaston's father and his sisters are very reluctant to accept Francie, her frumpish sister Delia, and the good-natured, homespun Mr. Dosson, who has indulgently brought his two daughters to Europe for an indefinite stay. With great patience, Gaston wins over his family; but, while Gaston makes a business trip to America, Flack "writes up" Francie's engagement, including a great deal of spicy detail about the Proberts. They are scandalized, and incredulous that Francie could have given such an interview under the illusion that they would be pleased. When Gaston returns to Paris, he first sides with his family and urges Francie to disavow her part in the affair. Francie now realizes that she made a horrible mistake, but she is too honest to deny her responsibility. She breaks her engagement with Gaston, and at last he sees that Francie means more to him than his family. The engagement is renewed, and Gaston comes to Francie in good American fashion—without a financial settlement from his family. Relieved, Francie's father comments: "Well, that makes me feel better."

If the ending of *The Reverberator* is as implausible as the rejection of Newman by the Bellegardes in *The American,* the light comedy tone of the novel seems congenial to the author. About intimate journalism, always a good subject for Jamesian satire, Flack gives this vision of the future development of his newspaper: "There are ten thousand things that haven't been done, and I'm going to do them. The society-news of every quarter of the globe, furnished by the prominent members themselves—oh, *they* can be fixed—you'll see!—from day to day and from hour to hour and served up at every breakfast-table in the United States—that's what the American people want and that's what the American people are going to have." Aside from Flack, who is too brash for subtle treatment, satire on both Americans and French is light and good-natured. When Gaston asks his father how he likes Francie, the old man (an expatriate American) replies: "She talks about 'Parus,' my dear boy." After Francie confronts the anguished Proberts and is rebuked by nearly every member of the family, the husband of one of Gaston's sisters accompanies Francie to her carriage, opens the door for her, and murmurs: "You are charming, mademoiselle—charming, charming!"[35]

X *"The Aspern Papers"* (1888)

Besides *The Reverberator*, James published in 1888 six tales, from twenty to fifty thousand words long. "The Aspern Papers," the longest of these, is often thought of as a short novel, but by James's definition it is "an anecdote" and therefore a tale.[36] In either category, it is one of James's most distinguished fictions. The origin of "The Aspern Papers" is an anecdote James heard in Florence early in 1887. Part of his notebook entry illustrates his working methods at this time:

> Hamilton (V. L.'s brother) told me a curious thing of Capt. Silsbee— the Boston art-critic and Shelley-worshipper; that is of a curious adventure of his. Miss Claremont, Byron's *ci-devant* mistress (the mother of Allegra) was living, until lately, here in Florence, at a great age, 80 or thereabouts, and with her lived her niece, a younger Miss Claremont—of about 50. Silsbee knew that they had interesting papers—letters of Shelley's and Byron's—he had known it for a long time and cherished the idea of getting hold of them. To this end he laid the plan of going to lodge with the Misses Claremont—hoping that the old lady in view of her great age and failing condition would die while he was there, so that he might put his hand upon the documents, which she hugged close in life. He carried out this scheme—and things *se passèrent* as he had expected. The old woman *did* die—and then he approached the younger one—the old maid of 50—on the subject of his desires. Her answer was—"I will give you all the letters if you will marry me!" H. says that Silsbee *court encore* (*Notebooks*, 71-72).

That Silsbee "is running yet" is the essence of this comic anecdote as James records it. In the situation he sees other possibilities, however, which readily appear as "The Aspern Papers" is reviewed. The scene of the story becomes Venice instead of Florence; and Jeffrey Aspern, a fictitious American poet, supposed to have come to Italy about 1820, takes the place of Shelley and Byron. Thus James, freed of hampering historical fact, can develop the idea which he himself projected into the situation of the anecdote. A young American publisher (never named in the story) has stopped in London on his way to Venice and has learned of an aged Miss Bordereau, also American, who is said to have known Aspern in her youth. It is likely that she still possesses letters written by Aspern which the publisher believes would make his fortune if he could publish them. A friend in Venice, Mrs. Prest, who knows Miss Bordereau and her niece, realizes that they need money. She therefore suggests that the publisher take rooms in their dilapidated old palace. The publisher meets the two ladies and, despite their suspicions, obtains rooms at a high rental. He makes little progress, however, and a casual expression of interest in Jeffrey Aspern puts young Miss Tita on her guard. The publisher perseveres by sending flowers and by occasionally inviting Miss Tita to ride with him in a gondola. One day she confides that her aunt does have letters of Jeffrey Aspern, and later Miss Bordereau herself shows a small oval portrait of Aspern done by her father. This she offers for a thousand pounds.

That night the old lady becomes seriously ill. The publisher, failing to persuade Tita to bring him the Aspern Papers, decides to hunt for them himself. He is apprehended by the old lady herself with a passionate, furious exclamation: "Ah, you publishing scoundrel!" In a spasm she then falls back into Miss Tita's arms. The young man leaves Venice for several days and learns on his return that old Miss Bordereau did indeed die. Miss Tita does not reproach him; she even gives him the oval portrait of Aspern. The papers, however, she will not show, believing that her aunt wished them destroyed. But there is a way, she points out. If the young man were not a stranger, if in short he were Tita's husband, then the letters could be shared. The price is too high. The young man records his feeling: "I couldn't, for a bundle of old tattered papers, marry a ridiculous pathetic provincial old woman" (NY XII, 137). Next day Tita seems strangely beautiful, and he is almost ready to pay the price. Then she tells him that she has at last destroyed the papers, burning them one by one. The oval portrait of Aspern still hangs above the publisher's writing table as a reminder of the chagrin he feels over the whole episode.

Thus the comic anecdote has been transformed into a serious story of rich texture. The nineteenth-century idealization of Shelley has been transferred to a fictitious American poet. The publisher's conspiracy is developed as a mean deception of two defenseless women and as a gross invasion of privacy. The charm of Venice is evoked, as, for instance, Tita sits with the publisher one evening in the garden: "we were still sitting there when I heard midnight ring out from those clear bells of Venice which vibrate with a solemnity of their own over the lagoon and hold the air so much more than the chimes of other places" (56).

Had James written only *The Portrait of a Lady* and "The Aspern Papers" in the 1880's his place in the development of fiction would be secure. As has been seen, however, he achieved a great deal more.

CHAPTER 4

The Tragic Muse (1889-1890):
Dramatic Years

IN JANUARY, 1889, appeared the first installment of *The Tragic Muse;* a novel of well over two hundred thousand words, it was to run serially in the *Atlantic* until May, 1890. In May, 1889, James noted that he had agreed to dramatize *The American* for Edward Compton, a rising young actor-manager in England.[1] Thus the invitation to become a dramatist came at a time when James was giving much thought to the stage, for in *The Tragic Muse* Nick Dormer, the painter, and Peter Sherringham, the diplomat, are both much concerned with Miriam Rooth, the talented young actress they meet in Paris. The novel therefore provides an approach to what many consider the strange and wasted years of James's dramatic experiment.

The complementary stories of the novel are interwoven. Nick Dormer, a handsome, brilliant young man, wants to be a painter but the tradition of his family pushes him toward a political career. Nick's father, now dead, has made the kind of friends that can help Nick. The widowed mother not only passionately desires a political career for her son; she sees that such a career will enhance the family's modest fortune and assist the marriage of Nick's two sisters. At the beginning of the novel, Nick has already served a short term in Parliament, but is now out of office. The Dormers are enjoying a holiday in Paris. Also in Paris is Julia Dallow, Nick's cousin, a wealthy and attractive widow of political influence. News comes that the incumbent for Harsh is dead, and Julia is ready to back Nick in a campaign for the vacant seat. Nick is reluctant, for his brief experience in the House has made him condescending toward a political career. He recognizes that he cannot be both a politician and an artist.

Without genuinely committing himself, Nick enters the campaign, wins the election, and finds himself more than ever attracted to Julia. Sensing his indecision, Julia postpones a formal engagement, but among their friends it is regarded as settled. A wealthy old family friend, Mr. Carteret, is ready to leave to Nick a substantial fortune, but he cannily wants the engagement definite. The temptation to secure Mr. Carteret's handsome legacy, however, rouses Nick's independence. He takes up painting again, and quarrels with Julia. As a result, he informs Mr. Carteret that both his engagement and his political career are ended; Carteret disinherits him. At the close of the novel, Nick is still not reunited to Julia, but she continues to be on friendly terms with his mother and sisters.

The other story concerns Julia's brother, Peter Sherringham. Peter is attached to the British embassy in Paris, and thus conveniently joins his sister and the Dormers in the opening chapters. By chance, an old Oxford friend of Nick's, one Gabriel Nash, a dilettante of the arts with no visible means of support, also turns up in Paris. Nash is interested in Miriam Rooth, a beautiful young girl who aspires to be an actress. Peter, who is passionately fond of the theater, is impressed with Miriam's beauty; and he takes her to a dramatic coach he knows. Despite Miriam's shallow, coarse manner, she captivates Peter. He realizes she is not the proper person for a diplomat to marry, and he attempts to escape her by taking a long leave in England and later by getting himself transferred to Central America. Returning to London for Miriam's triumphal performance of Shakespeare's Juliet, Peter passionately implores Miriam to marry him, only to discover that she has quietly married her stage manager three days before. Somewhat later, Peter turns to Nick's sister Biddy, who has waited for him adoringly throughout the novel.

Besides the family relationships, Miriam is the chief link between the two stories. Even before the affair between Miriam and Peter develops, Miriam attracts Nick as a fascinating model. Miriam likes Nick, but she is chiefly interested in the advantage of being painted by a man of Nick's social position. For a time a romantic interest between them seems possible, but it never develops. When Julia Dallow accidentally finds Miriam in Nick's studio and is obviously annoyed, Miriam is unconcerned. The quarrel that arises between Nick and Julia is none of her affair. There is in Miriam a kind of ruthless professional ambition and competence, as Mme. Carré, the Parisian dramatic coach, sees. Miriam wants success on the stage and she achieves it. Realistically, she accepts without complaint the convention that, though an actress may be sought out by the most talented and intellectual men, she may never enter a lady's drawing room.

Gabriel Nash, Miriam's original sponsor, wanders in and out of the story; he encourages Nick's interest in art, shares Peter's fondness for the theater, and pokes fun at middle-class respectability. "I work in life," he says loftily, when asked about his occupation.

He has visited "a delightful little spot" in Spain, "where a wild fig-tree grows in the south wall." When Nick asks him what he did there, Nash replies: "I lay down on the first green grass—I liked it." Nash can praise Nick's capacity for seeing, but, when Nick turns his painter's eye on Nash himself, Nash is uncomfortable; the picture remains unfinished, "gradually fading from the canvas."[2]

Nick is also seen to advantage in Chapter XV, when he proposes to Julia. Since it is so obviously to his interest to marry her, it must be shown that he does not propose for this reason. He and Julia row out on a little lake to an island where there is a little rococo, eighteenth-century pavilion. This odd place typifies the kind of detachment Nick longs for, but Julia, characteristically, takes little interest in it; she wants to talk politics instead. Their differences come out in a bitter-sweet way, and Nick's proposal is prompted by an affectionate sympathy which falls just short of real love.

The Tragic Muse is in the old sense a novel of events. Things happen. The two stories "turn out." It is also a novel of character analysis and of ideas. Painting, the theater, and art in general are central interests of the chief characters. What they say about these topics are natural comments that help to characterize. Yet there is no doubt that James saw possibilities for indirectly emphasizing views of his own. Gabriel Nash's airy estheticism, for example, is in part James's way of showing Oscar Wilde in a comic light. Madame Carré's belittling remarks of the British stage—Shakespeare is England's only playwright, she says—have something of James's own condescension toward the same stage at just the time he was to try to conquer it. Gabriel Nash speaks of "the essentially brutal nature of the modern audience" (57-58) and of the necessity for dramatists to defer to the rigid schedules of suburban trains. "What crudity compared with what the novelist does!" he exclaims. Peter Sherringham, although devoted to the theater, admits its faults in England: "The place is given up to abominable dialects and individual tricks, any vulgarity flourishes, and on the top of it all the Americans, with every conceivable crudity, come in to make confusion worse confounded" (161). Moreover: "In London the drama is already smothered in scenery; the interpretation scrambles off as it can."

These comments, of course, are in character, and they show the exaggeration natural to lively argument. Yet it is striking that in this long novel no one ever seriously defends the stage. Miriam's interest in it is governed by cynical ambition. And it is the omniscient author who makes the harsh comment on Miriam's triumphal representation of Juliet: "The great childish audience, gaping at her points, expanded there before her like a lap to catch flowers."[3]

I *Theater-Goer and Adapter*

If James had so low an opinion of the British stage, why then did he decide to write for it? Money was a prime consideration. As he recorded in his notebook Compton's request that he dramatize *The American*, he added: "Of how little money the novel makes for me I needn't discourse here." He spoke of "the novel" in a general way, and there are many references in his letters of this period to his lack of popular success in the 1880's. He seems to have reasoned that if lesser talents could make money in the theater, so might he. In 1890 he wrote his brother William that *The Tragic Muse* would be his last long novel (*Letters*, I, 163).

A more positive reason for turning dramatist, however, was James's life-long, passionate interest in the theater. His first auto-biographical volume makes much of his early delight. Writing about 1910, he recalled dozens of plays, actors, and theaters of the 1850's in New York: Dion Boucicault's comedies and melodramas; versions of Dickens; *Uncle Tom's Cabin;* Edwin Booth; Miss Julia Bennett, "fresh from the triumphs at the Haymarket"; and "Miss Kate Horn in Nan the Good-for-nothing"; Wallack's; Mr. Barnum's Lecture Room; and the National Theatre. The first article James submitted for publication (apparently it never appeared) was a tribute to Maggie Mitchell in *Fanchon the Cricket*, a translated German play James saw in Boston.[4]

Though his early magazine writing was largely book reviews and travel articles, he had published by 1890 more than twenty articles on the drama of Boston, New York, Paris, and London. There is in these articles a certain condescension. James comments with regard to a bad play in New York: "The public at large is very ignorant and very good-natured, and anything is possible." He finds Henry Irving "decidedly incomplete and amateurish." In 1880 he suggests that "the art of writing a play has become a lost one with the English race." On the other hand, James was always pleased by his frequent sampling of the Paris stage. He delighted especially in the comic art of Coquelin, once his schoolmate. Salvini's portrayal of Lear, seen in Boston (1883) he thought magnificent; his Othello (London, 1884) "a study of pure feeling." As early as 1878 James wrote to William: "My inspection of the French theatre will fructify. I have thoroughly mastered Dumas, Augier, and Sardou . . . and I know all they know and a great deal more besides."[5]

Before Compton's request for a dramatic version of *The American* in 1889, James had in minor ways tried his hand at the dramatic form. From 1869 to 1872 he had published three stories in dialogue —farces of the kind in which Howells was later to be so successful.

"Pyramus and Thisbe," for example, treats lightly and amusingly a flirtation between Catherine, a music teacher, and Stephen, a journalist, who live in the same rooming house. Catherine objects to his noise and tobacco smoke; Stephen has no taste for music. But when they find they must move from the rooming house, they decide they will house-hunt together. "Still Waters" and "A Change of Heart" are more elaborate in plot but equally artificial.[6]

These three short pieces, about twenty-five thousand words in all, may be regarded as finger exercises in dialogue. There is neither space nor time for character development. Resolution of situations must be contrived, with heavy reliance on asides and soliloquies. Apparently these pieces were never performed, though amateurs might have had fun with them. Occasionally James's wit flashes, and in the main the dialogue is clear and simple. It is easy to see why James would write these exercises in dialogue, harder to see why, even in his youth, he would publish them. "Still Waters," however, was a gift to charity, appearing in a publication for the benefit of French sufferers in the Franco-Prussian War.

James's next dramatic exploit was a version of "Daisy Miller," intended for the New York stage in 1882. It is not clear whether the idea of dramatizing this popular story originated with James. He did actively negotiate with Daniel Frohman, manager of the Madison Square Theatre, who rejected the play because he thought it too literary. Returning to London that summer, James failed to interest an English producer in the play. He finally sold the play to the *Atlantic Monthly* for a thousand dollars. It appeared serially in 1883 and in book form in 1884.[7]

The play *Daisy Miller* has generally been considered an inferior version of the story, and in particular the happy ending provided is objected to. Instead of Daisy's death and Winterbourne's belated recognition of her quality, their marriage is in prospect at the end of the play. Winterbourne's friend in Geneva, barely alluded to in the story, becomes in the play Madame de Katkoff. This lady is blackmailed by Eugenio, the Italian servant, into continuing her flirtation with Winterbourne. Eugenio, in turn, hopes to be rewarded for smoothing the path of Giovanelli to successful courtship of Daisy. Further complication is added by introducing Alice Durant as a cousin of Winterbourne; his aunt, Mrs. Costello, intends for her to captivate him. During carnival time, Alice becomes engaged to Charles Reverdy, a young American provided by the playwright for this purpose. Madame de Katcoff, before it is too late, confesses her perfidy to Winterbourne, who promptly rescues Daisy from Giovanelli.

Thus the quiet little story of Daisy Miller is transformed into a theatrical affair of considerable bustle. The attention so effectively focused on Daisy, as seen through Winterbourne's eyes in the story, is now dispersed among several characters. Two of the best scenes of the story—the snubbing of Daisy by Mrs. Walker and the evening meeting of Daisy, Giovanelli, and Winterbourne in the Colosseum— are only briefly reported in the play. Daisy's fever, induced by that evening in the Colosseum, is likewise incidental. No doubt these changes show a certain inventiveness, but they are clearly made in the interest of supplying the play with conventional action. The constant dependence on asides and soliloquies, even when they are trivial or easily avoidable, shows further how far James was willing to accept the theatrical conventions of the period. In the main, the dialogue is not only acceptable but best where it is merely adapted from the story. The charm of leisurely ruminations, and of James's evocative description of the visit to the Castle of Chillon, is sadly missing.

James's dramatization of *The American* was completed in the spring of 1890. James received two hundred and fifty pounds in advance royalties, and dreamed of fifteen hundred a week when the play reached London. After some twenty-five performances in provincial towns, with moderate success, the play ran in London for seventy performances. Christopher Newman occasioned some laughter when he appeared in the opening scene with "a Noah-ark coat of yellowish brown, with blue facings and mother of pearl buttons as large as cheese plates," and one reviewer objected to the "somewhat hysterical" acting of the young American girl who played the part of Claire de Cintré. Nevertheless the play was kindly received (*Plays*, 186).

The play, despite the happy ending provided, seems more melodramatic than the novel. Compression into four acts causes some awkward sequences. In the second act, for example, when Claire comes on stage for the first time, she is evidently already acquainted with Newman; in the novel, their meeting is an important incident. In the same act, Claire's brother the Marquis and her mother must, during a large party at their home, give Newman a conference in which they reluctantly accept him as Claire's suitor. Later in the act, Lord Deepmere talks with Claire, who he has reason to believe is still interested in him. When he discovers otherwise, he accuses the family of bad faith, and Valentin offers satisfaction in a duel. Unaware of this, the elder Bellegardes consider that they have made a mistake, and that Lord Deepmere, his fortunes repaired by his recent trip to England, is the better match for Claire. These shifts of action come abruptly, without the reflections allowed to Newman in the novel. The fourth act of the play is crowded with events. The funeral of Valentin, killed in the duel, must be reported. Mrs. Bread must explain to Newman how Madame de Bellegarde poisoned her late husband. Madame de Bellegarde must be accused. Newman must pardon her. And finally, in gratitude, Claire must announce that she will, after all, marry Newman.

II   Theatricals (1894)

James was thoroughly caught up by the rehearsals and the production of *The American*. Despite the anguish of suspense, even the small measure of success he achieved was exciting. He was still sure that he could conquer the stage. Between the autumn of 1890 (when *The American* was in rehearsal) and the autumn of 1892, he wrote four original plays. Unable to get them produced, he published them in two volumes entitled *Theatricals* in June and December of 1894. In his prefatory note James admitted that these plays were "conceived and constructed wholly in the light of possible representation" and that their publication instead was a "humiliating confession of defeat."[8]

In *Tenants,* Norman Byng, on leave from the army, is in love with his father's ward, Mildred. According to the terms of the guardianship, Mildred, now only eighteen, must not marry until she is twenty-two. Reminded of this by Norman's father, Sir Frederick, Norman and Mildred agree to postpone any formal engagement. At this point a Mrs. Vibert calls to arrange the rental of the dower-house of the estate, and she and her son become the "tenants" of the title. In the conversation of Mrs. Vibert and Sir Frederick it is revealed that they were once lovers and that he is the father of her son Claude, now twenty. Sir Frederick is apprehensive about having Mrs. Vibert as a neighbor, but her old charm persuades him. In Norman's absence, Claude Vibert courts Mildred; and Mrs. Vibert and Sir Frederick themselves contemplate marriage. Norman returns suddenly, much opposed to his father's marriage since he thinks Mrs. Vibert has plotted to aid Claude's suit for Mildred. As the two young men quarrel, Mrs. Vibert tells them they are brothers. Claude's affection for his mother, despite this revelation, leads Mrs. Vibert to give up all thought of marrying Sir Frederick. Instead she exacts from him his consent to the marriage of Norman and Mildred. Having brought the two original lovers into accord with Sir Frederick, the "tenants" depart.

Disengaged is an elaborate adaptation of the idea in James's story "The Solution" (1889-90). Captain Prime, a guest of Sir Montagu Brisket, appears to compromise Blandina, Sir Montagu's niece. Prime thereupon proposes and is accepted, much to the pleasure of Blandina's mother, who had planned the match. The problem, then, at the end of the first act, is to get the honorable Captain Prime "disengaged." This is managed through the resourceful and sympathetic Mrs. Jasper, who eventually becomes engaged to Captain Prime and neatly traps another man into engagement with Sir Montagu's niece.

The Album begins with the return of Mark Bernal, the lost heir, just in time to inherit the fortune of old Mr. Benedict. Grace Jesmond, Mr. Benedict's loyal secretary, is pleased to see the false heir thwarted, but her motives are misunderstood. Eventually she becomes engaged to Mark Bernal, and the false heir makes amends by gracefully giving up his claims. The "Album," a sketchbook, is a mere device by which the identity of Mark Bernal is established.

The Reprobate is about Paul Doubleday, a mild young man closely supervised by two guardians because of a single youthful escapade. A third guardian is to be added by the marriage of his stepmother to Captain Chanter. At the end of the play, three marriages are arranged through such devices as the arrival of Captain Chanter's old flame, who is also the woman involved in Paul Doubleday's youthful escapade, a stolen photograph, incriminating letters, and assorted misunderstandings.

These four *Theatricals—Tenants, Disengaged, The Album, The Reprobate*—are curious productions for James. They are filled with conventional characters: wards, guardians, the woman with a past, the charming widow, the widower, the unwelcome suitor, the conveniently ignorant servant. The plotting is intricate—too intricate for easy reading. How far stage representation would clarify relationships, as it sometimes does, is arguable. The managers who rejected these plays obviously thought it would not sufficiently do so. *Tenants* and *Disengaged* were seriously considered for production, and *Disengaged* and *The Reprobate* were years later produced before special groups. Allan Wade, a man of wide theatrical experience, produced *The Reprobate* with a distinguished cast in 1919 for the Incorporated Stage Society of London. This production followed James's text closely and was judged successful. A production of the same play later in Boston was captioned by a reviewer: "Blither in a Void" (*Plays*, 402-3).

Skeptical readers who approach the plays for the first time will be surprised to find the dialogue usually rapid and clear. It is sophisticated, as is appropriate to the characters and situations; but there is little expository padding and no straining for detachable epigrams. There are many passages which indicate that James's estimate of his ability to write plays was not so preposterous as his financial failure suggests. The most negative point is not James's failure to master the tricks of the trade—he mastered perhaps too many—but his failure to add anything original. The four situation comedies just analyzed have no comment on the social scene comparable, say, to Pinero's *The Second Mrs. Tanqueray* (1893), Wilde's *Lady Windermere's Fan* (1892), the plays of Henry Arthur Jones, or—above all—to the plays of Ibsen which were making their impact on the London public in the 1890's.

III   Guy Domville (*1895*)

Written in 1893, concurrently with the later *Theatricals, Guy Domville* was produced on January 5, 1895. Despite a disastrous first night, the play ran for a month, and James was paid about thirteen hundred dollars. George Alexander, the very popular actor-producer, lost nearly four times that sum. With his next play— *The Importance of Being Earnest*—Alexander's customary good luck returned. The text of *Guy Domville* was privately printed at the time, but it remained unpublished until 1949. Turning to the text today (*Plays,* 465-516), most readers will conclude that *Guy Domville* is less interesting than any of the four *Theatricals.*

Guy Domville, a dedicated young Catholic, plans to enter the Benedictine order. On the eve of Guy's departure for France, Lord Devenish, a family friend, arrives to notify him of the death of a kinsman and to press upon Guy his responsibility to take his place in the world, marry, and perpetuate the Domville name. Mrs. Peverel, to whose small son Guy has been an adored tutor, also urges Guy to take more time to consider his future. She assures him that Father Murray, to whom Guy feels committed, will understand the delay. Guy agrees to postpone his trip to France, saying: " 'Myself'—the self of yesterday? I seem suddenly to have lost it forever." In the second act, Guy is at the home of his kinswoman, Mrs. Domville, mother of the deceased heir. Mrs. Domville's daughter by her first marriage, Mary Brasier, reluctantly becomes engaged to Guy. Mary's heart, however, belongs to a young naval officer, who is disapproved by her family. The officer, George Round, contrives to talk with Guy and to engage him in a drinking bout that causes him to be absent from the engagement party that evening. In a short passage, George seems to have succeeded, for Guy exits tipsy and incoherent. George has also told Guy that Mary has long loved him. Mary joins George, but she is unwilling to elope with him until he tells her that Lord Devenish is her real father—a fact that explains his lordship's anxiety to marry off the girl. Guy then comes back on stage, completely sober, and aids the two lovers to elope. Guy himself then leaves, followed by Lord

Devenish. In the third act, Mrs. Peverel is once more rejecting the proposal of Frank Humber, a friend of Guy's. Lord Devenish arrives ahead of Guy, with news that Guy's marriage to Mary will not take place. Conferring with Frank, Lord Devenish warns him that Guy will now attempt to marry Mrs. Peverel. When Guy arrives, he learns of this interference from Frank, and is angered at Lord Devenish's continued meddling in his affairs. Guy has had enough of worldliness. He returns to his plan to enter the Benedictine order, and he commends Mrs. Peverel to his friend Frank.

The period of the play, 1780, is not reflected in any details of the text, and it serves only to make the play a costume piece. Guy's religious convictions are asserted, never really shown. Indeed, the renunciation of them in the first act and the return to them in the third both seem evidence of weakness rather than of strength. Frank Humber and Mrs. Peverel, favorably introduced in the first act, are completely absent in the second. Little Geordie Peverel, Guy's adoring pupil, never comes on stage. The drinking scene (later omitted) requires Guy to exit tipsily and within five minutes to return sober. The maneuvering of the last act requires Lord Devenish to be concealed and to overhear much of the dialogue for mere theatric convenience. The play retains a serious tone, with almost no relief. Though the theme of renunciation of worldly life for a religious order is one of great potential appeal, James does not seem at home with it. His interest in religious sentiment—his veneration of great cathedrals—is frequent and sincere in his fiction. He had, however, been brought up as a free-thinker, and he had little knowledge of intense religious experience. In a novel James could perhaps have made Guy Domville's dedication more substantial. In the play, this central motivation seems hollow. Lord Devenish is the stereotyped wicked nobleman, and the other characters are hardly more distinguished.

Considering these defects, the reception of the play was perhaps better than might have been expected. The first night seems to have been one of the most fully reported premieres in theatrical history. James's friends were many, and they were out in force—John Singer Sargent, Sir Edward Burne-Jones, and Edmund Gosse among others. Two prominent critics, William Archer and A. B. Walkley, were present. Three young men, not yet well known, were there as well: G. B. Shaw, H. G. Wells, and Arnold Bennett. Cultivated London respected James and wished him well in the theater.

In the gallery, however, were some roughs out for a lark (perhaps, it was later suggested, planted in the audience by unfriendly persons). When in the second act Mrs. Domville appeared in a tall black hat, someone called out the chorus line of a popular song: "Where did you get that hat?" The drinking scene was awkward. Toward the end of the play, when Guy exclaimed, "I'm the last, my lord, of the Domvilles," a voice from the gallery replied: "It's a bloody good thing y'are." James, who had nervously been watching an Oscar Wilde play at a nearby theater, entered the stage door just as *Guy Domville* was concluding. After customary curtain calls, the author was called for and Alexander pulled James out on the stage. The applause of his friends was drowned by the boos and catcalls from the gallery. For the shy James, it was a hideous experience. In one letter he refers to the whole *Guy Domville* episode as "one of the most detestable incidents of my life."

James's own habit of high-keyed expression has contributed to the impression that *Guy Domville* was far more of a catastrophe than it was and that he himself was shattered by the experience, which is very far from the truth. The first performance was on Saturday night. Monday night James attended, sitting in the gallery "where they were *lovely*." He reported "a remarkably good house," and he said the play went "like an enthusiastic and brilliant 1st." The four-week run was completed with no repetition of the first night's disorder. Reviews of the play recognized weaknesses such as those mentioned above, but of greater interest is the sturdy defense of the play and of James as a dramatist of promise. Shaw said flatly: "Mr. James's dramatic authorship is valid. . . ." A. B. Walkley contrasted *Guy Domville* favorably with Wilde's *An Ideal Husband*: "Mr. Wilde's play will not help the drama forward a single inch. . . . Mr. James's play is a defeat out of which it is possible for many victories to spring. . . ."[9]

IV The Other House (1894)

On December 26, 1893, James recorded in his notebook a three-page sketch of the characters and situations which the following year became a full-length play first known as "The Promise." Writing under the influence of Ibsen, James designed the leading feminine role for his actress friend Elizabeth Robins. Finding no producer for the play, he serialized it as fiction in 1896 under the title *The Other House*. In this form it had moderate success, and it remained in his mind as "a precedent, a support, a divine little light to walk by. . . ."[10] In 1909, with other dramatic ventures in hand, James spent some time in trying to turn the novel back into a play. It seems most unfortunate that *The Other House*, so close a contemporary of the ill-fated *Guy Domville*, was not produced in its stead. It would almost certainly have succeeded far better, and even today *The Other House* might justify presentation.

The central incident is the murder of a child to free the father, Tony Bream, from a promise made several years earlier to his dying wife that he would not remarry during the life of their daughter Effie. The rivalries and jealousies by which Rose Armiger is made capable of the murder are well developed, and the murder itself—an offstage drowning—is handled with a minimum of melodrama. The "promise" is explained in a prologue which introduces all the characters. Rose Armiger has lived for several years with Tony Bream and his wife, and she cherishes a secret passion for Tony. Rose faces two obstacles: the promise given by Tony to his dying wife, and Tony's more noticeable interest in another young woman. Nevertheless, Rose rejects Dennis Vidal, a young man whose new post in the foreign service has made possible their long-contemplated marriage.

Four years later the main action takes place. The situation is unchanged, except that Rose has lived elsewhere since Mrs. Bream's death. Mrs. Beever, a neighbor, has invited Rose to visit for a few days. Also invited is Jean Martle, long a friend of both families. Mrs. Beever's hope is to have her son marry Jean, but Jean feels only a friendship for him. It is Jean whom Rose recognizes as her rival for Tony Bream. At this point Dennis Vidal, Rose's old suitor, turns up, and Rose humbles herself to tell him she will now accept him. Dennis hesitates; and, while he does so, Rose sees a last desperate opportunity to disrupt the attraction between Jean and Tony. In the small stream between the two houses, Rose drowns little Effie Bream and contrives to throw suspicion on Jean. Tony Bream then confesses the crime himself in order to shield Jean. When it becomes clear that Rose is guilty, Tony realizes her motives and feels in some degree responsible. The circumstances of the murder and the presence of the family doctor make it possible to report the death as accidental. Rose goes away with Dennis Vidal, who temporarily accepts the role of fiancé to shield her. Jean and Tony are left more separated than ever. As Jean says of Rose, "It's her triumph!—that our freedom is *horrible!*"

Though not an "idea" play in the usual sense, *The Other House* is an intelligent treatment of violent crime erupting among restrained and well-bred people. Tony Bream is exposed as well-meaning but imperceptive. Mrs. Beever, the good neighbor who schemes to marry her son to Jean, is witty and shrewd; but she has too little imagination to see below the surface of things. Above all, the deathbed promise, so well intended and so honorably accepted, is a shocking extension of power over the living.

V   Summersoft (1895)—*"Covering End"* (1898)
The High Bid (1908)

Two plays and a story were based on the single situation of an old house, heavily mortgaged, rescued for its English owner by a wealthy American widow. The one-act *Summersoft* was written at the request of Miss Ellen Terry, who in 1895 was at the height of her career. James received an advance of one hundred pounds for the play, but when Miss Terry's plans altered and no use was made of it, James turned the play into the story "Covering End" (1898). In 1907, at the request of Johnston Forbes-Robertson, James converted the story into the three-act play *The High Bid*. On March 26, 1908, it was performed with some success at Edinburgh.[11]

The one-act *Summersoft*—the first version—is pleasant reading, and Ellen Terry's enthusiasm for it is understandable. Mrs. Gracedew, the American widow, would have made an excellent part for her; for Mrs. Gracedew is poised, sophisticated, and admirable rather than ridiculous in her zeal for old houses and furnishings. Coming to Summersoft, a country house open to the public, on a Sunday afternoon, she startles the butler by correcting his mistakes in describing the rooms and ornaments—back in Missourah Top, Mrs. Gracedew had read all about Summersoft. On the same afternoon, Captain Yule comes down to make his first inspection of Summersoft, a property he has inherited. It is so heavily mortgaged, however, that he sees no way to keep it. Prodmore, the real estate man who is showing the house, has suggested a way: if Yule will marry Prodmore's daughter and if he will change his politics so that he can stand for a conservative seat, the house can remain in the family. Cora Prodmore, an attractive young lady, is inside waiting for Captain Yule, having accepted her father's instructions with little outward resistance. Cora has met Mrs. Gracedew coming down on the train, and she likes her sufficiently to confide that she doesn't at all want to marry Captain Yule; she prefers a Mr. Buddle, to whom her father is opposed. Mrs. Gracedew, like a good American, encourages Cora's interest in Mr. Buddle, and she also kindly instructs Cora's father that he should give his approval. The implication is that he reluctantly does so.

All this is a mere backdrop for the affair of Mrs. Gracedew and Captain Yule. When Mrs. Gracedew learns that Cora is not going to marry Captain Yule, Mrs. Gracedew bargains with Prodmore, who very cleverly turns her enthusiasm against her by raising the price on the house. When she tells Captain Yule that she has arranged to buy the house, he eagerly proposes. Just then a new party of sightseers comes in. While explaining the portraits, Mrs.

Gracedew sees Captain Yule framed in an archway. Her curtain line is: "Oh, that's my future husband."

The High Bid, in three acts, makes no fundamental change in situation or sequence. The dialogue of *Summersoft* is almost wholly transferred to the longer work, but there are many more stage directions. Cora's young man now comes on stage (as in "Covering End," his name is now Mr. Hall Pegg). The butler and the sightseers are given more space. The first act ends shortly after Mrs. Gracedew comes on the scene; the second, after she has come to an understanding with Cora and knows that Captain Yule is fair game for her. The two intervals help to reduce the implausibility of two strangers like Captain Yule and Mrs. Gracedew becoming engaged in a single afternoon.

VI "The Chaperon" (1907)

Following a suggestion made by Pinero, whose *The Second Mrs. Tanqueray* was produced in May, 1893, James considered dramatizing his story "The Chaperon" (1891). In 1907, having just finished *The High Bid,* he dictated not only several pages of speculation about dramatic form for the story but also several passages of dialogue. This "Rough Statement," which runs to some twenty thousand words, offers interesting late evidence of James's increased ability to think in dramatic terms.[12]

Rose Tramore, the central figure of the story, has been brought up with her father and paternal grandmother because her mother ran away with another man. When her father dies, Rose announces her determination to go to her mother. She does so, despite the protests of her grandmother and of her suitor, Captain Jay. Rose, who lives contentedly with her mother, refuses invitations that come to her alone. While Rose and her mother are abroad, they meet Captain Jay. His respect for Rose's courage is so great that he accepts her mother, and Rose marries him. Thus Rose becomes "chaperon" to her mother.

As James thought of dramatizing this story, he considered carefully the way in which friends of the Tramore family could be included in the action to provide a richer social context for Rose's departure to live with her mother. He planned the first act around the occasion of Rose's coming of age, celebrated by family and friends. To heighten the effect of this occasion, he supposes it to take place about a year after the death of Rose's father, and thus a resumption of social life marks the end of the period of mourning. The "Rough Statement" dictated by James is a combination of speculations about the roles of various characters in developing the action, passages of dialogue (one of four pages), and careful planning of minute details of stage business. It is notable that nearly every speech in the dialogue is accompanied by stage directions to indicate the precise tone desired. "The Chaperon," had it been completed, might have come closer to effective social comedy than any of the finished plays.

VII   The Saloon (1908)

The Saloon is a dramatic version of James's story "Owen Wingrave" (1892); the title character of the story is a young man of a military family who is disinherited because of his refusal to enter the army. Symbolic of Owen's bravery and of the family tradition is his fatal encounter with the family ghost. With the production of The High Bid arranged for, James finished The Saloon early in 1908, showing it first to Granville-Barker and then to Forbes-Robertson, who was producing The High Bid. Neither producer was willing to take it. Later, James was asked to submit The Saloon to the Incorporated Stage Society, in which Shaw was involved. The society rejected the play, but Shaw wrote twice to James, urging him to revise the play by eliminating the seeming triumph of the ghost because it was meaningless and pernicious superstition. James, who replied with great good nature, insisted on the imaginative effect of the climax. Owen, he says, "wins the victory—that is he clears the air, and he pays with his life. The whole point of the little piece is that he, while protesting against the tradition of his 'race,' proceeds and pays exactly like the soldier that he declares he'll never be." Early in 1911 The Saloon was produced by Gertrude Kingston in the London Little Theatre. James was annoyed by reported liberties taken with the text, and especially with a visual representation of the ghost.[13]

VIII   The Outcry (1909)

The Outcry was James's last full-length play. After his many disappointments, it must have been singularly cheering to be invited to contribute a play to a London repertory season arranged in 1909 by American producer Charles Frohman. To be included with such distinguished contemporaries as Shaw, Galsworthy, Granville-Barker, Maugham, and Masefield was a flattering recognition that James's attempts in the theater had attracted favorable notice if they had not won popular success. For the theme of his play James chose the raiding of British art collections by wealthy Americans, treating the idea with seriousness but in a tone of sophisticated comedy. By December, 1909, the play was complete. Difficulties over revising the manuscript and casting the play dragged on. Suddenly in May, 1910, all theaters were closed because of the death of Edward VII. *The Outcry* was returned to James with a forfeit of two hundred pounds. The following year James turned *The Outcry* into quite successful fiction, as he had *The Other House*. In 1917, after James's death, the Incorporated Stage Society gave two performances of *The Outcry*.[14]

In *The Outcry* Lord Theign, possessor of a fine gallery of old paintings, is financially embarrassed by the debts of his older daughter, and is therefore tempted to sell some of his paintings to the wealthy American collector, Bender. A young art-critic, interested in Grace, Lord Theign's younger daughter, believes that one of the paintings attributed to Moretto is actually by Montevano and hence of much greater value (the artists' names being fictional). This proves to be true, but the controversy arouses an "outcry" against the sale of English art treasures to Americans. Even the Prince becomes interested, and Lord Theign finally bows to the wish of the public by giving the picture to the nation. Lord Theign also gives his consent for the marriage of Grace to the young art-critic. She has already rejected the proposal of Lord John, a young nobleman on whom her father had looked with favor. Meanwhile Lord Theign himself becomes engaged to Lady Sandgate, who has also been pressed by the American collector to sell one of her pictures.

The theme of greed is amusingly touched upon in *The Outcry*. The Moretto, which Theign is willing to sell to Bender, is not an interesting purchase at ten thousand pounds. Only when it takes on the much higher value of a Montovano does Bender become anxious. As the "value" is being discussed, the art critic asks: "Are you talking of values pecuniary?" It is Lord John who replies flatly: "What values are *not* pecuniary?" It is Lord John, too, who—because he has lost a marriage settlement through Grace's rejection of him—maliciously reports Lord Theign's contemptuous reference to giving his picture to the nation as if it were a bona fide offer. There is thus a special note of comedy in the final scene. Theign has just torn up the check left by Bender for Lady Sandgate's picture. Lord John precedes the Prince on his way upstairs to call on Theign. Grandly waving to the torn check on the floor, Lady Sandgate speaks the curtain line: "Lord John, be so good as to stop. . . . And please pick up that litter!" In this play, James had come a very long way from *Guy Domville*.

IX *Monologue (1913)*

An amusing trifle written for the monologuist Ruth Draper seems to have been James's last experiment with dramatic form. This untitled piece, unpublished until 1929, was never used by Miss Draper since she felt it impossible to conceal James's authorship, as he requested.[15] As a period piece this three-thousand word monologue would be effective today, and it should certainly find its way into anthologies. It is a deft and self-sufficient sketch of Mrs. Tuff, a wealthy American woman in London, who demands that an embassy official secure her a presentation at court to suit her own convenience. To an English friend who calls, she explains: "I seem to make them do what I want. What in the world *should* I make them do? . . . I don't at all subscribe to the pushing and fighting and rowing that your women seem to find necessary."

X *Conclusion: Henry James, Dramatist*

What is the significance of James's career as dramatist? He was not a success; for, in the rather arbitrary values of the theater, not to be a hit is failure. Yet failure seems too harsh a word. It is surely a misfortune that the first night of *Guy Domville* has become so common a tale, implying the total inadequacy of James as a dramatist. Readers who have been exasperated by James's deliberate fiction—and they are many—are flattered to find support for their adverse opinions in what appears complete rejection by London theater-goers. The boos from the gallery still drown out the vigorous defense by G. B. Shaw.

The first night of *Guy Domville*, however, is an outrageous over-simplification of James's connection with the theater. Despite that relative failure, the ablest producers and actors of the time continued to be interested in plays by James: Forbes-Robertson, Ellen Terry, Charles Frohman, Granville-Barker, Pinero, Barrie, and, of course, Shaw. James's effort was vigorous and sustained.

Of his plays, it is true, not one is up to the level of his best fiction, but *Summersoft, The Other House,* and *The Outcry* deserve to be far better known than the first night of *Guy Domville.* Beyond these durable achievements was James's discovery of "the divine principle of the Scenario" (*Notebooks,* 188)—of great importance in the development of his later fiction.

XI *Fiction Adapted for the Stage*

Though no play by James has been revived in recent years, nearly a score of professional adaptations of James's fiction have reached stage, screen, radio, or television. No comprehensive review of this aspect of the James revival is possible here, but the attention given to James in the modern theater is too important to ignore. Broadly speaking, even the weaker adaptations emphasize the current awareness that James's fiction turns on ideas and conflicts that are essentially dramatic, as that term is now understood. The great interest in psychology, both professional and popular, inevitably prepared people to appreciate the inner conflicts of James's characters. It is interesting that the fullest consideration of attempts to dramatize James is an essay by James Thurber, the great cartoonist and humorist, who was a sympathetic though sometimes skeptical admirer of James.[16]

John L. Balderston's *Berkeley Square* is a very free adaptation of the incomplete *The Sense of the Past*, the story of a modern man who steps back into the eighteenth century. Produced in 1926 in London, it was successfully revived in 1929 with Leslie Howard as star. In 1928 *The Tragic Muse* was dramatized in London. One of the hits of the 1947 New York season was *The Heiress*, based on *Washington Square*. Originally a failure, the play by Ruth and Augustus Goetz was turned into a success by producer Jed Harris; Wendy Hiller starred as Catherine Sloper and Basil Rathbone as her father. The movie version of this play featured Olivia de Haviland, with Montgomery Clift in the part of Morris Townsend, her lover. In 1952 Dodie Smith put *The Reverberator* on the London stage with only moderate success under the title *Letter from Paris*. Four years later a radio version attracted favorable notice. William Archibald's dramatic version of *The Portrait of a Lady* ran only four performances in 1955. James himself, once asked to dramatize the novel, said that he saw no play in it. Tallulah Bankhead played the lead in *Eugenia*, a not very successful version of *The Europeans* in 1957. Bertram Greene's *The Summer of Daisy Miller* was moderately successful in May, 1963.

"The Turn of the Screw," one of James's most popular stories, has also been most successful in stage adaptation. William Archibald's *The Innocents*, 1950, was called by *Life* "the most frightening play Broadway has seen in years." It was revived in New York in 1959, and in London in 1961. Ingrid Bergman played the governess in a Startime television performance in 1959, and Deborah Kerr played that part in a British film of 1961. In 1954 Benjamin Britten based an opera on the story.

In 1947 "The Aspern Papers" was turned into a melodramatic film called *The Lost Moment*. A much more faithful adaptation for the stage by Michael Redgrave was regarded as one of the best plays of the London season of 1959-60. Redgrave himself played the young publisher, perversely named "H.J.," and Florence Robson the part of old Miss Bordereau.

The Wings of the Dove, adapted by Guy Bolton in 1956 as *The Child of Fortune* ran for only twenty-three performances, despite a Jed Harris production. In January, 1959, a television version by Meade Roberts was surprisingly effective. In 1962 Douglas Moore produced an opera based on the story.

It is not surprising that many of these adaptations failed, for the works of James have qualities almost impossible to stage. The movement of James's stories is characteristically slow, deliberate, and reflective. Yet with reasonable faithfulness to situations and character values, *The Heiress, The Innocents,* and Redgrave's *The Aspern Papers* have provided drama that asked no favors from general audiences and that required no previous knowledge of author or of story. James himself, one is persuaded, would be pleased that indirectly he has achieved the success in the theater that his own plays never won for him. He would also be pleased by the willingness of notable actors and actresses to appear in plays based on his stories.

CHAPTER 5

Fiction: 1891-1900

JAMES'S LIFE from 1890 to 1895 was largely devoted to the dramatic projects described in the preceding chapter. There were, naturally, interruptions and distractions. Each summer James went to the Continent, except in 1895. A number of deaths touched him closely: J. R. Lowell and Wolcott Balestier, 1891; his sister Alice, 1892; Constance Fenimore Woolson and Robert Louis Stevenson, 1894. The disappointment over *Guy Domville* early in 1895 was soon pushed aside by other concerns. In February, Sidney Colvin asked advice about publication of Stevenson's letters. James replied: "Publish them—they make the man so loveable" (*Letters,* I, 236). In March, James visited friends near Dublin. Part of the summer he spent near Torquay, a resort on the south coast of England. In 1896 he was bicycling in Sussex. That year he discovered Lamb House in Rye, and the following year moved there, first as tenant, later as owner. He continued to spend much time in London, especially during the winter season; and it was in Cheyne Walk, Chelsea, that he died. Lamb House, however, was his settled home and the familiar address on his letters.

In 1896 there was a welcome visit from the old friend of his youth, Oliver Wendell Holmes. In 1898, James's friendship with H. G. Wells began. In 1899 William James and his wife came to Europe for two years, and Henry spent much time with them. As the new century approached, James was disturbed by the war between the United States and Spain, which seemed imperialistic to him. He deplored the jingo spirit he found in Theodore Roosevelt. The Boer War in South Africa was another shadow. In 1901, like all the world, James felt older as he contemplated the death of Queen Victoria: "the Queen's magnificent duration had held things together magnificently, beneficently together and prevented all sorts of accidents. Her death, in short, will let loose incalculable forces for possible ill." In this comment, written to an American friend, he suggested that Americans, too, wear mourning for the Queen: "for she was nice to us."[1]

The thoughtful speculations in James's notebook for February and March, 1895, register his pleasure at returning to fiction with its larger freedom. Actually, he had not entirely deserted fiction during the years of dramatic writing. From 1891 through 1895 he published nineteen stories, totaling more than a quarter of a million words, a considerable achievement for five years even if the plays are written off as a total loss. Among these stories are some of his most familiar titles: "The Marriages," "The Real Thing," "Greville Fane," "The Middle Years," and "The Altar of the Dead." Besides these new stories, he published collections of new and old material in 1892, in 1893 (three volumes that year), and in 1895. In the later years of this decade, he concentrated his energies on fiction. In rapid succession came *The Spoils of Poynton, The Other House, What Maisie Knew,* "The Turn of the Screw," *The Awkward Age,* and twenty more short stories—all this by 1900. The essential toughness of James's nature and his thoroughly professional attitude are never shown more clearly than in the accomplishments of these five years immediately following his relative failure in the theater.

I   The Spoils of Poynton (*1896*)

On the surface, *The Spoils of Poynton* is a family quarrel over possessions. Poynton is the family estate of Mrs. Gereth, a widow who with her late husband furnished the place with a sort of intense personal artistry. Owen Gereth, her only son, has little taste for the fine things of Poynton, and he is about to marry Mona Brigstock, a girl who looks possessively rather than appreciatively on Poynton as her future home. It is understood that when Owen marries, his mother will leave Poynton, taking with her "what she requires." Just before the marriage is to take place, however, Mrs. Gereth practically strips the house; she crams furniture, pictures, tapestries, and rare ornaments into Ricks, her new residence some distance away. Owen is offended, and Mona far more so; for she now makes the return of the "spoils of Poynton" a condition for her marriage to Owen.

Mrs. Gereth enjoys the company of Fleda Vetch, a young woman of exquisite taste but of small fortune. Fleda, in the opinion of Mrs. Gereth, is the proper young woman for Owen to marry; and she makes it clear that for Fleda she would willingly return all that has been taken from the old place. This is the situation at the end of Chapter Seven, which marks the first third of the story. Owen, who is rather slow-witted and who has seen little of Fleda, must now negotiate with his mother through Fleda, since he and his mother are not on speaking terms. Fleda, who sympathizes with Owen's difficulties, agrees that his mother has gone much too far. Owen is quickly attracted to Fleda, and her sympathy turns to passionate affection. She has two scruples: she will not accept Owen unless and until he is "free", and she will not be bribed by the knowledge that Mrs. Gereth stands ready to return the "spoils" if Fleda is to be mistress of Poynton.

The love affair between Fleda and Owen progresses through meetings in London while Fleda is away from Ricks, but Mrs. Gereth scents out developments. Convinced that Mona has withdrawn and that Owen will marry Fleda, Mrs. Gereth suddenly sends back the furnishings of Poynton. Ironically, this gives Mona the face-saving victory she has sought, and she holds Owen to his promise. Learning this, Mrs. Gereth finds Fleda at her sister's:

"He has done it," said Mrs. Gereth. . . . "It's the end."
"They're married?"
"They're married."
Fleda came to the sofa in obedience to the impulse to sit down by her; then paused before her while Mrs. Gereth turned up a dead grey mask. A tired old woman sat there with empty hands in her lap (NY X, 236-37).

Some months later, while Owen and Mona are traveling abroad, Owen writes Fleda that he would like her to have whatever she chooses from Poynton; the servants have been instructed, and she is to go at her convenience to select what she likes. Just before Christmas, Fleda visits her sister in London, and one morning she goes to Poynton. Alighting from her train at the village, she smells smoke. The station master tells her that Poynton had burned during the night and that nothing was saved: "It's not a place for a young lady, nor, if you'll believe me, a sight for them as are in any way affected" (266). Fleda takes the next train back to London.

So Poynton and its spoils are gone. They are the pretexts of the story. The real story is Fleda's love for Owen, her scrupulous unwillingness to take advantage of him, and her capacity to keep the affection and respect of the coarse-grained Mrs. Gereth, whose ruthlessness is so clearly exposed as the reality behind her pretentions of artistic taste. What Fleda lost—and what Owen lost—is shown in one of James's most convincing love scenes. Owen has found Fleda at her sister's in London. He proposes marriage to her, and she confesses that she has long loved him. But, she asks, is he *free* to marry her?

"You must settle that with Mona. You mustn't break faith. Anything's better than that. You must at any rate be utterly sure. She must love you—how can she help it? *I* wouldn't give you up!" said Fleda. She spoke in broken bits, panting out her words. "The great thing is to keep faith. Where's a man if he doesn't? If he doesn't he may be so cruel. So cruel, so cruel, so cruel!" Fleda repeated. "I couldn't have a hand in that, you know: that's my position—that's mine. You offered her marriage. It's a tremendous thing for her." Then looking up at him another moment, "*I* wouldn't give you up!" (196-97).

Only two days before James recorded in his notebook the anecdote that was to result in the play *The Other House*, he had set down the anecdote on which *The Spoils of Poynton* was based.[2] The dramatic conflicts between Mrs. Gereth, Owen, Fleda, and Mona form a subtler theme than the story of child-murder in *The Other House*, and certainly a far more substantial idea than is found in any of the four *Theatricals* then engaging James's attention. When he turned back to the idea of *The Spoils* in May, 1895, James first thought in terms of a three-act play. By August he seems to have adopted the narrative form, but he still discussed the story in terms of scenes. Thus *The Spoils of Poynton* is an important transitional work, and its undeniably dramatic quality is a direct result of James's projects for the theater. The story has been attacked on various grounds: the "spoils" remain vague; the quarrel over them is trivial; the character of Fleda is flawed. Such objections seem directed against James in general rather than against this particular story. The vagueness of the "spoils" directs attention away from them to the persons concerned. The trivial basis of the quarrel has a similar effect: not the cause, but the result of the quarrel is important. Fleda, though the pattern of her behavior is virtuous renunciation, is not idealized, but left with a human ambiguity.

II What Maisie Knew (*1897*)

An anecdote of a child whose divorced parents remarried gave James the idea for *What Maisie Knew*.[3] Like *The Spoils of Poynton*, this novel is developed chiefly by dramatic scenes. The presence of a child who grows from six to thirteen in the course of the story forces James to rely heavily on implication in the dialogue. The fact that Maisie "had fewer names than conceptions" is a further difficulty in interpreting her view of adult situations. Despite the great interest of the theme, the subtle treatment makes great demands upon the reader, who would often welcome the actor's voice and demeanor as aids to interpretation. The difficulty of James's method, however, kept him from disaster on the shoals of sentimentality. Maisie's plight, portrayed with a fine sympathy, never fails to combine intellectual and emotional appeal.

Maisie is the daughter of Beale and Ida Farange, whose divorce is granted at the beginning of the story. Since Maisie lives part of the time with each parent, she is used by each to abuse the other.

Beale instructs his daughter to tell her mother that she is "a nasty horrid pig"; Ida in turn asks Maisie to tell her father that "he lies and he knows he lies." In due course, Beale marries Maisie's governess, Miss Overmore, who will henceforth be referred to by James as "Mrs. Beale." Ida, meanwhile, marries Sir Claude. After a series of other liaisons, Mrs. Beale and Sir Claude part company with Maisie's parents. By this time, the stepparents have become interested in each other, partly because of their concern for Maisie. The stupid but affectionate Mrs. Wix, employed by Ida as governess for Maisie, stays with her; and Mrs. Wix welcomes Sir Claude's continued interest in Maisie. If Sir Claude will only devote himself to little Maisie, Mrs. Wix thinks, he will be "saved."

At the end of the story, Mrs. Beale joins Sir Claude, Maisie, and Mrs. Wix in France. Sir Claude's intention to live with Mrs. Beale, though neither yet has a formal divorce, scandalizes Mrs. Wix, who wishes to take Maisie back to England with her. Sir Claude urges Maisie to give up Mrs. Wix. Maisie, now thirteen, offers her terms: she will give up Mrs. Wix if Sir Claude will give up Mrs. Beale. It is clear that Maisie, unlike Mrs. Wix, is not scandalized by Mrs. Beale's presence. To her, Sir Claude and Mrs. Beale are both "free." She does see Mrs. Beale as a rival, however, a threat to her future with Sir Claude. When Sir Claude refuses to give up Mrs. Beale, Maisie and Mrs. Wix take the next boat for England. The reader, like Mrs. Wix, still has "room for wonder at what Maisie knew."

What did Maisie know? James's failure to give a clear answer to this question is, paradoxically, the essential success of the novel. For Maisie, a child exposed to a torrent of adult experience, would "know" much more than she could understand. She herself would be unable to say just what she knew and just what it meant. Maisie's conversation with the mysterious Captain, one of Ida's lovers, is an example. Maisie and Sir Claude have by chance met Ida and the Captain in the park. While Ida and Sir Claude quarrel, Maisie is left with the Captain, who seems genuinely fond of Ida and who is kind to Maisie. As Maisie says goodbye to him, she asks:

> "You *do* love her?"
> "My dear child—!" The Captain wanted words.
> "Then don't do it only for just a little."
> "A little?"
> "Like all the others."
> "All the others?"—he stood staring.[4]

Now if Maisie fully understood about "the others" she would realize that reference to them should be avoided. Maisie is attracted to the Captain. She knows that her mother and Sir Claude have fallen out of love. Perhaps the Captain will please her mother permanently. This childlike hope is convincingly expressed as Maisie unwittingly tells the very thing that will put the Captain on his guard; indeed, only four chapters later, her mother refers to the Captain as "the biggest cad in London." But Maisie is not wholly naïve, either. After her talk with the Captain, Sir Claude asks her what he said. Since the Captain's conversation dealt with his intention to have Maisie come and live with him and Ida, Maisie, who shrewdly guesses the plan would be displeasing to Sir Claude, gives only vague answers to his questions. The mixture of naïveté and shrewdness in this single situation is most convincing.

In the bitter quarrels that are central to the action, James nowhere relies upon physical violence to get his effects. The corruption of human affection furnishes sufficient horror. Terrible are the scenes in which the natural parents of Maisie use crafty stratagems to get rid of her. Beale takes the child to the home of the hideous "Countess" late at night; and, while they wait for her, he tells Maisie that he and the "Countess" are going to America. Would Maisie go with them? Twice the child assents: "I'll do anything in the world you ask me, papa." When the "Countess" enters, she is delighted with Maisie, as Beale intended she should be. Then in front of Maisie, he lies, saying flatly: ". . . she declines to have anything to do with us." In a parallel scene, Ida asks Maisie to choose between going to South Africa with her and staying in London. When Maisie, hoping to please her mother, refers to the kind things the Captain had said about her, Ida gives her "one of the looks that slammed the door in her face."

The two parents have hardly a redeeming trait except what is conferred by Maisie's anxious efforts to please them. In contrast, the stepparents are more agreeable. Sir Claude, in particular, takes a genuine pleasure in Maisie's company. There is even conviction in Mrs. Beale's final defense against Mrs. Wix's disapproval: "What in the world's our connection but the love of the child who's our duty and our life and who holds us together as closely as she originally brought us?" Maisie, however, instinctively and rightly distrusts the possessiveness of Mrs. Beale and the weakness of Sir Claude.[5]

III *Shorter Fiction: Family Themes*

Nearly half of the short stories of the 1890's deal with courtship, marriage, separation, and the plight of children. Thus they are variations on the general themes of *The Other House, The Spoils of Poynton,* and *What Maisie Knew.* These stories are also a kind of preparation for James's long novel, *The Awkward Age* (1898-99). Without pressing the distinction too rigidly, most of the stories turn on an analysis of situations; a smaller number permit a memorable emphasis of character values.

"Lord Beaupré" (1892), for example, is a situation story. Mary Gosselin is a willing party to a pretended engagement to Lord Beaupré as a friendly protection of the young man from husband-hunters, and thus blocks the possibility of a true romance between them. "The Wheel of Time" (1893) is a different kind of reversal: a plain girl is jilted by a young artist; years later, her son jilts the daughter of the artist. "Glasses" (1896) is narrated by an artist, who on vacation finds Flora Saunt, a beautiful young girl, as a subject for a portrait. Although something is wrong with her eyes, she indignantly denies it, for she loathes the idea of wearing glasses. Her portrait attracts the attention of Dawling, a kind but unattractive man. When Flora later goes blind, Dawling marries her. The friend who introduced the artist-narrator to Flora no longer sees the girl. She cannot bear the thought of the beautiful girl's blindness.

"The Given Case" (1898-99) is a double demonstration of duty imposing the renunciation of love. The story, just under ten thousand words, lacks the length necessary for the development of the six characters involved. In "The Great Condition" (1899), a woman refuses to tell about her past until after her marriage. Her fiancé, too suspicious to accept this condition, loses the lady to another man. Later the first man meets the lady, who tells him there was absolutely nothing to conceal; the condition had been a test of his affection. A remark by a mutual friend points the moral in Jamesian phrase: "What I don't grasp . . . is your liking her so much as to 'mind' so much, without by the same stroke liking her enough not to mind at all." "Paste" (1899), as James himself comments, is a variant on Maupassant's famous story, "The Diamond Necklace."

"The Special Type" (1900) refers to the kind of woman who will for a fee allow herself to be compromised to give grounds for a man's divorce. The artist-narrator suggests his model, Mrs. Dundene, to an American friend, Frank Brivet. All goes well, and eventually the divorce is arranged. The woman Brivet now wants to marry asks the artist to paint Brivet's portrait, and he does so. Meanwhile Mrs. Dundene has grown fond of Brivet, and knowing that he will not marry her, also asks the artist for a portrait of Brivet. The artist, who appreciates her spirit, gives her the painting already finished. That Mrs. Dundene's relationship with Brivet was innocent is evident from her comment: "I never saw him alone."

In contrast to Mrs. Dundene, "The Two Faces" ("The Faces," 1900) shows in Mrs. Grantham the venom of the woman scorned.

Lord Gwyther, who has married a young girl brought up in Germany, seeks Mrs. Grantham's aid in helping his bride launch herself properly in London society. Mrs. Grantham, formerly quite intimate with Lord Gwyther, manages to have the bride ridiculously overdressed when she makes her first appearance. A friend notes the contrast between the exquisite beauty of the young girl's face and the pathos of her expression as she realizes "what's been done with her." "Europe" (1899) is a variant on the theme of the early "Four Meetings" (1877): the natural desire of American girls to go to Europe.

"Miss Gunton of Poughkeepsie" (1900) is the story of a broken engagement to an Italian Prince. "Covering End" (1898)—already discussed in connection with dramatic versions of it in 1895 and 1908—combines the amusing development of an artificial situation with the attractive character of Mrs. Gracedew, the wealthy American widow who "saves" the old country house by marrying its poverty-stricken young owner. The effect of the story, either as fiction or as drama, is contrived. There is little opportunity given or taken for insight into important motivations.

Of far greater depth than these analyses of special situations, "The Pupil" (1891) is an extremely perceptive treatment of the relationship between a brilliant adolescent boy and his tutor. The Moreen family travels about, living in a high style but never paying its bills. The insecurity of this life deeply affects young Morgan. He and Pemberton, the new tutor, quickly take to each other; but Morgan becomes apprehensive that Pemberton will leave, like all the other tutors, when he finds he will not be paid. At last Pemberton does leave to take another position. When Morgan falls ill, Pemberton is sent for. On his arrival, Pemberton finds that Mrs. Moreen has in effect tricked him into coming, so that he can once more take responsibility for Morgan. The boy has long realized that his parents are "awful frauds,—poor dears," but his mother's deceit of Pemberton and her shameless request that Pemberton take full charge of Morgan at his own expense are too much for him. When Pemberton and Morgan return from an afternoon walk, the servants have departed, and the open trunks in the passage signify that the family must move out of its lodgings at once. The irresponsibility of the parents is thus exposed in a glaringly public way before Pemberton, who is Morgan's only friend. When Mrs. Moreen repeats the proposal that Pemberton must now look after Morgan, the boy at first feels some pleasure at the prospect. Then he sits down quickly, turns livid, and dies in the arms of his mother and Pemberton, as the father stands by.

"But I thought he *wanted* to go to you!" wailed Mrs. Moreen. "I *told* you he didn't, my dear." Mr. Moreen was trembling all over and was in his way as deeply affected as his wife. But after the very first he took his bereavement as a man of the world (NY XI, 577).

By showing relentlessly all that Morgan's home was not, James implies—perhaps with a recollection of his own childhood—all that a home should be. The gay comradeship between Morgan and Pemberton forms an interesting contrast to the serious undertone and main action of the story.

"The Marriages" (1891), another story of deep psychological insight, is startling when it is remembered that the story antedates modern psychology. A young woman, Adela Chart, learns of the probable remarriage of her father. Adela's worship of her dead mother and, below the surface, her almost incestuous possessiveness toward her father make her violently opposed to the marriage. She takes the unusual step of warning Mrs. Churchley, her father's intended bride, that her father and mother never got on well together—an obvious untruth. The engagement is broken off, and later Adela goes to the lady and confesses her lie. The astute Mrs. Churchley informs her that she never believed the tale; but disliking Adela, she had broken the engagement because of her. A subordinate action involves Adela's brother in such a way as to emphasize Adela's emotional conflicts. A contrasting story, already discussed in the preceding chapter is "The Chaperon" (1891), which James seriously attempted to dramatize. In this story a daughter has the insight to appreciate the position of her mother, ostracized because of her divorce, and the courage to take her mother's part successfully: with her daughter as chaperon, the mother gains a limited social acceptance.

"Brooksmith" (1891) is the one story by James which centers in a servant, and thus gives a glimpse below stairs. It is an unusual glimpse, for Brooksmith is an unusual butler in an unusual household. Brooksmith serves an elderly bachelor whose charm and culture attract a circle of remarkable friends. Brooksmith's association with the guests is thoroughly discreet; but, as James permits him to say to the narrator of the story, one of the circle of friends, the conversation was "quite an education." When Brooksmith's master dies, the friends feel a great loss, but for Brooksmith himself the loss is greatest. He explains to the narrator: "Mr. Offord was *my* society, and now, you see, I just haven't any. You go back to conversation, sir, after all, and I go back to my place. . . " (NY XVIII, 364). The narrator attempts, without much success, to find a suitable place for Brooksmith. As time goes on the butler is occasionally seen as an extra servant for large parties. Eventually he drops from sight. This brief story, so sparse in event, so rich in insight, anticipates by many years the *New Yorker* sketch—the glimpse into private life which lies beyond the reach of mass journalism, treated with taste that avoids the banalities of the feature story.

As in "Brooksmith," the angle of vision for "In the Cage" (1898) is unusual for James. The girl who sits "in the cage" takes telegrams from customers and assesses the charges. She speculates silently on the personal affairs of the fashionable people to whom the telegrams relate. Captain Everard, a handsome young man who communicates constantly by telegram, attracts her in particular. One evening as she walks past the entrance of his apartment, he recognizes her, and a conversation follows. He thanks her for the pains she always takes with his telegrams, and she quite directly tells him she has postponed transferring to another office so that she may continue to serve him. This extraordinary conversation is carried on without a hint of impropriety: Everard is polite; the girl (who is never named) "keeps her place."

Though this story leans heavily on an involved and artificial plot, there is also a strong character interest. The young woman is memorable, and she must have been attractive to James, for the story runs to forty thousand words. She quite sees the class difference between herself and Captain Everard's gay world, yet he represents something she can appreciate. She is too intelligent to indulge in romantic expectations, but merely serving him by handling his telegrams is a pleasure. Even to help him remove an obstacle to his marriage with another woman was something. As she looks toward her own humdrum marriage, she is neither rebellious nor vindictive.

In all these briefer treatments of family themes, there is a visible limitation more important than brevity. The structure, even of his best stories—"The Pupil" and "The Marriages"—lacks the variety and completeness so apparent in *The Spoils of Poynton* and *What Maisie Knew*. In the situation pieces James practiced adeptly the art of fiction. He did not advance it.

IV The Awkward Age (1898-99)

It is Nanda (Fernanda) Brookenham's "awkward age" that is chronicled in this elaborate novel. Her entrance into society has been delayed as long as possible by her attractive and ambitious mother, "Mrs. Brook." Entrance into society, of course, means courtship. Nanda is courted by the wealthy Mitchy, whom she rejects; and by the handsome Vanderbank, who despite encouragement never brings himself to a proposal. Nanda's friend, Little Aggie, carefully brought up in the Continental style, marries Mitchy in obedience to her mother's ambitious plan; and she soon separates from him. Everywhere in the society Nanda enters, she finds intrigue and selfish impulse. The marriage of her own parents is a hollow arrangement, and Vanderbank, Nanda's favored suitor, has been her mother's lover for years; he cannot give up Mrs. Brook for Nanda. Generous by nature, Nanda is hurt by what she sees and experiences. Little Aggie learns quickly to play the cynical social game. Harold, Nanda's younger brother, becomes a sponger, a liar, and a petty thief before he is of age. Thus in this single novel, James gathered together many themes that formed the substance of his other fiction in the 1890's.

The story is told in ten books, each bearing the name of one of the characters in the little circle that Nanda enters. The heavy proportion of dialogue is deliberate—partly because of James's fondness for the dramatic method, and partly because of his acknowledged adaptation of the French "dialogue romance" then current. The dialogue is clever, but extremely allusive and often circuitous; it demands close attention and a quick alertness to implication.

After Vanderbank's final call on Nanda, Mr. Longdon comes to see her. From the vaguely worded message left for him by Van, Longdon realizes that his plan for Nanda's happiness has failed. "It would be easier for me," he tells her, "if you didn't, my poor child, so wonderfully love him." When Nanda tries to deny this, she breaks down: "Her buried face could only after a moment give way to the flood, and she sobbed in a passion as sharp and brief as the flurry of a wild thing for an instant uncaged; her old friend meantime keeping his place in the silence broken by her sound and distantly—across the room—closing his eyes to his helplessness and her shame. Thus they sat together while their trouble both conjoined and divided them" (NY IX, 540).

Then Nanda agrees to go and live with Longdon permanently. She has concluded she will never marry, and he implicitly agrees. At any rate, life in her mother's house is now hardly possible. She has at last found a father—Edward Brookenham having long ago abdicated that relationship.

V Ghostly Tales

It was in the 1890's that James gave greatest attention to the most unusual category of his fiction: the ghostly tales. Among his early tales, already discussed, are four which may be so classified: "The

Romance of Certain Old Clothes" (1868); "De Grey: A Romance" (1868); "The Last of the Valerii" (1874); and "The Ghostly Rental" (1876). These stories were written much under the influence of Hawthorne, and today they seem old-fashioned; even among the early tales, they are not the best. From 1876 to 1891 James's fictional mood was realistic. "The Aspern Papers," with its powerful suggestion of a dim past, is almost the only evidence of the witchery of the ghost story. Professor Edel, in his collection of James's ghostly tales, emphasizes as influences not only the peculiar psychic experiences of Henry James, Sr., but William James's long concern with such phenomena.[6] In the later nineteenth century there was great interest in hypnotism, and a wide pseudo-scientific concern with spiritualism, evidenced in Mrs. Browning and William Dean Howells, to name only two of the many writers who might be cited. The scientific approach to psychic phenomena, though of great interest to Henry James and to his reading public, did not appeal to him as a fruitful literary method. In one of his prefaces he dismisses the psychical case as not of a nature "to rouse the dear old sacred terror" of the ghost story. Elsewhere he said that the ghost story had always been for him "the most possible form of the fairy tale." Such comments imply that the ghostly tales are to be taken as fairy tales—flights of poetic imagination—enriched by whatever insights into human motive the author finds appropriate.[7]

"Sir Edmund Orme" (1891) is the story of a jilted lover. Mrs. Marsden, now a widow, tells the narrator of her broken engagement with Sir Edmund. Since his spirit appears to her from time to time, usually near her daughter, Mrs. Marsden is apprehensive for her daughter's safety. The narrator, who has been in love with the daughter for some time, marries her. Mrs. Marsden dies, secure in the belief that the narrator will protect her daughter. This trust is justified, for after Mrs. Marsden's death the ghost is seen no more. By implication, the ghost has seen to it that the daughter did not jilt her lover, as Mrs. Marsden had Sir Edmund. The ghost in this story may easily be taken as an illusion based on a guilty conscience. Mrs. Marsden's emotions are real enough.

"The Visits" (1892), though not precisely a ghost story, turns on an unexplained mystery. Louisa Chantry confides to the narrator, a friend of her mother's, that she has "said things" to Howard Brandon for which she is ashamed. Swearing the narrator to secrecy, Louisa later dies. What Louisa said remains a mystery, and the effect of the story is that of a psychological aberration beyond rational explanation. James does not comment on this story in his notebooks or prefaces.

Other "ghost" stories of the period include "Owen Wingrave"

(1893), the story of a young man who renounces the family profession of military life and dies confronting the family ghost. Dramatized in 1908 as *The Saloon,* the story has been discussed in the preceding chapter. "The Friends of the Friends" ("The Way it Came," 1896) is introduced as the diary of a dead woman, recording a courtship broken off by psychic visions. "The Third Person" (1900) is an amusing tale of an English spinster to whom the ghost of an ancestor appears. The ancestor had engaged in smuggling, and his ghost desires that the spinster do likewise. The soul of caution, the spinster complies: she brings in from the continent an undeclared Tauchnitz volume.

"Maud-Evelyn" (1900) carries loyalty to the dead to the pitch of a hypnotic spell. Marmaduke, refused by Lavinia, vows never to marry. In Switzerland he meets a couple who have lost their only daughter, Maud-Evelyn, and have made a religion of her memory. Marmaduke is touched by their devotion, and for several years he associates himself closely with them. When they die, he carries on the worship of the dead girl's memory. He even comes to believe that he is married to Maud-Evelyn. Later, when Lavinia sees Marmaduke again, she is deeply impressed by his devotion. This story, like a scientific experiment, pushes a normal aspect of human emotion to the breaking point of belief. Yet it was to have a brilliant sequel when in *The Wings of the Dove* Kate Croy divines Merton Densher's deep loyalty to the memory of Milly Theale.

"The Altar of the Dead" (1895) is a much more sympathetic treatment of the bond between the living and the dead than that in "Maud-Evelyn." George Stransom mourns the death of the girl he had hoped to marry; and, though not himself a believer in religion, he gives an altar to the church where his lost love is buried. On one of his customary visits to her grave, he notices a woman in mourning. In time they become acquainted, and he finds that she, too, knew Acton Hague, an enemy whose betrayal Stransom has never forgiven. Under her influence he is able at last to grant her request for "just one more candle." The phrase is intended for Acton Hague, but, as Stransom himself is dying, it applies also to himself. He dies in the comforting arms of the unnamed lady.

The "religion of the dead" in this story recalls James's own emotion as he read aloud William's letter at their father's grave in 1882. With no settled religious belief, Henry James saw in the memory of the dead a kind of immortality deeply influential on the living.[8] Some readers find "The Altar of the Dead" a morbid story, for the concern with the dead isolated both George Stransom and the lady from the world. The whole of their lives, however, is not rendered in the story. The narrative focuses sharply on a relationship with the dead which finds some parallel in the lives of all sensitive people. The strange coincidence of the meetings between the two mourners and the slow, deliberate development give "The Altar of the Dead" a special depth.

VI *"The Turn of the Screw"* (1898)

It is in the light of James's other ghostly tales that "The Turn of the Screw" should be read. The ghost story, James says, is the fairy tale; it is not the marvelous but the effect on character that interests him. Characterized disarmingly by James as "a potboiler" (*Letters,* I, 299), but often reprinted as a masterpiece of short fiction, "The Turn of the Screw" is James's most expert and most popular ghost story. For long it was taken at face value as a story of actual apparitions seeking to exert an evil power on two children at the remote, lonely estate to which their new governess is sent. After a few introductory pages, the governess herself is the narrator of events at Bly, through a manuscript written in her own hand. Since Edmund Wilson's comments of 1934, discussion has centered about the reliability of the governess and about James's purpose in so contriving the story that doubt of her reliability is not only possible but probably mandatory—is, in fact, intended as the "real" interest of the story.[9]

The governess begins by describing her welcome at Bly by Mrs. Grose, the housekeeper, and by little Flora, one of her charges, a beautiful and well-mannered little girl. The next day she receives a letter from her employer in London, enclosing a communication from the headmaster of little Miles's school. It is stated that Miles, who is coming home for the usual holidays, may not return to the school. Questioning Mrs. Grose about Miles, the governess gets no information, but she does learn that the previous governess left Bly and died under mysterious circumstances. Miles, who duly arrives, is "incredibly beautiful," like his sister Flora. The governess confides to Mrs. Grose that for the present she will say nothing to anyone about the letter from the school. Shortly after, the governess sees a man standing on the tower of the house. A few days later, the same figure appears to her outside the window. The governess divines that the apparition is looking for "someone else." When she describes the figure to Mrs. Grose, after this second appearance, the housekeeper recognizes it as Quint, the dead valet of the master of the estate.

Occupied as the governess is by the mystery of Miles's misconduct at school, she concludes that the apparition was looking for Miles. Mrs. Grose confides that Quint was "much too free" with everyone. The governess now sees her mission: she must protect the children. It is, she comments, "a magnificent chance." Her sense of the danger is confirmed when near the lake she sees a strange woman, and is convinced that Flora recognizes her. Hence the strange figure must be the spirit of Miss Jessel, the previous governess. The present governess sweeps aside the doubts of Mrs. Grose, but she learns that Miss Jessel was infatuated with Quint and that Miles knew this. When Quint appears a third time, on the stairs, the governess records: "I had, thank God, no terror. And he knew I hadn't . . ." (NY XII, 222). Then she discovers Flora's bed empty; when Flora returns a moment later, the governess is sure Flora has seen Quint. Thereafter, the governess keeps nightly watch. Once she sees Miss Jessel on the stair, and one night she finds Flora's bed empty again. Flora is looking out the window, and on the lawn is Miles, sought by "a person on the tower." When the governess questions Miles, he merely says his going outside was a trick, pre-arranged with Flora. The governess is now convinced that Quint, Miss Jessel, and the two children are meeting secretly. When Mrs. Grose asks why they meet, the governess replies: "For the love of all the evil that, in those dreadful days, the pair put into them. And to ply them with that evil still, to keep up the work of demons, is what brings the others back" (237). When Mrs. Grose urges the governess to appeal to the children's uncle, she refuses; she has been strictly ordered by the uncle not to communicate with him.

In the autumn Miles asks about returning to school, but he will give no explanation of why he was dismissed. Then for the third time Miss Jessel appears to the governess. When she tells Mrs. Grose of this, the housekeeper asks her once more to send for the children's uncle. A few days later, Flora is missing, and is found at the lake by Mrs. Grose and the governess. When the governess sees Miss Jessel (a fourth appearance), Mrs. Grose cannot see anything. Flora, witness to the argument between the two women, turns on the governess: "I don't know what you mean. I see nobody. I see nothing. I never *have*. I think you're cruel. I don't like you!" (281). The governess interprets this as proof of Miss Jessel's possession of the child. Back at the house, Mrs. Grose moves Flora's things from the governess's room, and she reports that Flora is in bed with a fever.

The governess now orders Mrs. Grose to take Flora to her uncle. At this point Mrs. Grose is half-convinced that spirits are really at work, for Flora in her delirium speaks of "horrors." Mrs. Grose also informs the governess that Miles has intercepted the governess's letter to the guardian. Perhaps, thinks the governess, almost with relief, it was for stealing letters that Miles was dismissed from school. After Mrs. Grose and Flora leave, the governess talks with Miles about the missing letter. Through the window, she sees Quint once more, just outside the window. The governess keeps Miles's back to the window, while Miles readily confesses that he did indeed take the letter in order to see what the governess said about him. He admits that the letter said nothing about him. The governess then asks him with some intensity if it was for stealing letters that he was dismissed from school. No, Miles says, not for that, but because he "said things." Feeling that she has at last won the boy's confidence, the governess shrieks to the figure at the window: "No more, no more, no more!" Surprisingly, Miles asks, "Is she *here*?" Assured that it is not Miss Jessel, Miles asks, "It's *he*?"—meaning Quint—but apparently Miles cannot see Quint, for his last spoken word is "Where?" The governess catches the boy to her tightly: "it may be imagined with what passion; but at the end of a minute I began to feel what it truly was that I held. We were alone with the quiet day, and his little heart, dispossessed, had stopped."

Considering the governess's narrative by itself, it seems clear that she alone saw the four appearances of Quint and the four appearances of Miss Jessel. That the children "saw" rests in each case on the governess's inference and assertion. Mrs. Grose never saw the figures. Just before she takes Flora away, Mrs. Grose does have a degree of belief, but it is fully explainable by the weeks of queer behavior, especially that of the governess. It is notable that the other five servants (mentioned in the introduction) are not involved. A puzzling detail is that the governess has never seen Quint, nor heard details of his appearance, seemingly; yet when she describes the apparition, Mrs. Grose recognizes it as Quint. The suggestion that in some way—perhaps in the village—the governess had learned about Quint is plausible. If she had, she would certainly not have mentioned it, for a logical explanation of her experience is something she never seeks. In short, the governess's story seems to be the account of a woman in the grip of hallucinations, so vividly described that they *seem* true, not only to her, but to the housekeeper, to the reader, and finally to little Miles. It is the unbalanced condition of the governess, then, that frightens Flora and results in her being taken away.[10]

If this interpretation of the governess's story is accepted, then the function of the brief introduction is clear: it is to provide a realistic frame which encourages the reader to proceed on the assumption that he is being given a documentary, a *true* account. On Christmas Eve, someone has told the story of an apparition that had appeared to a child and then to the child's mother. Douglas, one of the listeners, confides to a companion that he knows a story that touches two children. No one else, he says, has ever heard this story: "It's beyond everything." Besought to tell the dreadful story immediately, Douglas explains that he has a manuscript, and must send to town for it. The manuscript, he says, was written by a woman dead now for twenty years, once his sister's governess. Someone guesses that the woman must have been in love. Yes, says Douglas, but not with him, and the story won't tell with whom. The manuscript arrives, and by way of introduction Douglas explains that it is the narrative of a parson's daughter who answered the advertisement of a handsome and wealthy bachelor in Harley Street. Through the death of a brother and sister-in-law this gentleman had become the guardian of two young children, now looked after on his Essex estate by his housekeeper, Mrs. Grose. The previous governess had died. Questioned about her death, Douglas refuses to add anything, saying that the circumstances will come out in the governess's narrative—though they are never fully given. The young lady, he goes on to say, was somewhat taken aback at the prospect of having full charge of the little girl and holiday responsibility for the boy. The salary was generous, however, and after two days she accepted the position. It is pointedly added that she never saw her employer again.

The tone of the introduction hints of strange matters to come, but in itself is most matter-of-fact. By failing to speculate or explain further, Douglas creates the impression that the governess's story is to be trusted. Moreover, Douglas says of the governess that "she was the most agreeable woman I've known in her position." At the death of Miles, the climactic event, no one among the listeners thinks of picking up the loose ends of the introduction. What *did* happen to the governess next? How did she become the governess of Douglas' sister? What did the guardian do with regard to Miles's death and Flora's departure? What happened later to Flora? And what was Mrs. Grose's later view of events? It is precisely the proof of James's skill that no one raises these questions, so appropriate to a genuinely realistic story. In Coleridge's phrase, James has caused his readers to suspend their disbelief.[11]

VII *Shorter Fiction: Writers and Artists*

In 1890 James was forty-seven. All his adult life he had been a professional writer, and he had personally known a great many writers in America, England, and France. Little interested in acquiring a scholarly knowledge of literary men of previous eras, James was very sensitive to the problems writers experienced in his own time. Though James's letters do not usually concentrate on literary matters, his notebooks show a persistent curiosity about literary themes and treatment. Over the years, his conversations with such diverse men as Howells, Turgenev, Stevenson, and Wells must have brought out many odd ideas and bits of information. Habitually, too, James reflected on the interesting parallels between the writer and the painter. In the 1890's, sixteen stories center on the special problems of writers and artists. As in James's stories on other themes, some are merely clever statements or developments of situation; others touch deeper values of character and idea.

"Nona Vincent" (1892) depends almost wholly on situation and contrivance. A young dramatist is worried about the actress who plays the part of Nona Vincent in his new play. Only after a woman friend visits the actress does she get the part right. Each of the two women thinks the dramatist is in love with the other, but he marries the actress. There is less emphasis of stage atmosphere than might be expected in the only story of this period directly related to the stage.

"The Private Life" (1892) is an almost allegorical treatment of a playwright whose plays are written by his double and of a public man who so completely lives in the public eye that, when he is in his room, he ceases to exist. The story is said to have been suggested by the career of Robert Browning, a very ordinary man in public, and by Sir Frederick Leighton, a superb public figure.

"Sir Dominick Ferrand" (1892) turns on the temptation faced by a journalist who discovers papers related to the late Sir Dominick Ferrand, a public figure of sufficient reputation that the vague hint of scandal in the newly discovered papers will be worth a sizable fee from a magazine called *The Promiscuous*. Dr. Edel groups this story with the "ghostly tales" of James, finding a suggestion of mesmeric power in the papers themselves.

"Collaboration" (1892) is a satirical comment on the idea that art has no country. The narrator invites to his studio a German musician, an American, a French poet, a French lady and her daughter. The French poet and German musician begin to collaborate on an opera, but the hatreds of 1870 break up the engagement of the French poet and his French sweetheart. Her mother cannot tolerate the poet's association with a German, since her husband had died in the Franco-Prussian War.

"The Coxon Fund" (1894) was suggested to James by James Dykes Campbell's life of Coleridge, which appeared the previous year. The story, however, is not to be taken in any literal sense as an evaluation of Coleridge. In the story the great irresponsible, talkative writer figures as Mr. Saltram, who is watched over by the Mulvilles, modeled on Coleridge's quasi-guardians, the Gillmans. In this story James ridicules both the writer who cannot work systematically and the sentimental admirers who persist in shielding him from the harsh necessities of life.

"The Figure in the Carpet" (1896) involves much discussion of the inner meaning of Hugh Vereker's fiction. The narrator reviews one of his novels; later, when he meets Vereker himself, the author hints at a meaning not perceived by the critic. A friend of the narrator, who excitedly discovers the secret, dies before revealing it. What the inner meaning is remains a frustrating mystery. James may be laughing at critics, or pretentious authors, or both.

"The Real Right Thing" (1899) and "The Abasement of the Northmores" (1900) treat the difficulties of biography. Withermore is flattered by the opportunity to write the biography of Ashton Doyne, whose relationship with his wife proves to be a problem. After Withermore works for some time with Mrs. Doyne, important documents are unaccountably lost, and eventually the project is given up. The story illustrates James's distrust of biography as a dangerous invasion of private life. In "The Abasement of the Northmores" Mrs. Hope cooperates with Lord Northmore's widow by returning his lordship's letters to her husband. When the letters are published, the book is badly received. Mrs. Hope, gathering her husband's letters together, has a single copy printed, to be published only after her death.

"The Tone of Time" (1900) is a revelation of rivalry between two women, revealed by a portrait. The narrator, asked by Mrs. Bridgenorth to paint a certain type of man to serve as portrait of her late husband, turns the commission over to Mary Tredick, a woman copyist. Free to do as she likes, Mary paints from memory a portrait of the man she herself had lost. When she takes the portrait to Mrs. Bridgenorth, it turns out to be the man Mrs. Bridgenorth expected to marry. The copyist refuses to let her have the portrait, guessing that it was Mrs. Bridgenorth who caused her to lose the man. After both women die, the artist-narrator inherits the picture.

The theme of the artist as failure, so effectively treated in "The Madonna of the Future" (1873), is more lightly touched in two stories of 1900. In "Broken Wings" a painter and a young woman who writes plays meet and fall in love. Gradually each discovers that the other is a failure. They decide, good-naturedly, to face defeat together, but the story ends: "And now to work." In "The Tree of Knowledge" Peter Brench dislikes the sculpture of his friend Morgan Mallow, though he is fond of Mallow himself. Brench warns Mallow's son against a career in art, but the boy goes to Paris anyway. There he learns not only that he is a duffer in art, but also that his sculptor-father is a duffer. Talking with his mother when he returns, the boy finds that she has long realized that her husband has no talent. When Peter Brench learns of this conversation, he realizes that his own secret love for Mrs. Mallow is now hopeless.

Much more important are several stories that treat the relation of reality to art, the nature of popular success, the dedication of the sincere writer, the limitations of editorial policy, and "the dreadful fatal too much" of the life that floods in on the writer.

"The Real Thing" (1892) ironically states the idea that Impressionism is a sounder principle of creative art than literal Realism. The artist-narrator illustrates the point by the sad case of Major and Mrs. Monarch, genteel people in need of money, who ask to serve as models for illustrations of novels that deal with genteel life. The artist tries them, but he finds they lack the flexibility of his professional models, who know nothing of good society. In the opinion of a friendly critic, it is the new models who are ruining the artist's style. When they are discharged as models, the Monarchs offer to work as servants; but the artist pays them to go away. The "real thing" was limiting; it encouraged copying rather than creation. Details stifle the creative mind; suggestion stimulates it. The posing of this idea, the humorous contrast between the Monarchs and the vulgar professional models, and the pathos of the shabby-genteel couple have made this one of James's most frequently reprinted stories.

"Greville Fane" (1892) is an ironic comment about a type of popular woman novelist, combined with a bitter exposure of her ungrateful children. When Mrs. Stormer, whose pen name is Greville Fane, dies suddenly, the narrator is asked to write a feature article about her. This narrative tells what he cannot put in his feature article: the shallowness of Greville Fane's stories, the pathos of her personal life.

"The Next Time" (1895), like "Greville Fane," is an ironic representation of the popular press as the enemy of artistic quality. The narrator, a critic with a taste for subtlety and a revulsion against the "age of trash triumphant," has for many years praised the work of Ray Limbert, only to witness book after book fail with the public. Meanwhile, Mrs. Highmore, a great popular success, persuades a magazine editor to serialize Limbert's *The Major Key;* and, on the hope of its success, Limbert marries Mrs. Highmore's sister. *The Major Key,* however, is also a failure. Despite his efforts to be popular, Limbert died a failure: "There was some obscure interference of taste, some obsession of the exquisite."

"The Death of the Lion" (1894) is a slightly different treatment of the popular writer. The narrator is a journalist who tells ironically of his assignment to "do" Neil Paraday, the novelist. At a literary party in the country, Paraday becomes ill and dies, leaving to the narrator the task of bringing out his unpublished manuscript. The manuscript, however, has been lost by one of the admirers who borrowed it. Perhaps, the narrator concludes, "some brutal, fatal ignorance has lighted kitchen fires with it" (154).

In "The Middle Years" (1893) the novelist Dencombe rests at Bournemouth just after the publication of his latest book. He becomes acquainted with a young doctor, the personal physician of a wealthy countess, and a great admirer of Dencombe's work. When Dencombe falls ill, the young doctor deserts his wealthy patron to take care of the author, and he is disinherited by the countess. Though Dencombe deprecates the young doctor's devotion, he is touched by it. Just before the author dies, a favorable review of his new novel comes in. Many details seem to echo James's personality. Dencombe is described as "a passionate corrector, a fingerer of style." As he lies ill, he turns the pages of his novel, thinking: "Ah, for another go, ah, for a better chance!" Just before he dies, Dencombe himself answers that vain hope in a speech that has been much quoted, so applicable is it to James: "A second chance—*that's* the delusion. There was never to be but one. We work in the dark— we do what we can—we give what we have. Our doubt is our passion, and our passion is our task. The rest is the madness of art."[12]

"John Delavoy" (1900) is a fictional posing of the problem of restrictive editorial policy. An article on John Delavoy is first commissioned, then rejected on the ground that Delavoy's novels are too indelicate for readers of this family journal. The editor in this story is represented as the absolute slave of his undiscriminating readers. "The Great Good Place" (1900) is told about a writer, but it has a wider application. George Dane wakes up one morning to confront a pile of unfinished work, stacks of mail and newspapers, a disagreeable luncheon engagement, and even a guest for breakfast. It is the guest's arrival that produces a strange transition. At the touch of a hand, Dane feels transported to "the Great Good Place," a kind of monastic retreat. When he asks a gentleman where they are, the following dialogue occurs:

"I shouldn't be surprised if it were much nearer than one ever suspected."
"Nearer 'town,' do you mean?"
"Nearer everything—nearer everyone."

Later, Dane reflects that part of his present bliss is the absence of identity in "a world without newspapers and letters, without telegrams and photographs, without the dreadful fatal too much."

Suddenly Dane realizes that "his hour seemed to strike," and soon he is back in his familiar room. The young man invited for breakfast smiles at him and explains that Dane seemed very tired and has slept all day. Dane looks around his room, "which seemed disencumbered, different, twice as large. It *was* all right." What did James mean by this fantasy? Perhaps nothing more than the importance of preserving some inner resource, some privacy into which the round of daily concerns does not enter. That this is a peculiarly intense problem for a writer is obvious.[13]

VIII *Retrospect*

In 1900 James was fifty-seven. The 1890's had for him been untouched with *fin de siècle* decadence. If he had failed as a dramatist, it was not for lack of energy. Indeed, the failure was far from absolute, and during the years of dramatic experiment (1891-95) he had concurrently achieved a quarter of a million words of fiction, all of it competent, some of it distinguished. The dramatic method so painfully learned, enabled him in the later 1890's to achieve such sharply new work as *The Spoils of Poynton, What Maisie Knew,* and "The Turn of the Screw." To turn back to such earlier masterpieces as *The American, The Portrait of a Lady,* and "The Aspern Papers" is to realize how insistently James experimented, how rapidly he learned. In 1900 others might regard his career as over. For himself, he was supremely confident that "the best was yet to be." And so it was.

CHAPTER 6

The Major Phase and the
Last Years: 1901-1916

FOR THE FIRST TEN YEARS of the new century, James maintained an extraordinary rate of production. From 1901 through
1904 he published a novel a year: *The Sacred Fount, The Wings of
the Dove, The Ambassadors,* and *The Golden Bowl,* sufficient in
themselves to make a novelist's reputation. Meanwhile he dictated
the two-volume life of Story, the American sculptor (1903); and he
assembled *The Better Sort* (1903), a volume of eleven stories, six
of them written in this period. Then in 1904 came his ten-month
trip to America, with an itinerary that carried him to California and
to Florida, and included a number of public lectures, something of
an ordeal for James. Back in Lamb House in August, 1905, James
settled down to revise articles on his American observations for
The American Scene (1907) and to work concurrently on the New
York Edition of his novels and tales. Thorough revision of twenty-
four volumes of fiction, with elaborate prefaces, took the better part
of two years. Before James finished this large project he had once
more turned to plays. As outlined in a previous chapter, he turned
"Covering End" into the full-length *The High Bid;* he dramatized
"Owen Wingrave"; and he wrote *The Outcry.* Seven more short
stories appeared from 1908 to 1910, the last he was to write. Also
he published some twenty critical and travel pieces.

   The American Scene clearly exposes James's growing alienation
from American life. As he traveled about the eastern seaboard, he
experienced a rich nostalgic reminiscence of the America of his
youth, a reminiscence that was to have freer and happier expression
in the later autobiographical volumes. At the same time, as he made
brief visits to New York City, Boston, and Chicago, James felt a
revulsion at the new lines of development. He speaks of himself
repeatedly as "the restless analyst," but he could not find a way to
come to terms with what he saw. The result is a shrillness of tone,
as in this remark: "To make so much money that you won't, that
you don't 'mind,' don't mind anything—that is absolutely, I think,

the main American formula." James was perhaps uneasily aware that his consideration of the American scene was too limited, too narrowly based. James's essays on American writers, recently collected by Professor Edel, show a far more sympathetic under-standing of American life than the book based on the American trip of 1904-05.[1]

I The Sacred Fount (*1901*)

Despite the fact that *The Sacred Fount* immediately precedes the novels comprising the so-called major phase of James, this work is least relished by James enthusiasts. It is a first-person narrative; and, as in "The Turn of the Screw," an important clue to understanding the story lies in the estimate made of the narrator. The title comes from a passage toward the end of the second chapter; the narrator is explaining how Guy Brissenden, a young man who has recently married an older woman, seems to have aged so rapidly, while his wife seems younger than ever: " 'One of the pair,' I said, 'has to pay for the other. What ensues is a miracle, and miracles are expensive. What's a greater one than to have your youth twice over? . . . Mrs. Briss had to get her new blood, her extra allowance of time and bloom, somewhere; and from whom could she so conveniently extract them as from Guy himself? She *has*, by an extraordinary feat of legerdemain, extracted them; and he, on his side, to supply her, has had to tap the sacred fount.' "[2] It then occurs to the narrator that Gilbert Long, his companion, is involved in a similar relationship, ostensibly with Lady John.

This idea of the psychological effects of relationships platonic or otherwise becomes an obsession relentlessly pursued by the narrator through discreet spying and a bewildering series of conversations with guests at the weekend party. Greatly impressed with his own cleverness, the narrator discounts surface impressions. It seems to him unlikely that Lady John, a boring woman, could really have stimulated Gilbert Long. Noting the vivacious Mrs. May Server, the narrator theorizes that she may really be the one. It develops, how-ever, that there is some attraction between Mrs. Server and Brissenden. But is this a pretense designed to distract attention from a real affair between Brissenden and Lady John? Or is Brissenden being used by Mrs. Server to deflect attention from her interest in Long?

In pursuing these possibilities, the narrator finds himself some-what emotionally involved with Mrs. Server and then with Mrs. Brissenden. The latter is herself interested in the narrator's theories, but is finally revolted by them, especially when she gets what she believes is the truth from her husband. In a late evening rendezvous with the narrator, Mrs. Brissenden flatly tells him he is crazy. As she sees it, Lady John is, after all, the real interest of Gilbert Long. Thus the narrator is brought back to the hypothesis stated in the first chapter, except that the supposed "change" in Gilbert Long has never really occurred. As for Mrs. Server, Brissenden himself has told his wife about his attachment—presumably innocent—for Mrs. Server. The narrator's "palace of thought" is thus, as he says, reduced to "a house of cards." The narrator goes to his room, looking forward to his departure the next morning. He feels the need of "escape to other air."

In its substance, *The Sacred Fount* is the least rewarding of James's novels. The characters are virtually cut off from the molding forces of their lives, and it is difficult to distinguish them—even more difficult to take any real interest in their designs. There is some satisfaction in the final discomfiture of the narrator, for his obsession with gossip is above the keyhole level only in its well-bred language. The atmosphere of the weekend party—the formal dinner, the evening musicale, the art gallery, tea on the terrace, the walks in the woods, the outdoor benches inviting private conversations—is agreeably rendered; but it is more pleasantly available in other stories. Perhaps James's purpose was a satiric contrast between the beauty of the setting and the vapid, malicious people who enjoy it. The surface of life is wonderfully polite and delicate. The intimacies just below the surface hint constantly of adultery, though such involvement is never asserted. The "love" the narrator thinks he feels for Mrs. Server is more akin to what Henry Green pictures in his novel *Doting:* a self-indulgent and temporary titillation.

For form and structure, *The Sacred Fount* may be respected if not admired. Only a master technician could have achieved it. The reader can see enough of the pattern, even in his most bewildered moments, to be sure that a pattern exists. If he sees the novel in the perspective of James's later career, he will take on faith the details hard to fit into place. And he will rightly feel that hardly anyone else writing before 1901 could have written *The Sacred Fount.* James's comment in a letter to Howells that he intended to write only a short story is significant. Having invented the obsessed narrator, James found that he needed an elaborate maze of maneuver to allow the narrator to expose himself. Of the many observations on this unusual novel, one of the most appropriate is that of Bliss Perry at the time of publication: "*The Sacred Fount* makes me feel insufferably stupid, like talking to some confoundedly clever woman who is two or three 'moves' ahead of you in the conversational game. . . . Only a woman would let you catch up, and James doesn't."[3]

II   The Ambassadors (*1903*)

Though published later, *The Ambassadors* was written a full year earlier than *The Wings of the Dove*. Unsuccessful attempts to sell serial rights for *The Wings of the Dove* led to its appearance in book form several months before serial publication of *The Ambassadors* began in the *North American Review*. In the preface to the New York Edition of *The Ambassadors* James thought it "quite the best, 'all round,' of my productions." It was not, James thought, the best of his novels to read first;[4] but his high opinion, widely though not universally supported, has made *The Ambassadors* a test case. If the intention, methods, and values of this novel are granted, the whole body of James's work is vindicated. To the extent that reservations are made in judging *The Ambassadors*, James's whole artistic career is called in question.

A bald statement of the story seems damaging enough. Lambert Strether, a widower of fifty-five and a minor literary man, goes to Europe at the request of his patroness and fiancée, Mrs. Newsome of Woollett, Massachusetts. Mrs. Newsome's son Chad has been abroad for some time and is now living in Paris. His mother thinks it time for the young man to come home and to assume responsibility in the family business. Chad's unwillingness to leave Paris has been set down to some entanglement with a woman, and Strether's purpose as ambassador is to persuade the young man of his duty to give up the woman and to return to Woollett.

Strether's recollection of Chad is not favorable; but, when they meet, Strether is much pleased by Chad's improved manners. When Strether meets Chad's friend, Mme. de Vionnet, a charming lady separated but not divorced from her husband, Strether is even more impressed. Mme. de Vionnet has a young daughter, and Strether naturally assumes that Chad is in love with the daughter. Soon the daughter marries, however, and it is clear that Chad is interested in Mme. de Vionnet herself. Unexpectedly, Strether meets Chad and Mme. de Vionnet in the country, and the circumstances force the conclusion that the attachment is not so innocent as had appeared. Strether now feels that Chad has a responsibility to Mme. de Vionnet; when Chad begins to talk, finally, of going home, Strether feels that Chad is callously abandoning the lady. Meanwhile, Strether's delay in getting a decision from Chad has resulted in the dispatch of other "ambassadors" from Woollett: Chad's married sister, Sarah Pocock; her husband, Jim Pocock; and Jim's sister Mamie, the family choice for Chad to marry. The Pococks, particularly Sarah, represent the Woollett insensitivity which life in Paris has gradually revealed to Strether. After meeting Mme. de Vionnet,

Sarah denounces Strether for daring to introduce that lady. At the end, Chad has not yet given up Mme. de Vionnet, though he seems likely to; and he has not accepted Mamie. Strether, through his sympathetic appreciation of Mme. de Vionnet, seems to have forfeited the chance to marry Chad's mother, though he does not seem to feel this a shattering loss.

The reader who turns to *The Ambassadors* from active sport or business, from consideration of political and social problems, will strongly doubt whether four hundred pages of Jamesian rhetoric are necessary to expose an adultery which any worldly minded person would have been certain of to begin with. Strether's dawdling progress argues a nature either too innocent or too stupid to merit such elaborate analysis. Yet such an approach ignores a great deal. James sees human character and personality as the real end of life. Actions and choices, conversations and silences, give clues as to what people *are*. To draw the right inferences can never be easy or swift, either in life or in a fiction faithful to life. The realities are seldom spectacular, but to the observant mind they need never be dull. The constant companion, the new acquaintance, the old friend seen in new surroundings, silently pose the fascinating questions: what is he like; what did he mean; how has he changed. When "she" is substituted for "he," or when the two are combined, the questions become even more fascinating. These questions, which in life occupy the attention momentarily or haphazardly, in James's novels—and particularly in *The Ambassadors*—receive a sustained and disciplined scrutiny. The results, if patiently examined, are illuminating.

The novel begins at the hotel in Chester, where Strether is to meet Waymarsh, an old friend, a successful lawyer, separated from his wife and traveling rather disconsolately about Europe. Strether's relief at finding his old friend not yet arrived tells us something of their opposite natures. It also gives an opportunity for Maria Gostrey to make Strether's acquaintance, rather forwardly, but still discreetly. She, too, is acquainted with Mr. Waymarsh, and overhears Strether's inquiry. Maria, an American in her middle thirties, describes herself as a "companion at large" for traveling Americans. She quickly puts Strether at his ease. As they walk about the old city, she catches him looking at his watch: "You're doing something that you think is not right." To this he replies, "Am I enjoying it as much as that?" Then he confesses his inability to enjoy the present without preoccupation; Woollett, he adds, "isn't sure it ought to enjoy" (NY XXI, 16). Thus the first chapter lays the basis for a later meeting in London, and for frequent meetings in Paris, in which Strether can state to this perceptive woman his problem with Chad, and progressively analyze its complications. To say that Maria Gostrey is a foil for Strether is to underrate her charm. Waymarsh more nearly fits that term, for when he appears at the end of the first chapter, he is described as "joyless."

In Paris, Strether's meeting with Chad is plausibly postponed. Chad is away, and Strether, cautiously reconnoitering, meets Chad's companion, Little Bilham. From Bilham, Strether derives the impression that Chad must be much improved from the awkward boy who had left Woollett. Attending the opera with Maria, Strether first sees Chad, and takes the opportunity to blurt out that he has come to take Chad straight home. Chad's suave and good-humored, though indecisive, reply pleases Strether. Chad continues to be kind, and at a garden party contrives that Strether meet Mme. de Vionnet and her daughter. Strether is captivated. Calling on her a few days later, Strether is fully appreciative of the part she has played in Chad's development. When she urges him to speak well of her to Mrs. Newsome, Strether promises, "I'll save you if I can."

Thus, in the first half of the novel Strether has reversed his opinion and intention. He has rejected Woollett's view that the woman in the case must necessarily be bad. He accepts Bilham's word that the attachment between Chad and Mme. de Vionnet is "virtuous." At this point the Pococks arrive as fresh ambassadors from Woollett. Mme. de Vionnet takes the initiative by calling on Sarah. Sarah is polite but reluctant to return the call. A little later she demands to see Strether alone. Sarah insists in this interview that Strether has insulted both her and her mother in defending Mme. de Vionnet; she also insists that Chad's development in Paris is not fortunate but "hideous." Since Sarah is so direct and recent an ambassadress from Mrs. Newsome, Strether can only conclude that his own relationship with Mrs. Newsome is at an end. The Pococks leave for Switzerland, taking with them Waymarsh, who is attentive to Sarah, and Little Bilham, to whom Mamie is attracted. It is after the Pococks leave that Strether meets Chad and Mme. de Vionnet in the country and concludes that their attachment, after all, is not "virtuous."

What Strether makes of his experience is brought out in final scenes with Mme. de Vionnet, Chad, and Maria Gostrey. Mme. de Vionnet's humiliation is painful to Strether, and he gently rebuffs a seeming proffer of serious affection from her. Chad is indecisive: he is "not a bit tired" of Mme. de Vionnet, but he is tempted by the advertising end of the business back in Woollett. Strether makes no judgment of their adulterous relationship, except to insist again

on Chad's obligation. What seems implied, however, is that along
with the undoubted "good" of the relationship there was something
of callousness, deception, and hypocrisy.

Strether's final interview with Maria, the last chapter of the novel,
repeats two ideas with the implication of finality. Chad is likely to
go back to Woollett; so, in a sense, Strether will have been a
successful ambassador, after all. Nevertheless, he sees his relationship with Mrs. Newsome as ended. Not even Chad can change that.
"Too much has happened," Strether explains to Maria. "I'm different
for her." But Mrs. Newsome has not changed: "She's more than ever
the same. But I do what I didn't before—I *see* her." Since Strether
does not go home, then, to Mrs. Newsome, why should he go at all?
"There's nothing, you know," says Maria, "I wouldn't do for you."
Despite Maria's undoubted charm for him, and the charm of her
beautifully appointed apartment, Strether rejects Maria. To be
"right," he says, he must not "out of the whole affair, to have got
anything for myself."[5]

Strether's rejection of Maria has been much criticized. Has not
James, in order to get a theoretical perfection of design, abandoned
nature as well as the desires of his readers? From first to last,
Strether has hardly passed an uncomfortable moment in Maria's
company. The dialogue between them is an extraordinary blend of
comedy and communion. Why should Strether reject the delightful
Maria? Professor Cargill argues (320) that Strether's rejection con-
ceals the fact that he is more strongly attracted to Mme. de Vionnet
than to Maria. Since he cannot tell Maria this, he takes refuge in a
dialectical statement of his position, which he knows she will admire
despite her own disappointment. This theory is possible, but many
readers will not find it plausible. Strether, though delighted with
Mme. de Vionnet, has seen her so steadily and so approvingly in
relation to Chad that Strether's personal interest in her is hardly a
love interest. Certainly, too, after Strether sees the pair in the
country, he feels a pity for Mme. de Vionnet. He can say goodbye
to her tenderly, as he does; but it seems unlikely that he will long
for her when he returns to Woollett—or elsewhere in America. The
companionship with Maria is a different matter. She has become
almost a staple in his life. To do without her will be a deprivation.
Why, again, should he reject her?

There is a clue early in the final chapter. Strether comments on
the happiness of her Paris home: "What's this . . . but a haunt of
ancient peace?" In reply she wishes she could make him treat it
"as a haven of rest." Strether's next comment has perhaps not been
given its full weight: "It wouldn't give me—that would be the
trouble—what it will, no doubt, still give you. I'm not . . . in real

harmony with what surrounds me. You *are*. I take it too hard. You *don't*. It makes—that's what it comes to in the end—a fool of me" (320). Strether's education has been immense, but it has not been complete. He sees, as Maria does not, that he can still be more at home in Woollett than in Paris. He has, in his phrase, *had* Maria. There is enough self-reliance in him to reject the domination which marriage to her might imply.

There is another aspect to his scruple: his only logic, he says, is not "out of the whole affair to have got anything for myself." This results from his continuing respect for Mrs. Newsome, whose overshadowing presence is felt throughout the novel, even though she never directly appears. She is of all the characters the easiest to misjudge. As the embodied spirit of Woollett, she seems almost designed as the focus for the reader's scorn—almost, but not quite. After all, Strether's love for Mrs. Newsome is presupposed. It is a middle-aged affection. Strether is a widower of fifty-five, whose wife died before he was thirty, and his one child some time after. Mrs. Newsome is a widow of ten years. For an unspecified time, she has been Strether's patroness, the backer of his literary review. Strether always speaks of her with great respect. He willingly became her ambassador on her own terms and, probably (James does not say), at her expense. With regard to Chad, Mrs. Newsome shows some lack of tact, and she can even telegraph Strether to come home at once. Yet when the Pococks are expected, Chad himself says: "Mother's worth fifty of Sally!" Strether is aware of a sharp contrast between mother and daughter:

> Mrs. Newsome was much handsomer, and while Sarah inclined to the massive her mother had, at an age, still the girdle of a maid; also the latter's chin was rather short, than long, and her smile, by good fortune, much more, oh ever so much more, mercifully vague. Strether had seen Mrs. Newsome reserved; he had literally heard her silent, though he had never known her unpleasant. It was the case with Mrs. Pocock that he had known *her* unpleasant, even though he had never known her not affable (73-74).

As he describes Mrs. Newsome's limitations, her inability to understand the letters he has written, Strether betrays no irritation, no malice. Had he done so, acceptance of Maria Gostrey might have been easier. Yet had he been capable of expressing malice, Maria's interest in him would have been diminished. Part of Strether's "rightness," of his very capacity to see, was his patience, his generosity of mind. There is in his relation to Maria Gostrey something of a parallel to the decisive qualities of character built into

Longmore and Euphemia in James's early story, "Madame de Mauves."

The development of *The Ambassadors* is of particular interest, not only because the novel is important, but because the relevant information is unusually full. On October 31, 1895, James recorded that William Dean Howells had recently told their mutual friend, young Jonathan Sturges, "Live all you can, it's a mistake not to." In several paragraphs, James then set down the basic idea for *The Ambassadors*. Returning to the idea about 1900, James wrote a twenty-thousand word "project" or scenario, specifying the structure later embodied in the novel. This statement, dated September 1, 1900, was sent to Harpers as a basis for placing the novel as a serial, and was thus preserved in the publisher's files. In serial form, certain chapters were omitted because the novel exceeded the intended length. These chapters were restored when the novel appeared in book form. The Preface to the New York Edition adds comments on the intention and execution of the novel. Taken together, this material makes *The Ambassadors* one of the most fully documented of important fictional works. It illustrates James's own analytical methods in writing, and encourages the analytical approach to critical evaluation. From the "project," for example, it appears that James first intended to have Strether meet Waymarsh before he met Maria Gostrey. This was reversed in the finished novel and to great advantage. Opportunities for such comparisons are great; they explain, in part, the continuous attention given to *The Ambassadors*.[6]

A bibliographical detail of exceptional importance is the reversal in the sequence of two chapters, unnoticed by James, in the New York Edition. The error persisted in American reprints and was undetected by two generations of James critics until pointed out in 1950. The chapters in question are the first two in the eleventh book (Chapters XXVIII and XXIX). Once the point is raised, it is clear that Strether's evening visit to Chad properly precedes Strether's call on Maria Gostrey the next day. That this error was so long undetected is embarrassing to some critics who praised the structure of the novel on the basis of an erroneous text. The error was not James's, however; and the proper sequence, now established, is his design.[7]

The germ idea of the novel, Strether's comment, "Live all you can, it's a mistake not to," has perhaps been overstressed. Taken out of context, it is an echo of Emerson (through Howells) which leaves unspecified what "living" means. That James realized this fact is evident from his incidental use of the idea in other stories. In "The Bundle of Letters" (1879), for example, James's intention is ironic when sophisticated, stuffy Louis Leverett writes from Paris to a Boston friend: "The great thing is to *live*, you know—to feel, to be conscious of one's possibilities; not to pass through life mechanically and insensibly, like a letter through a post-office." The idea sounds well, but there is some doubt whether the callow youth comprehends it. In *The Ambassadors*, too, "living" is a term to be given value by intuitions which James could nourish but could not inventory.

III The Wings of the Dove (1902)

The idea for *The Wings of the Dove* James first sketched out in November, 1894, even considering the possibility of making it into a play. But the roots of the idea go back to his acquaintance as a young man with "Minny" Temple. Her long illness and her death in 1870 cast a long shadow in James's life. "Farewell to all that she was," he wrote William. "How much this was, and how sweet it was." As late as 1914 he devoted the eloquent last chapter in *Notes of a Son and Brother* to Minny's memory.[8]

In the novel the fictional character modeled on Minny Temple is Milly Theale, an immensely wealthy American girl. Since all the members of her immediate family are dead, Milly clings with special devotion to her friend and traveling companion, Mrs. Susan Shepherd Stringham (often alluded to as Susan Shepherd). It is not until the third of the ten books of the novel that Milly and her companion are introduced. They are traveling in Switzerland in early spring, but Milly wishes to go on to England. Mrs. Stringham writes immediately to Mrs. Maud Lowder, her schoolgirl friend years ago in Switzerland. Thus it is that, when Mrs. Stringham and Milly arrive in London, they become part of Mrs. Lowder's social circle.

Two members of this circle are Kate Croy, Mrs. Lowder's niece, and the young man she is in love with, Merton Densher. It is with the problems of these two young people that the first two books of the novel deal. Kate's mother is dead; her irresponsible father refuses to let her share his precarious lot; and her sister is married to an impoverished curate. Because of Kate's intelligence and beauty, Mrs. Lowder (Aunt Maud) takes the girl into her opulent home, virtually on condition that she will have nothing to do with her family. Aunt Maud's idea is to marry Kate to a man of fortune and social position. At present the chief possibility is Lord Mark, toward whom Kate is coolly polite. Aunt Maud disapproves of Merton Densher as a suitor, simply because he is a journalist with no money or prospects. Kate and Densher are thus forced to see each other quietly and furtively. Toward the end of the second book, Densher is dispatched to America for several months on a journalistic assignment. There he meets Milly Theale several times before she and Mrs. Stringham go abroad. When Densher returns from America, Milly is already in London and a part of Aunt Maud's circle. Milly, aware of Aunt Maud's plans for Kate, gains the impression that, while Densher loves Kate, she does not return his affection. So sure is Milly of this that, even when she meets the couple unexpectedly in the National Art Gallery, she suspects nothing. Mrs. Lowder, anxious to please Milly, makes Densher welcome because of their previous acquaintance. This arrangement has obvious advantages for Kate and Densher. Meanwhile, Lord Mark tries unsuccessfully to attract Milly.

The latter half of the novel skillfully exploits these conflicts between appearance and reality, between the innocent and generous Milly and the schemes of nearly every one else. It is soon evident that Milly is much attracted to Densher. He in turn finds her agreeable, and is the more considerate since it becomes known that Milly is mysteriously ill of some ailment for which the finest doctor in England can find no cure. When the ladies—Milly, Mrs. Stringham, Kate, and Aunt Maud—decide to spend some weeks in Venice, Densher also goes there, ostensibly to write a book. It is there that Kate directly proposes that Densher marry Milly, wait for her death, inherit her money, and then be "free" to marry Kate herself. The deception will be benevolent, since it will give great happiness to Milly. Densher, who has been a reluctant partner in the deception already practiced, consents only on condition that Kate come to his rooms that night. This she does. Their intimacy, however, intensifies the difficulty of Densher's pretense with Milly. After Kate and Aunt Maud return to London, Densher is one day refused admittance to Milly. Later, Mrs. Stringham explains that Milly "has turned her face to the wall," signifying that she has lost the will to live. It comes out that through another caller, Lord Mark, Milly has learned that Densher loves Kate. Lord Mark has told Milly this in the hope that Milly will reconsider his own rejected suit. It is Mrs. Stringham who urges Densher to deny to Milly his love for Kate. Densher does see Milly once more, but he cannot make the denial. To Kate herself, he later asserts that, had he made the denial, he would have stuck to it; that is, he would have given up Kate.

The final maneuvers of Kate and Densher, back in London, are intricate and full of meaning. Before news of Milly's death arrives, Densher asks Kate to marry him at once: "Our marriage will—fundamentally, somehow, don't you see?—right everything that's wrong . . . (NY XX, 347). Kate demurs. All has gone well, she says. Their triumph, their real freedom, is at hand. A few days later, on Christmas morning, news comes of Milly's death. To Kate, Densher takes this news, and also—unopened—a letter from Milly received the night before. Kate agrees that the letter from Milly undoubtedly contains news of a generous bequest. Densher offers Kate the document, to do with as she will. Kate, sure of the contents, but sure also that Milly's last letter will have a great emotional impact on Densher, throws the letter on the fire, unopened. As they watch it burn, it is Kate who speaks: "You'll have it all . . . from New York" (387).

After two months, legal papers arrive from New York, apparently confirming Kate's prophecy. These papers, too, Densher sends to Kate. This time she opens the envelope and learns that the legacy is indeed generous. When Kate brings the papers to Densher, he will not let her tell him the amount of the legacy. He is disappointed that she has opened the letter. His own intention had been that they would send it back, unopened. He now tells Kate that he will marry her without the money. If she refuses, he will not marry her, but will make over the whole amount to her. Densher's insistence causes Kate to infer that Densher is now in love with Milly's memory, and this Densher will not deny. The final lines must be quoted in their monosyllabic brevity. Densher says to Kate:

> "I'll marry you, mind you, in an hour."
> "As we were?"
> "As we were."
> But she turned to the door, and her headshake was now the end.
> "We shall never be again as we were!" (405).

In these final lines, an important distinction is made. Densher, by his refusal to touch the money, clearly asserts that the game of deceiving Milly should never have been begun. Kate sees only that she has lost the game. It is of secondary importance that, according to Densher's promise, Kate will now get the money Milly left to Densher.

In *The Wings of the Dove*, there is much to praise, little to object to. For many readers it is the most satisfying of the three James novels of the early 1900's. It has substantial themes: the conflict between innocent trust and social stratagem; the conflict of America and Europe. The central characters—Milly, Densher, Kate—are fully developed and convincingly interrelated. Milly, confiding with Mrs. Stringham, explaining her aloneness to her doctor, fencing with Aunt Maud when the older woman wants her to do some discreet spying on Kate, Milly luxuriating in the beauty of Venice—this is a varied Milly, quite substantial enough to escape ethereal abstraction. But the ethereal quality, sensed by everyone, is expressed by Kate: "You're a dove." Milly accepts the comparison as an illumination:

"*That* was what was the matter with her. She was a dove" (NY XIX, 283).

Kate herself is a casualty in a ruthless social warfare. In the opening chapter, when she offers to leave Aunt Maud and throw in her lot with that of her father, she is convincingly generous in an unsentimental way. In her early relations with Densher, she is frank at least with him. Had Aunt Maud been sympathetic enough, the reader feels, she could have enabled the love affair of Kate and Densher to prosper. In the beginning, Kate is attracted to Milly, and even warns her: "drop us while you can." The deception Kate proposes to Densher is in the beginning an innocent accommodation to circumstances. It is in Venice that her plan becomes seriously corrupt. Even at the end, Kate saves at least her dignity. She has intelligence enough to see her failure, though not the spirit to turn disaster into triumph. Densher himself is another of James's passive young men, yet James makes his struggle real. In his last scene with Kate, Densher is perhaps too theatrical, if the passage is taken out of context. Read at the very end of the long novel, the scene has weight and finality.

The minor characters—Mrs. Stringham, Aunt Maud, Lord Mark, Kate's father and sister, Sir Luke Strett (the doctor)—add fullness to the picture of life, and incidentally a great deal of light humor blended with the serious major theme. Mrs. Stringham is the New England type such as James had displayed in *The Bostonians;* she reads her *Transcript*, attends her concerts, and conscientiously visits the Public Library. For such a lady, Europe was, as James assures us, "the great American sedative." Aunt Maud sadly contemplates the dying Milly, and the girl's passionate desire to live: ". . . why in pity shouldn't she, with everything to fill her world? The mere *money* of her, the darling, if it isn't too disgusting at such a time to mention that. . . ." One feels that to Aunt Maud it would never be out of place to mention money. Yet James makes of Aunt Maud a gracious person, another in his gallery of dominating older women. As for Lord Mark, Milly is allowed to characterize him: "You're familiar with everything, but conscious really of nothing. What I mean is that you've no imagination."[9]

The principal objection to *The Wings of the Dove* is its length, a little over two hundred thousand words. It is a little longer than *The Ambassadors*, not quite so long as *The Golden Bowl*. Various parts of *The Wings of the Dove* could be omitted or compressed, but in almost every case there would be a loss. The first chapter, about six thousand words, presents Kate's quarrel with her father. Since the father never directly appears in the novel again (though his new misfortunes are vaguely alluded to in the last book), it is arguable that this chapter could be omitted, perhaps with brief explanation elsewhere of Kate's relation with her father. Yet the chapter is an arresting one, and the favorable impression it leaves of Kate heightens the effect of her later corruption. The third book, which shows Milly and Mrs. Stringham in Switzerland, is unnecessarily expansive, yet the relation between these two women is a special bond that merits full representation.

The middle books—four through seven—take a hundred thousand words to tell the London maneuvers after Milly's arrival, with a brief account in the seventh book of the arrival in Venice. It is doubtful whether every dialogue and every long paragraph of exposition is essential. And the last three books, though they include some very fine scenes, do rouse the suspicion that Milly's death is delayed for the author's convenience rather than from natural causes. At the time James wrote *The Wings of the Dove,* however, he was nearly sixty; and to judge by the best scenes, he was clearly at the height of his powers. If James thought, as he surely did, that he needed the space he used, then the length should not be set down to mere whim or to long-windedness.

IV The Golden Bowl (*1904*)

The least popular of the three major late novels is *The Golden Bowl.* Yet the novel has been highly praised as the subtlest and most masterly of all James's fiction.[10] The situation has great interest and possibilities. Maggie Verver and her widowed father are very wealthy Americans who live in England. As the novel begins, Maggie marries an Italian nobleman, Prince Amerigo. The three live happily together until it appears to both Maggie and her father that, since their own tie has been so close, it might be well for him to marry again, so as not to be overdependent on his daughter. Charlotte Stant, whom all have known for some time, seems appropriate, and she gladly accepts Mr. Verver's courteous proposal. Unknown to Maggie, however, Charlotte and the Prince have once been lovers. After Charlotte marries Mr. Verver, the continued close relationship between Maggie and her father has the effect of throwing the two former lovers together once more.

Maggie gradually feels some jealousy of Charlotte, but she has no real grounds for suspicion, and she struggles with her doubts as foolish and ungenerous. Through a strange coincidence (the purchase of a golden bowl once admired by Charlotte and the Prince), Maggie learns the truth and confronts the Prince. In doing so, she is much aware that a real quarrel will hurt her father as much as herself—perhaps even more. Therefore she employs almost superhuman restraint and decorum. The Prince neither confesses nor denies. Maggie leaves any further move to him, but she is acutely interested in whether he tells Charlotte. Maggie herself never does, and, when Charlotte asks for an explanation of Maggie's coolness, Maggie denies that their relationship has changed. Finally, Charlotte persuades Mr. Verver to move back to America, and their departure concludes the novel. Maggie leaves the way open for the Prince to have a final meeting alone with Charlotte; but, when he says to Maggie that he intends to tell Charlotte that both he and Maggie have lied to her, Maggie replies:

"She isn't to know."
"She's only to think *you* don't—?"
"And therefore that I'm always a fool? She may think," said Maggie, "what she likes" (NY XXIV, 356).

The Prince follows Maggie's wish. The four spend the evening together. When Charlotte departs with Mr. Verver, the Prince has the last speech of the novel. To Maggie he says: "I see nothing but you."

Thus Maggie, with extraordinary patience and restraint, has saved her marriage. Yet the novel is not a demonstration that she should have done so; it is an analysis of what she did do. There is for Maggie loss as well as gain. She loses her father, though no open break occurs, and Mr. Verver seems quite unaware of the quiet struggles around him. Maggie loses Charlotte, for, despite her protests to the contrary, Charlotte comes to think that Maggie hates Mr. Verver's marriage. Above all, Maggie's sweet, compliant nature is shown to have its devious, unlovely sides. She did accept the Prince as a kind of present from her father. She did manage her father's marriage with her own convenience as partial motivation. She is capable of deceiving the Prince, Charlotte, and even her father; without her deception, indeed, it is not clear how she could have saved her marriage. The crown of her deception comes when Charlotte tells her that she has persuaded Mr. Verver to return to America. Charlotte, with her own marriage to save, believes that this decision represents a failure for Maggie, and she tries to make Maggie admit it. Maggie does admit it, but the chapter ends with a significant comment on Maggie: "Yes, she had done all." She has carried off the most difficult strategy. She has silenced her enemy forever by making her own victory appear to be a defeat (318).

In the development of the story, James has many triumphs of his own. One is the provision of Colonel and Mrs. Assingham, old friends of all four of the major characters. Mrs. Assingham serves as confidante to Maggie, and her role is complicated by the fact that she knows more about Charlotte than she can tell. She can't tell, that is, because her knowledge is mere inference, which could of course be wrong. Fanny Assingham's struggles to believe, against her instinct, that all will be well with the two remarkable marriages are revealed through discussions with her husband, a sturdy, rather obtuse and phlegmatic man. Their dialogues are some of James's best comedy.

In the main action the use of the golden bowl itself as a link is ingenious. The shopping trip of Charlotte and the Prince, just before his marriage, is a memorable sequence. Charlotte proposes the trip, telling the Prince she would like to buy him a present. They look in an antique shop at a crystal bowl, overlaid with gold leaf. Charlotte is much tempted to buy the bowl, despite the high price, but the Prince discovers a crack in it and dissuades her. Four years later, Maggie drops into the same shop, sees the same bowl, and purchases it. Later, the shopkeeper comes to her home to explain that he overcharged her; he has now recalled that a lady and gentleman once looked at the bowl and discovered a flaw in it. In Maggie's reception room the shopkeeper recognizes photographs of the Prince and Charlotte. Maggie sends for Fanny Assingham and explains the strange situation. Fanny, still hoping that all will come right, dashes the bowl to the floor. At that moment, the Prince enters the room. It is a scene that could easily become stereotyped melodrama. Instead, the restraint of Maggie and the delaying tactics which both she and the Prince adopt quickly restore the interest in motive; attention quickly shifts from the sensation of the physical action.

The novel, carefully structured in five parts, is comparable to the five acts of a play. The inspection of the golden bowl by the Prince and Charlotte closes the first book; Charlotte's acceptance of Mr. Verver, the second; the association of Charlotte and the Prince at the Matcham party (Maggie and her father having stayed at home) concludes the third; the breaking of the golden bowl, the fourth; the departure of the Ververs, the fifth. Aside from the Assinghams, who act as reflectors, or as a dramatic chorus, attention centers on the two married couples. The major emphasis is on the Prince in the first three books and on Maggie in the last two. Only a very great writer could develop from this simple basic design so many complex variations.

With such advantages of design, character, and situation, why does the novel disappoint so many readers? It is very little longer than *The Wings of the Dove,* but it makes greater demands on the attention. The small number of characters, all of them preoccupied with each other, limits the range of dialogue, and puts an emphasis

HENRY JAMES

on subtleties of implication. There is so little external movement that the dialogue often seems static and unduly prolonged. The long passage between Maggie and her father in the tenth chapter is an illustration. Mr. Verver consents to invite Charlotte to visit them, as Maggie suggests. More is accomplished in this chapter than the reaching of this simple decision, but the general effect is that father and daughter have a narrow range of interests.

Too often, large blocks of exposition and analysis seem obstacles to the reader rather than interesting supplements to his direct observation. For example, the second part begins with three chapters—thirty pages—virtually without dialogue. These chapters explain rather than present Adam Verver, usually in paragraphs of five to seven hundred words. There is very little in this elaborate analysis to account for Adam Verver as the builder and possessor of an enormous fortune. Farther on, the departure of Charlotte and the Prince on their little side-trip on the way home from the party at Matcham is followed by thirty pages of guessing by the Assinghams and then by thirty more of analysis representing the impact of this event on Maggie. After the breaking of the golden bowl, there is similar analytical elaboration. At every point the careful reader can see what James is doing and why he is doing it. Yet reasons are not sufficient in art. For most readers, the effect is some degree of exasperation at the slowness of movement, the exhaustiveness of analysis.

Finally, a reason for adverse reactions to *The Golden Bowl* is the limited appeal of the characters. It is difficult to believe in the "American City" to which Adam Verver takes Charlotte at the end of the novel, or to believe in the immense fortune this unobtrusive, passive man is said to have amassed. The beautiful objects with which Verver surrounded himself are as unknown to the reader as the spoils of Poynton in James's earlier story. The Prince is said to be interested in old Italian books. It is mentioned once that Charlotte and Maggie attend various charitable activities. Maggie alludes gently to the selfishness of their lives, but it is Charlotte who lays bare the reality: "Isn't the immense, the really quite matchless beauty of our position that we have to 'do' nothing in life at all?" (NY XXIII, 289). These people care nothing even for sport. They are bound up so completely in their eventless lives that there is nothing to give perspective even to their judgment of their own feelings. It is a hothouse air they breathe, with a faintly incestuous aroma. Yet when all is said, readers who follow the novel to the end find some of James's sharpest perceptions, some of his most delicate touches.

V Shorter Fiction: American Themes

American characters and situations, so important in James's fiction during the 1880's, were virtually ignored in the 1890's. James's preoccupation with English life—illustrated in *The Spoils of Poynton*, *What Maisie Knew*, and *The Awkward Age*—was reflected in the short stories as well. The three major novels, of 1902-04, however, all deal with Americans in Europe; and three situation stories of the same period are concerned with the same subject. The trip to America in 1904-05 gave James ideas for four of his last and best pieces of short fiction.

The title character in "Mrs. Medwin" (1901) is English, but it is to the American Mamie Cutter that she turns for help in getting social recognition. Mamie, popular herself, makes something of a business of social wire-pulling. In the midst of her negotiations in behalf of Mrs. Medwin, Mamie is annoyed by the appearance of her ne'er-do-well half-brother Scott. Unexpectedly, Lady Wantridge, the English lady who thus far has refused to meet Mrs. Medwin, drops in to see Mamie and is charmed by the gay, irresponsible Scott. Mamie is quick to seize her opportunity to bargain: if Lady Wantridge wants Scott for her party in the country, she must ask Mrs. Medwin, too. Good-naturedly her ladyship consents, and Mrs. Medwin gratefully sends a generous check to Mamie. This story of social maneuver is a cynical but amusing comment on the pretensions of English society, which are more savagely exposed in "A London Life" and in *The Awkward Age*.

"Flickerbridge" (1902) is the story of an old-fashioned English spinster and her home—Flickerbridge—which is discovered by Granger, an American artist, in an odd way. Granger is ill in London, and his American sweetheart, an enterprising young writer for newspapers, recommends that he look up a distant kinswoman. When Granger does so, he is captivated by the peace and quiet of the old place and by the kindness of the old lady. When the young newspaperwoman from America sends word that she is coming, Granger leaves, warning the kind owner of Flickerbridge that the resulting publicity is sure to ruin the old place. Merely by staying in Flickerbridge for a few weeks, Granger has come to see his American sweetheart in a new way. "We're not engaged," he explains, as he takes his leave.

"Fordham Castle" (1904) brings together by chance two Americans traveling in Europe under assumed names. A. F. Taker is going about as C. P. Addard, for whom he has made up a splendid past. When he confides this to a Mrs. Vanderplank, she reveals that she is actually Mattie Magaw. Taker's wife and Mattie's daughter, who regard them as social handicaps, have asked them to disappear temporarily. Meanwhile it develops that Taker's wife and Mattie's daughter have met at Fordham Castle, and the older woman has helped the girl to become engaged to Lord Dunderton. "Mrs. Vanderplank" is invited to attend the wedding. Ruefully, Mr. Taker reflects that he is still "dead."

The setting of "Julia Bride" (1908) is New York. The beautiful Julia's desire to marry the highly respectable Mr. French is handicapped by "her own six engagements and her mother's three nullified marriages—nine distinct little horrors in all." After many stratagems the story ends with Julia contemplating "her certain ruin." "The Jolly Corner" (1908) expresses the revulsion James felt at the rapid change, the harsh modernity of American cities. In a remarkably effective modern ghost story, Spencer Brydon, expatriate, returns to New York and confronts in the old family home the man he might have become. "Crapy Cornelia" (1910) is another story of a middle-aged man much influenced by his past. He is subtly persuaded by his old friend Cornelia not to marry a wealthy widow, as he had planned. This story might easily become conventionally sentimental. James keeps the dialogue gay, and his descriptive touches contrasting old New York with the present are witty.

"A Round of Visits" (1910), the last story James published, is about another New Yorker who has lived long abroad. Mark Monteith comes back to look after some business and finds he has been cheated by an old friend, Phil Bloodgood, who has absconded. At a party Monteith is reminded of Newton Winch, another old friend, now quite ill. When Monteith calls, Winch confides that he is another Phil Bloodgood, but one who has not fled from the scene of his crimes. Their talk is nevertheless friendly. When Monteith leaves, he notices a revolver near the bed, and he puts Winch on his honor to do "nothing." Coming out of the room, Monteith meets two officers on their way to arrest Winch. Then a shot is fired in the bedroom, and Winch is found dead. When one officer asks, "Don't you think, sir, you might have prevented it?" Monteith replies: "I really think I must practically have caused it." The sight of Monteith, the very absence of a quarrel, strained Winch's spirit to the breaking point.

VI The Whole Family (1908)

Though not a short story, James's contribution to *The Whole Family* may be treated as such. *The Whole Family* is a collaborative novel, written by twelve authors and published serially in *Harper's*

Bazar, a woman's magazine, without identification. The book form of the novel lists James as the author of chapter seven, "The Married Son." Howells had led off with the first installment, showing the father of the family passing on to his neighbor the news of his daughter's engagement. Various complications arise, and the story develops through successive misunderstandings and preposterous events. Peggy, the heroine, throws over her original fiancé and elopes with a college professor. James's chapter, "The Married Son" presents Charles Edward's attempts to prevent his sister from marrying. He thinks that her engagement is a mistake, and that it may interfere with his plans for going abroad the coming year to study art—his means of escape from the family business of manufacturing plated ware. This chapter is a reminder that James,, despite his eminence, could turn his attention to a trifling commercial venture, partly to please the editor of the magazine, Elizabeth Jordan, and partly to gain a fee, four hundred dollars. There are, however, some unmistakably Jamesian touches in the chapter; for example, Charles Edward's contrast of his father and mother: "Poor Mother, who is worth all the rest of us put together, and is really worth two or three of poor Father, deadly decent as I admit poor Father mainly to be. . . ."[11]

VII *Shorter Fiction: Writers and Artists*

James's later stories dealing with writers and artists lack the seriousness of purpose seen in such earlier stories as "Greville Fane," "The Middle Years," and "The Madonna of the Future." In "The Beldonald Holbein," for example, the title refers to a fine portrait which gives fame to the unattractive sitter, a companion to the beautiful Lady Beldonald. The artist, who tells the story, had been sought out by Lady Beldonald to paint her own portrait as a means of attracting attention. Because the "Beldonald Holbein" overshadows Lady Beldonald, she sends the unattractive companion away.

"The Story in It" (1902) relates a courtship carried on in terms of a literary argument. Maud Blessingbourn defends to Mrs. Dyott and their friend Colonel Voyt her fondness for French novels. She gets, she thinks, "more life for her money" in these novels than in others. The Colonel, who has the conventional contempt for literature, is sure that drama and romance reside only in vice. Maud disagrees. After he leaves, Maud confides that she is in love, and Mrs. Dyott shrewdly guesses that the Colonel is the object of her affection. Later, when Mrs. Dyott tells this to the Colonel, he is much interested. But he can see no "story" in it. This amusing dialogue—

it is little more—is a light statement of James's fundamental conviction that there is a "story" in every relationship.

"The Birthplace" (1903) is satiric of the hero-worship associated with literary shrines. Though Shakespeare is never mentioned, it is clear that his is the birthplace of which the schoolmaster Gedge becomes custodian. At first the appointment seems ideal. Soon, however, Gedge becomes bored and indignant at the irrelevant and doubtful "facts" he is supposed to repeat over and over to uncomprehending tourists. His skepticism nearly loses him his job, and he decides he must learn to lie if he can. He does learn: "I daresay, if we looked close enough, we should find the hearthstone scraped by his little feet." Gedge's reward is a higher salary.

"The Papers" (1903) is a satire on journalistic publicity. A young man and woman, writers for the "papers," are aware of how Sir A. B. C. Beadel-Muffet keeps himself in the public eye. The mysterious disappearance of this gentleman creates an opportunity, they think, to gain publicity for a man named Marshal by allowing him to disclose certain "facts" regarding Beadel-Muffet. The scheme fails, however, because of the reappearance of the baronet, but no explanation of his absence is given. The young journalists abandon the "papers," marry, and consider writing a play or a tale.

"The Velvet Glove" (1909) is a comment on literary taste. John Berridge, a successful author, is asked to read a story written by a young woman admirer and to write a preface for it. After he reads *The Velvet Glove*, he refuses to write the preface: "You are Romance," he says; "don't attempt such base things."

"Mora Montravers" (1909) is the story of a strong-minded young girl who runs away with an artist. Her aunt and uncle insist on marriage. The artist is willing, but not eager; for he rightly suspects that marriage may lead Mora to lose interest in him. Later the artist calls, explaining that Mora now wants a divorce. The aunt is indignant, and now takes the artist's side. He should retain the marriage settlement, if Mora does divorce him. Throughout the story, Mora's aunt and uncle see the various situations in ironic contrast.

VIII *Two Love Stories*

Two of James's finest stories are unusual variations on the perennial theme of love; but they are so unusual that the phrase "love story" seems ironic when applied to them. In subtlety and in deliberate effect "The Beast in the Jungle" (1903) and "The Bench of Desolation" (1909-10) have something of the quality displayed by the three major novels of 1902-04. The first is of love recognized too late; the second, of love persisting in spite of alienation.

"The Beast in the Jungle" is the story of John Marcher. In the opening pages he meets May Bartram at luncheon; it turns out that they had met years earlier, and May remembers the meeting well, for Marcher had confided on that occasion his dread that some "beast in the jungle" would destroy him. Instead of laughing at him for this extravagant fear, May now agrees to watch with him for this mysterious fate. Since Marcher has confided his fear to no one else, his fear forms a bond between them; and, over the years which follow, their association is very close. Eventually May falls ill and dies, but before she dies she tells Marcher: ". . . you've nothing to wait for more. It *has* come." When he does not comprehend, she adds: ". . . your not being aware of it is the strangeness *in* the strangeness" (NY XVII, 110).

Even after May's death, Marcher does not comprehend. A year later, returning to her grave, he notices another mourner at a recent grave in the churchyard. Suddenly he feels the absence of deep emotion in his own life, and he sees at last the beast of his jungle: ". . . he had been the man of his time, *the* man, to whom nothing on earth was to have happened" (125). Nothing in James surpasses the lightness of touch, the delicacy of movement of this nearly eventless story. May Bartram's love, never spoken and never perceived by Marcher until too late, is slowly evoked with a shy strength. May is indeed the more convincing character; for Marcher is almost an allegorical representation of insensitivity, caution, and inaction—a cumulative selfishness all the more horrifying because it is so well bred.

"The Bench of Desolation" is compounded of jealousy and loyal devotion pushed to a preposterous but affecting extreme. Because Herbert Dodd has jilted her, Kate Cookham threatens to bring action against him. He agrees to pay her four hundred pounds, mortgaging his house and his bookstore to do it. Dodd then marries Nan Drury, and in the years that follow, ill fortune pursues him. He loses his bookshop and becomes a clerk. His two children die, and finally Nan herself. One Saturday afternoon Dodd goes to his customary bench in the seaside park. Nearby is a well-dressed lady, who turns out to be Kate Cookham. Diffidently, she asks Dodd to take tea the next afternoon at her hotel, saying she has something important to tell him. Out of curiosity, he agrees to come; he warns her, however, that he can never pay the balance of his debt. On Sunday, Kate reveals that she is ready to repay all his money, with interest. Moreover, she remarks that she never had grounds for a legal suit, and knew it; Dodd, it seems, had never sought legal advice. Overcome with the memory of the needless bitter years of struggle to pay what he had promised, Dodd leaves the hotel without the money. A week later, Dodd is in the park again, contemplating his situation as a combination of fairy tale and nightmare. There Kate finds him, and gives him the bank book showing deposits of twelve hundred and sixty pounds. She is ready to say goodbye, when his questions detain her. It comes out that her initial jealous hatred of him was soon overpowered by contrition for what she had done to him. The money is to make up for that. How she saved it and the details of her life, she wisely says she will never tell him, just as she may never hear the details of his trials. Though the past cannot be canceled, these two middle-aged people can now accept each other: "I can take care of you," says Kate. To which Dodd replies, "You have." The story concludes: "She was beside him on the bench of desolation."

"The Bench of Desolation" makes heavy demands on credulity, and the fact that James based the story on a supposedly true anecdote (*Notebooks*, 330-32) is no adequate defense. The reader must accept several improbabilities: that Dodd, threatened with a suit, would not get legal advice; that Kate Cookham could by undisclosed means accumulate the twelve hundred pounds; that after his years of suffering, Dodd could forgive her; and that a reunion of the two could be so quickly brought about. To be sure, the law is so complex that people often act on inaccurate notions of it, and besides, Dodd wanted no scandal. The means by which Kate accumulated the money are, James might say, another story. Dodd's acceptance of the money results from the fact that his sufferings have devitalized him instead of making him vindictive. Moreover, the sum of money offered was, to a man in his circumstances, considerable. There is, incidentally, no hint of a bribe; the money is offered as a free gift, and Dodd's wonder at this overshadows his initial sense of affront. In life, the reconciliation might have occupied many meetings, but the end-result of reconciliation is conceivable. The literal plausibility of such matters is of less importance than the treatment. Here James triumphs. The despair of Dodd's years of struggle is convincing. The meetings between Dodd and Kate show an interesting opposition of temperaments. The ending, far from being "happy" in the conventional sense, implies a future freighted with memories of a somber past. That love and hate are often commingled is commonplace, but seldom have they been shown more strangely or more touchingly mixed than in "The Bench of Desolation."

IX   *Last Years: 1910-16*

In 1910, William James and his wife Alice came to England, primarily because of William's health. Henry himself was unwell, but he accompanied them to Germany. When William did not improve, Henry returned to America with them. In his summer home at Chocorua, New Hampshire, William James died on August 26. A few days later, Henry wrote to the friend both he and William had known in their youth, Thomas Sergeant Perry: "I sit heavily stricken and in darkness—for from far back in dimmest childhood he had been my ideal Elder Brother, and I still, through all the years, saw in him, even as a small timorous boy yet, my protector, my backer, my authority and my pride. His extinction changes the face of life for me—besides the mere missing of his inexhaustible company and personality, originality, the whole unspeakably vivid and beautiful presence of him" (*Letters*, II, 167).

Henry James remained in America until August, 1911. He helped his sister-in-law, Alice, with various family concerns; and, as they talked together, the tide of reminiscence was strong. Alice urged him to "write these things," and thus began the autobiography which Henry left unfinished. He dictated most of it in London with a stack of William's letters to jog his memory.

In the years following William's death, Henry's activities continued almost unabated, with many cheering signs of recognition and appreciation. Before he left America, Harvard awarded him an honorary degree; and in the following year, 1912, Oxford conferred an honorary doctorate. In 1911, James's play *The Outcry*, now turned into a novel, was moderately successful. Early in 1912, James wrote a long open letter to be read at a celebration of William Dean Howells' seventy-fifth birthday, praising many specific works of his old friend and honoring the consistent distinction of a long career. In the spring, James was invited to deliver a lecture before the Browning Society in London, his chosen subject being "The Novel in *The Ring and the Book*." For James's seventieth birthday, in 1913, nearly three hundred of his English friends arranged to have his portrait painted by Sargent, a gesture James much appreciated. In 1913 and 1914 appeared the first two volumes of his autobiography: *A Small Boy and Others* and *Notes of a Son and Brother*. In the autumn of 1914 came *Notes on Novelists*, a collection of critical papers of the preceding twenty years. Though James wrote no short stories after 1910 and only a dozen new critical pieces, he had turned once more to the writing of a long novel, *The Ivory Tower*. Left incomplete, this work was published after his death.

War with Germany came in August, 1914, and with its coming, James's literary activity virtually stopped. James was seventy-one, and, like most people of his years, he found the brutality of the attack on Belgium inconceivable. The war seemed to negate all that had made his life worth living. To one friend he wrote: ". . . the appalling blackness of it all, and the horror of having lived to see it!" Referring in the same letter to "the good old days," he added, "if any days can be called good that were so villainously leading up to these."[12] James's Lamb House servant went off to war, and James spent much time in London to be closer to the news. He talked with wounded Belgians and Grenadier Guards at a hospital. He took a convalescent soldier to his own dentist, and put up over-night in his Chelsea rooms a volunteer from Rye. James interested himself in the American Volunteer Ambulance Corps, organized by the son of his old friend, C. E. Norton. Hugh Walpole, then serving on the Russian front with the Red Cross, was one of James's correspondents. To Edith Wharton (engaged in war work in France), James wrote a letter condemning the damage to Rheims Cathedral—a letter that was read to the Académie Française and later published. To the New York *Times* he gave an interview on "the decent and dauntless people of England." He wrote articles on the war refugees. Several of these wartime pieces were later collected in *Within the Rim* (1919). The last writing James did was his introduction to Rupert Brooke's *Letters from America;* James had first met Brooke in 1909, and he considered the young poet's death in 1915 symbolic of the tragic waste of the war.

Thus James was deeply and daily touched by the conflict. Eager for the United States to come in on the side of England and France, he was constantly irked by President Wilson's policy of neutrality. This feeling, supplemented by the inconvenience of being a war-time alien subjected to various regulations, led James to become a British citizen on July 26, 1915. Two letters to his nephew, Henry James, Jr., explain his decision, one he had never previously contemplated since he had established residence in England in 1876. Mr. Asquith, the Prime Minister, joined three other Englishmen in sponsoring James's application for citizenship.

An unfortunate episode of the war years was the quarrel between James and his younger friend H. G. Wells. From about 1898 until 1915 Wells and James found much to admire in each other. Gradually, however, Wells moved toward a journalistic conception of the novel and away from James's concern with form. Partly as relaxation from the war, Wells published a satirical book called *Boon,* a copy of which he sent to James. In it the Master found himself called by one of the characters, "the culmination of the superficial type." There followed the famous jibe at James's style: "a magnificent but painful hippopotamus resolved at any cost, even at the cost of its dignity, upon picking up a pea which has got into the corner of its den." James wrote Wells with sad dignity, regretting that so old a friend and so good a writer thought so ill of his work. Wells replied, half apologizing; *Boon*, he said, was "just a waste-paper basket." James had the last word, pointing out that publication is not a proper substitute for a wastepaper basket, and stating eloquently his conception of fiction as an art: "It is art that *makes* life, makes interest, makes importance, for our consideration and application of these things, and I know of no substitute for the force and beauty of its process." But he concluded that the "bridge that made communication possible" between himself and Wells had collapsed.[13]

In December, 1915, James suffered a stroke. William's widow, her eldest son, Henry James, Jr., and a daughter came from America to look after him. During the illness, James's nephew wrote to a family friend that his uncle's mind wandered a great deal in the past and that he sometimes seemed to think William was there with him; the nephew added, "there never was a gentler more considerate and careful patient."[14] The king's honors list in January, 1916, included the award to James of the Order of Merit, the decoration being brought to his bedside by Lord Bryce, an old friend. On February 28, Henry James died, a few weeks before his seventy-third birthday. Following cremation of the body, a funeral service was held in Chelsea Old Church on March 3.

X The Ivory Tower (*1917*)

James's last attempt at an American novel seems to have been begun about 1908; at least from a project of that date come many of the names of characters. After many interruptions, James took up the idea again, dictating a "scenario" of twenty thousand words, later published with the fragmentary novel. Of the ten books planned, three were completed. With the coming of the War in 1914, James found it impossible to continue work on *The Ivory Tower*.

The scene of the novel is Newport. Rosanna Gaw is about to inquire about the health of her neighbor Frank Betterman. On the Betterman lawn she finds her father, Abel Gaw, "perched like a ruffled hawk," also waiting for news about his former business partner. The two men had been estranged for many years, but Rosanna has just recently managed a reconciliation. Now Betterman is dying. Arriving to see Betterman, as the story opens, is Graham Fielder, son of his half-sister. Young Fielder grew up in Newport and so is known to Rosanna and her friends, but for many years Fielder has lived abroad. He is welcomed by his uncle, who tells him: "You utterly loathe and abhor hustle! That's what I blissfully want of you. . . ." Betterman wants to leave his fortune to a man of taste who will know how to use it. Fielder, he thinks, is his appropriate heir.

Later that afternoon, Fielder calls on Rosanna Gaw, who is to inherit her father's fortune of twenty millions, a far greater sum than Betterman possesses. Rosanna gives Fielder a letter from her father. Fielder hesitates to open it at the time, and instead slips it into the drawer of an ivory tower. This ornament, to which the title refers, Fielder has been admiring, and Rosanna presents it to him.

Not long after Fielder's arrival, Mr. Betterman and Mr. Gaw die on the same day. The young friends of Rosanna and Fielder speculate on their futures. Among these friends are Gussie and David Bradham, rich and dominating; Horton Vint, a rejected suitor of Rosanna; and Cissy Foy. Books three and four are taken up with Fielder's attempts to learn the business details of his inheritance. In his ignorance, Fielder seeks advice from Horton Vint, who had once saved his life in Switzerland. Meanwhile, Fielder becomes interested in Cissy Foy, not realizing that Cissy is in love with Horton Vint, their attachment being inconspicuous because they lack the money to marry. Fielder eventually discovers their love affair, and about the same time he learns that Horton Vint is defrauding him. Probably at this point, though James does not specify, the letter from Abner Gaw (put aside in the ivory tower) informs Fielder that his uncle's fortune was made by means worse than those Vint has employed. In this state of disillusion, Fielder is brought together with Rosanna once more. The marriage of Fielder and Rosanna seems too conventional an ending for James, but no clear alternative is indicated.

The scenario for *The Ivory Tower* is not an orderly plan, book by book. It is rather a series of speculations about motives, interrelationships of characters, and their depiction. The problem of structure is central, and the solutions remain flexible in the statement. Questions are frequent. Alternatives are compared. It is obvious that Fielder's situation is to illustrate the pull between the instincts of a "non-producer," as James calls Fielder, and the responsibilities of wealth. There is much in James's previous work that impinges on this idea. The situations of the novel are so special, however, that for many readers it would be too little connected with the economic struggle as they experience it. Yet the completed chapters of *The Ivory Tower* are solid, and James's excitement in the scenario is contagious. It is evident that at seventy he thought readily and creatively in fictional terms.

XI The Sense of the Past (*1917*)

When James found that, because of the war, he could no longer concentrate on the problems of *The Ivory Tower,* he turned back to a manuscript begun in 1899 as a sequel in fantasy to "The Turn of the Screw." The success of that masterly ghost story in 1898 had interested two publishers in the possibility of other fantasies, but the scheme had been given up after James had written some thirty thousand words. From late in 1914 until his final illness in December the next year, James worked intermittently on *The Sense of the Past.* Posthumously published, the manuscript of seventy-five thousand words is supplemented by some twenty thousand words from James's notebooks.

The central figure of the novel is Ralph Pendril, a young American of studious tastes who has just been rejected by a wealthy widow whom he has long loved. The rejection is kind and not completely final. Since Ralph has just inherited property in England, Mrs. Coyne predicts that, once he goes there to claim it, he will never return to America. Ralph's chief inheritance is an old house in London. His mind is caught up by the old furniture and portraits, and he feels a strange kinship with one ancestor whose portrait is prominently displayed. So extreme is this sensation that he calls one day on the American ambassador to explain that he is "not himself." The ambassador listens courteously, and betrays no surprise at Ralph's strange story. When Ralph returns home, his butler tells him that Miss Midmore is waiting. Entering the parlor, Ralph finds Molly Midmore, materialized from her portrait, welcoming him from America, as she actually had his ancestor in 1820. Without hesitation, Ralph finds himself explaining his recent arrival and apologizing for not having asked permission to call. Molly's mother soon enters, and there is pleasant, hospitable talk. Soon Molly's brother Perry joins the group. A younger sister, Nan, is in the country, but Ralph "knows" about her. Then Sir Cantopher Bland, a suitor rejected by Nan, comes in. He is a rather supercilious man, somewhat patronizing to Ralph. A love match between Ralph and Molly, based on their long correspondence while Ralph was still in America, is more or less assumed; and there is sufficient reference to Ralph's property to make him uncomfortable. Now, unexpectedly, Nan arrives from the country, and Ralph's insistent reaction is: "She's *modern.*" James's story breaks off here.

James's notes of 1914 make clear his intended development of the story. Ralph Pendril's engagement to Molly is to be broken because of her gradual distrust of him, for he combines in a strange mixture the 1820 man and the 1910 man. Nan, however, is sympathetic, and to her Ralph reveals his secret. She confesses that she had loved the 1820 man without being loved in return. Now, aware that Ralph loves her, she can consciously and willingly wait for him in the distant future. Meanwhile, Aurora Coyne is vaguely disturbed about what may have happened to Ralph. She goes to London and consults the ambassador. He agrees to investigate. When the ambassador arrives at the old house, the Ralph who emerges is back in the world of 1910. The ambassador, of course, immediately explains Aurora's arrival. Though James specifies that Aurora herself is not to be brought directly on the scene, the novel was to end with the anticipation of Ralph's engagement to her.

The idea of a modern man stepping back into an earlier time has interesting possibilities, as John Balderston's *Berkeley Square,* freely adapted from James's story, was to show. James's own story and projected plan, however, seem obtuse. James is not interested in an objectively historical reconstruction of the past, and the feeling of strangeness, so powerful in "The Turn of the Screw," is in this story very weak. Ralph's conversation with the ambassador about "not being himself" seems merely odd. The Aurora Coyne story, mildly interesting in the opening scenes, has too little connection with what follows. The one solid idea—that the freedom of choice of the modern world be contrasted with the arbitrary custom of 1820—is represented only in the projected event of Nan's sacrifice. There is little preparation for this emphasis, and not even the incidental ornament of satire at the expense of either period. Perhaps the most moving thing about the story is James's excitement: ". . . don't I in fact find myself just leaping and snatching at the idea which answers all my questions of procedure and has my perfect solution just locked up and waiting within it?" (NY XXVI, 339). To the end, James was fascinated by the endless possibilities of his fictional ideas.

The two posthumously published novels add little to James's stature. Even had World War I not interrupted his creative activity, or had he survived the war to live on into the 1920's, it is doubtful whether either of these novels would have been major productions. They are important, as James said of Thackeray's incomplete *Denis Duval,* because of the man that wrote them. James's work was done in 1910, it may be said. He had learned his craft so well, however, that it continued to be a resource in his declining years. In the unsolved problems of the posthumous novels, we feel, as James did, the excitement of intelligence and imagination at work.

CHAPTER 7

Henry James: Man and Stylist

JAMES has been the target of some very clever caricature. Max Beerbohm began "The Mote in the Middle Distance" with this sentence: "It was with the sense of a, for him, very memorable something that he peered now into the immediate future, and tried, not without compunction, to take that period up where he had, prospectively, left it." The exaggerated use of parenthetical phrases, the piling up of abstractions, the absent-minded rhythm, and the frequent effect of total fog do remind one of James at his worst. Wells's comparison of James's style to a hippopotamus trying to pick up a pea is memorable, if more malicious. Carolyn Wells begins her paraphrase of a limerick in the Jamesian manner: "She luminously wavered, and I tentatively inferred that she would soon perfectly reconsider her not altogether unobvious course." Here the adverbs and the "not altogether unobvious" are recognizable echoes of conspicuous qualification. That these parodies have some truth in them is illustrated not only by passages of the fiction but by Edith Wharton's wonderful story of James's inquiry for directions in Windsor. After directing at a passerby a long sentence of bewildering and unnecessary explanation, James continued: "in short, my good man, what I want to put to you in a word is this: supposing we have already (as I have reason to think we have) driven past the turn down to the railway station (which in that case, by the way, would probably not have been on our left hand, but on our right), where are we now in relation to. . . ." At this point Mrs. Wharton cut in with a request that James inquire directly for King's Road. To this the passerby replied, "Ye're in it."[1]

There is in all this more than a ray of truth; but the image conjured up is hard to associate with the historical Henry James. The feckless shadow in the parodies, even the actual James in Mrs. Wharton's automobile, it seems, could never have been known to family and friends as Harry James; could never have ridden horseback in Rome; gone boating with a man who played the banjo; ridden a bicycle; helped his servant put out a fire at Lamb

House in the middle of the night; or written to a friend, after an attack of shingles: "I had had, saving your presence and that of my secretarial friend, a regular hell of a night. . . ." Nor would he have had the wit to add of the doctor that he had "the attitude of mere rapt and supernatural contemplation."[2] Above all, the James of caricature, the legendary "Master," could never have written the nearly five million words of fiction, the plays, the critical prose, and conducted the business negotiations for the hundreds of magazine contributions and the dozens of books. The historical James did all these things.

To turn to photographs of James is to form an image of a man capable of such accomplishments. The boy of sixteen or seventeen, with finely shaped head, serious, deep-set eyes, and firm, full lips looks like a person who could dream and put his dreams to work. The bearded man of forty-two is balding; he has a high dome-like forehead and a vigorous profile. As was mentioned in Chapter I, the 1912 portrait by Sargent shows a strikingly Churchillian head, the facial expression stern, the shoulders massive. It represents a man who could have done what James had done by 1912. Photographs taken in James's later years all give this impression of physical power and intellectual keenness.

With the image rather than the caricature in mind, some recent interpretations of James may be briefly considered. Professor Edel, in the three volumes of his biography, has emphasized some negative factors in the relation of Henry James, Jr., to his family. Professor Edel believes that Henry, Sr., was an unstable man, whose manner of life raised doubt in the mind of Henry, Jr.; that the mother, at the same time, was forced to show a managerial decisiveness which is reflected in the large number of such women in Henry, Jr.'s fiction; and that Henry, Jr., was overshadowed during his youth by William, his impulsive older brother. Henry's resentment, it is suggested, was released in fictional portraits of officious older brothers.[3] In short, the fulsome affection of the published letters does not wholly conceal the existence of psychological frictions in this remarkable family. That frictions did exist seems very likely; frictions exist in all families—and a family that included seven strong-minded individuals could hardly escape some irritations. The extraordinary feature of the James family, however, remains the bond of affection among its members.

As for the father of the family, it is sufficient testimony to his essential strength of character that not one of the five children at any time "revolted" from his authority or became alienated from him. If anything, there was an overdependence on the father. The five children may have been baffled by the frequent moves of their youth, but they enjoyed their travels; and, as adults, they all continued to travel a great deal. The children were puzzled by their father's lack of regular occupation, and they were not attracted to the tattered volumes of Swedenborg over which he pored. As adults, however, both William and Henry, Jr., paid respectful tribute to "father's ideas" and to the permissiveness of the household they remembered. In the sixth chapter of *Notes of a Son and Brother,* Henry, Jr., speaks of "our father's unsurpassable patience and independence" in his daily routine of writing. With regard to "Father's Ideas," the son remembers "the color and savor they gave to his talk." Even more significant, he says: "It was a luxury, I today see, to have all the benefit of his intellectual and spiritual, his religious, his philosophic and his social passion, without ever feeling the pressure of it to our direct irritation or discomfort."[4] The *Autobiography* of John Stuart Mill (1806-73) provides a useful contrast. Mill's father, too, was a student, but to his son he was a ceaseless, strict master. In later years, Mill never lost his respect for his father's character and achievements, but there is little of the tenderness so evident in the relation between Henry, Sr., and his children. *The Education of Henry Adams* presents a similar contrast to the James household.

As for the mother, too little is known to controvert Henry's moving tribute to her after her death. That she was "the keystone of the arch" has perhaps something of the conventional tribute of sons to mothers. Yet the published letters between mother and son give reality to the convention. Henry's letters, in particular, show nothing of overdependence, petty irritation, or pique. When Henry justifies his expenses abroad in 1869-70, he does so with dignity and a desire to explain. Above all, the letters to his mother, as to other members of the family, are lightened by a good humor that is the best evidence of a happy, "normal" family feeling. Such a managerial type as Mrs. Touchett in *The Portrait of a Lady* can hardly be thought of as a "portrait" of Mrs. James, except that the son may have speculated about what his mother might have been like had her natural affection been left out of her nature.

A few days after William's death, Henry wrote to T. S. Perry, their mutual friend, that William had been "the Ideal Elder Brother" (*Letters,* II, 167). A few years later in *Notes of a Son and Brother* occurs this passage: "Whatever he might happen to be doing made him so interesting about it, and indeed, with the quickest concomitance, about everything else, that what I probably most did, all the while, was but to pick up, and to the effect not a bit of starving but quite of filling myself, the crumbs of his feast and the echoes of his life."[5] Does not such a passage indicate that

William dominated his younger brother? Are not elder brothers usually shown to a disadvantage in Henry's fiction? Was not William's criticism of Henry's fiction tinged with envy because of Henry's earlier success? Did not Henry resent the failure of William to sympathize with his artistic development?

A partial answer to these queries is to read the opinions of the two brothers about each other conveniently assembled in *The James Family*. It is true that William criticized Henry's early stories for "a want of blood" (vitality), and he was sometimes patronizing. But he apologized for his "rather law-giving tone," and in *The American* he recognized with a chuckle that he had served as a model for the "morbid little clergyman," as he and Henry had traveled together. The general tone of William's comments on the fiction is intelligently appreciative. The fact that Henry lived abroad after 1875 made William anxious to communicate what he felt were typical American responses. Even in later years, in objecting to what he considered the over-subtlety of *The Wings of the Dove* and of *The Golden Bowl*, William admitted "touches unique and inimitable" in the first and "brilliancy and cleanness of effect" in the second. Henry accepted William's strictures with respect, sometimes agreeing, sometimes not. With regard to *The Wings of the Dove*, he simply said, "One writes as one *can* . . . my stuff, such as it is, is inevitable for me." In 1905 Henry seemed impatient when he said: ". . . I'm always sorry when I hear of your reading anything of mine, and always hope you won't—you seem so constitutionally unable to 'enjoy' it, and so condemned to look at it from a point of view remotely alien to mine in writing it. . . ." The dominant tone of the letter, however, is affectionate.[6]

As for William's own writing, which came late, Henry admired it. In the letter just quoted, he said, "And yet I can read *you* with rapture. . . . " And he chided his brother for not sending him copies of papers he had recently seen on the desk of a mutual friend. In 1902 Henry read *The Varieties of Religious Experience* with "rapturous deliberation." In 1909, *A Pluralistic Universe* was a statement of pragmatism he could approve: "As an artist and a 'creator' I can catch on, hold on, to pragmatism and can work in the light of it." That there was from time to time annoyance and irritation between the two brothers is not surprising—and not very important. What is surprising, and of lasting importance, is the extraordinary degree of generous appreciation and affection maintained for so long by two men so different in temperament and vocation. The generosity of spirit they displayed must have come in no small part from their father and mother. When all is considered, to have grown up in the James household offered great advantages.

With a minimum of rivalry, both William and Henry used these advantages well.[7]

Professor Anderson, taking a different tack altogether from that of Professor Edel, has argued that Henry James, Sr., furnished to Henry, Jr., so complete a set of moral ideas that the novelist was in effect sealed off from the social thought of the later nineteenth century. So thorough was the novelist's assimilation of his father's ideas that the three great novels of the later years are described as a trilogy with almost allegorical purpose: "*The Ambassadors* has for its subject the failure of the law, and its correspondent 'church' is New England's, here standing for the elder James's 'Jewish' church. *The Wings of the Dove* treats the redemption of an individual by an exemplary savior, Milly Theale; the correspondent church is 'Christian.' *The Golden Bowl's* subject is the regeneration of mankind, and its correspondent church is that of the new Jerusalem announced by Swedenborg." Such a characterization of these novels is a serious distortion of their texture and of the temper of the mind of Henry James. To read the son's critical essays and then to turn back to the father's *Moralism and Christianity* (1850) is to see how very far the son was from the schematic intellectual patterns of his father.[8]

Professor Anderson's statement of his case, if exaggerated, may still point to some important truth. That the novelist drew from his father and from Emerson some faith in Transcendental ideas ("the bootstrap myth," Anderson calls it) is surely true. This is why James's stories deal so constantly with individual choice and so little with blaming society for individual misfortune. There was advantage, as Professor Anderson points out, in James's customary selection of situations in which the economic factor is unimportant or subordinate. The emphasis of the story may then be upon the "real" motives which lie below and beyond economic interpretation. The quality of "moral spontaneity" James found in Minny Temple was central in the individualism of his own point of view. Professor Anderson is right in saying that this was "American" and that James is misread when he is viewed as alienated from his native country. In *The Ambassadors,* we are meant to approve Strether's advice to Little Bilham: "Live all you can." And we are expected to agree with Madame de Vionnet when she says to Strether: "What it comes to is that it's not, that it's never, a happiness, any happiness at all, to *take*. The only safe thing is to give. It's what plays you least false." With Emerson, these ideas were powerful, luminous abstractions. With Henry James, Sr., they were a System. With the novelist they are concrete discoveries.[9]

I *The Style*

Caricatures and parodies of James create the impression that James's style was mostly mannerism, that most of the mannerism was bad, and that with time it grew worse. The Jamesian style, however, was carefully wrought out over a period of fifty years and under the constant pressure of editorial demands. That the style had virtues is evident from the fact that, with three exceptions, all of the fiction before 1900 was published in magazines. From 1900 on, *The Ambassadors* and nineteen stories appeared in magazines. Besides the acceptance of his fiction for magazine publication, there are hundreds of travel pieces and critical articles, many solicited by editors.

The style of James's early fiction, and of his critical work as a whole, is, within the conventions of the time, straightforward. Long expository paragraphs were customary, as a glance at bound volumes of the *Atlantic Monthly* or *Cornhill* will show. James begins "The Story of a Year" (1865) with this sentence: "In early May, two years ago, a young couple I wot of strolled homeward from an evening walk, a long ramble among the peaceful hills which inclosed their rustic home." The literary flourish, "I wot of," aside, the sentence moves directly and literally. *The Portrait of a Lady* (1880-81) begins even more simply: "Under certain circumstances there are few hours in life more agreeable than the hour dedicated to the ceremony known as afternoon tea." And *Washington Square* (1888), though heavier and more bookish, is quite conventional in its opening sentence: "During a portion of the first half of the present century, and more particularly during the latter part of it, there flourished and practiced in the city of New York a physician who enjoyed perhaps an exceptional share of the consideration which, in the United States, has always been bestowed upon distinguished members of the medical profession." *The Wings of the Dove* (1902) shows the later style at its simplest: "She waited, Kate Croy, for her father to come in, but he kept her unconscionably, and there were moments at which she showed herself, in the glass over the mantel, a face positively pale with the irritation that had brought her to the point of going away without sight of him."

These samplings are minute, but they help to focus the conclusions offered in a perceptive study of James's sentence structure.[10] Limiting himself to the period of 1901 through 1904, Professor Short finds that James's sentence length is not excessive. In the first chapter of *The Ambassadors*, for example, it averages 35.3 words a sentence; or, if grammatically complete groups are counted as sentences, only 25.3 words a sentence. Difficulties in reading the later James come not from the length of the sentences but from James's indulgence in unusual sentence order, parentheses, special emphasis of connecting words, and seemingly deliberate ambiguity in placing modifiers. Beyond these characteristics, Professor Short finds frequent use of rhetorical devices such as alliteration and balance. From *The Golden Bowl* he quotes: "When they were so disposed as to shelter surprises the surprises were apt to be shocks."

The well-selected examples in Professor Short's article persuasively illustrate his conclusion that James's stylistic devices "contribute a heightened tension to a prose which, for all its own peculiar artifice, forever threatens to become devitalized by its own preciosity." Those whose taste approves James will italicize the first clause; those who dislike James will take comfort in the final one. In either case, the way James's style actually works is much clarified by the analysis given. It should be noticed, however, that James retained, even in the late period, a command of the short direct sentence. The ending of *The Wings of the Dove,* for instance, includes exactly two hundred words in the last twenty sentences: the longest, very simple in structure, is thirty-seven words. The vocabulary, too, is extremely simple; the eighteen words of more than one syllable are familiar ones, like "memory" and "again." Yet few passages in James convey a richer complexity of meaning.

This same passage in *The Wings of the Dove* is an excellent refutation of the charge that James's characters all "talk like Henry James." Kate Croy and Merton Densher talk in an individual way, and many other stories furnish striking examples of dialogue free from Jamesian mannerism. There is excellent mimicry in the correspondents in "A Bundle of Letters" (1879) and in "The Point of View" (1882). Caroline Spencer in "Four Meetings" (1877) and Daisy Miller in the story of the next year are both young American girls; one is serious, the other flirtatious. The narrator in "The Aspern Papers" (1888) is quite unlike Dencombe in "The Middle Years" (1893). The butler in "Brooksmith" (1891) and the girl clerk of "In the Cage" (1898) are well-realized types. May Bartram in "The Beast in the Jungle" (1903) and Kate Cookham in "The Bench of Desolation" (1909) talk neither like Henry James nor like each other. Additional illustrations of James's sensitivity to the rhythm and idiom of a wide range of speech might be cited from the novels.

Other features of James's style that call for brief comment are his vocabulary, his fondness for abstract words, and his command of figurative language. There are, it is true, certain Jamesian words and expressions that become mannerisms. Characters in his stories "ring out," "wind up," and "hang fire" with noticeable regularity. Favorite qualifiers and intensives are "beautiful," "splendid," "immense," "lovely," "abominably," "horribly," "appalling," and "vulgar." Often James will write in the French manner, "of a neatness" instead of "neat." Such expressions are usually playful, part of a conversational game. Acquaintance with James's letters helps a reader catch this tone of verbal play. Occasional bookish words like "obsequiosities," "osseous," and "matutinal" are humorously intended. On the whole, James's vocabulary is simple, even colloquial.

James's heavy dependence on abstract words may be illustrated by quoting the first paragraph of *The Ambassadors*, with abstract nouns italicized:

> Strether's first *question*, when he reached his hotel, was about his friend; yet on his *learning* that Waymarsh was apparently not to arrive till evening he was not wholly disconcerted. A telegram from him bespeaking a room "only if not too noisy," reply paid, was produced for the enquirer at the office, so that the *understanding* they should meet at Chester rather than at Liverpool remained to that *extent* sound. The same secret *principle*, however, that had prompted Strether not absolutely to desire Waymarsh's *presence* at the dock, that had led him thus to postpone for a few hours his *enjoyment* of it, now operated to make him feel he could still wait without *disappointment*. They would dine together at the *worst*, and, with all *respect* to dear old Waymarsh—if not even, for that *matter*, to himself—there was little fear that in the *sequel* they shouldn't see enough of each other. The *principle* I have just mentioned as operating had been, with the most newly disembarked of the two men, wholly instinctive—the fruit of a sharp *sense* that, delightful as it would be to find himself looking, after so much *separation*, into his comrade's face, his *business* would be a trifle bungled should he simply arrange for this *countenance* to present itself to the nearing steamer as the first "note" of Europe. Mixed with *everything* was the *apprehension*, already, on Strether's part, that it would, at *best*, throughout, prove the note of Europe in quite a sufficient *degree*.[11]

The italicized nouns in this paragraph are not at all unusual words, yet each requires the reader to supply from his own experience a "referent"—to use the semanticist's term. To note these abstract terms, however, is merely to begin the analysis of this aspect of James's style. The reader who comes to this paragraph for the first time finds "Strether" and "Waymarsh" quite as abstract as "principle," "enjoyment," and "disappointment." Who these gentlemen are will be explained in due course, but for the present their names must be carried in the mind as a focus for various associations and distinctions. The relationship between Strether and Waymarsh is a special one. It is not flatly stated that Strether was glad his friend was delayed; instead, the reader is told of "The same secret principle . . . that had prompted Strether not absolutely to desire Waymarsh's presence on the dock. . . ." That he "did not absolutely desire" is, perhaps, half way between "desiring" and "not desiring." Moreover, Strether's reluctance about seeing Waymarsh is clearly not dislike; Strether's "enjoyment" of the meeting has merely been postponed by a change of meeting place. In the fifth sentence the mysterious principle "operating" to produce these events is again alluded to, and it is now described as "wholly instinctive." The unexplained "business" of Strether, it seems, would be "a trifle bungled" should he see Waymarsh immediately. Waymarsh is to be *a* "note of Europe," but there is danger of his becoming *the* "note of Europe."

It is evident that James's method in this paragraph is, in the specific sense of the word, "Impressionistic." It is not the facts of the meeting with Waymarsh that are important; it is how Strether feels about the meeting. How he feels can not be directly stated: it has to be hinted. The reader, in turn, must see the implications of the hints given, and he must hold them in suspension so that succeeding paragraphs can fill them out. The care with which the qualifications are made creates confidence that a line of direction is being established. Suspense is created as to where it will lead. Thus the heavy reliance on abstract terms is dictated by the aim; it is not a mere stylistic blemish. It is no accident that the James revival came at the very time when the study of verbal meanings—semantics—was becoming popular. Just when Stuart Chase was insisting in *The Tyranny of Words* (1938) that an abstract word was meaningless unless visibly equipped with a referent, the Jamesian "impressionism" was getting a new and serious hearing. Indirectly, James operated to supplement Chase's limited view of language and meaning.[12]

James was early conscious of "impressionism" as his method. In "The Art of Fiction" (1884) he says that a novel is "a personal, a direct impression of life." Further on, James defines experience as "an immense sensibility," capable in a man of genius of converting "the very pulses of the air into revelations." Such an intuitive approach to writing led James to value most highly those aspects of a situation which lie beyond a provable proposition. It should be added that James's impressionism was not derived from French impressionistic painting, which did not interest him. The increasing emphasis on science—on the provable—turned the word "impressionistic" into a derogatory term in the 1920's, and partly explains the decline of James's reputation at that period. Similarly, the James revival has been accompanied by an increasing skepticism regarding science as a complete guide to life or as a means of "ultimate" truth. It was James's peculiar service to show that "impressionism" could be precise, could be disciplined.

An important part of Jamesian "impressionism" is the use of figurative language. When in the fifth sentence of the paragraph quoted from *The Ambassadors* the reader is told that the mysterious "principle" is "the *fruit* of a *sharp* sense," two figures give concrete associations to an idea that still remains abstract. Similarly, Waymarsh's "countenance," not yet described, is compared to a "note," not wholly displeasing but capable of becoming monotonous. Most readers have noticed James's extreme fondness for figurative language, and many have set it down to his mere loquaciousness. The figurative language is more than ornamental, however; it is essential if the abstraction of impressions is to be given the force of concreteness. The figures enrich the reader's experience, and to a remarkable degree they minimize the complaint of vagueness.

Recent studies present convincing evidence of the variety and resourceful use of imagery in James's fiction. Not only a given image, but a series of images in a given passage may be shown point by point to contribute to the general effect. And this skill in the handling of imagery developed steadily toward the symbolism of the later novels. The repeated comparison of Milly Theale to a dove goes far beyond ornament; it is an essential revelation of Milly's inner quality.[13]

It is not too much to say that for the best situations of his fiction, James's style is brilliantly effective. It makes demands, but it confers rewards; and the style has far greater variety than is generally believed. It is a disciplined, an intellectual style. Unlike most of his nineteenth-century contemporaries—Stevenson, for example—James does not try to sweep the reader off his feet by emotional fervor. Deep feeling James does provide in such memorable passages as the endings of *The Portrait of a Lady, The Awkward Age, The Wings of the Dove* and in many of the stories; but the feeling is within the limits of discriminating intelligence. The style in such passages bears little resemblance to the parodies. It is the style of a very great writer, skilled by long diligence to convey the insights of a gifted observer.

James's travel books, criticism, autobiography, and letters won for him a solid reputation in an age of great prose writers. These non-fictional works deserve to be read for their own merit, as well as for their illuminating commentary on his fiction. Mannered as it often is, James's prose falls more agreeably on the modern ear than the prose of such great contemporaries as Arnold, Carlyle, Ruskin,

Stevenson, Wilde, and—to name an American—James Russell Lowell. In accent as in idea, James is one of the greatest of the nineteenth-century men who made the transition to the twentieth century.

II *James's Revisions*

The New York Edition of the novels and tales (1907-09) is important for two reasons: it provides prefaces to many of the most familiar and interesting works; and it provides a revised text, one usually regarded as definitive and followed in most subsequent reprints. James's revisions were stylistic, not structural, but they were conspicuous enough to raise objections. Early readers who remembered the original version of *The American* (1876-77) and *The Portrait of a Lady* (1880-81) disliked what they considered an intrusion of the later style. Scholars, impressed with James's highly conscious art and critical method, have increasingly found in the textual variants a subject for comment rare in the study of fiction.[14]

In his first preface, that to *Roderick Hudson*, James compares the process of revision to the painter's "tentative wet sponge" and varnish bottle. The purpose was to restore and refresh, not to alter the original intention. James's feeling as he looked over his early fiction is memorably recorded by his secretary: ". . . he confessed that the difficulty of selection was mainly the difficulty of reading them at all. 'They seem,' he declared, 'so bad until I *have* read them that I can't force myself to look at them except with a pen in my hand, altering as I go the crudities and ineptitudes that to my sense deform each page.' But when he had managed, by dint of treating each page as a proof sheet, to read the earlier stories, he was relieved to find them, as a rule, really much better than he had feared. They were perhaps not, after all, he decided, the disgrace to his more mature artistic self that he had been persuaded they must be."[15]

James's own interest in the process of revision has accentuated the impression that he was essentially a fussy writer more concerned with detailed refinements than with the fundamental strength of substance. The elderly author of "The Middle Years," Dencombe the "passionate corrector, the fingerer of style," naturally comes to mind. This picture is but part of the truth. As has been emphasized in this book, James was a prolific writer; his output would have been impossible without a rapid, fluent style. He was one of those numerous nineteenth-century novelists who could send off to the publisher the early chapters of a novel before the last were written. He once told Constance Fenimore Woolson, perhaps with teasing exaggeration, that he never "copied" his work, meaning that he did not need to make a fair copy of his manuscript.[16] The chief association, then, with James's revision, should be energy rather than fussiness. Few poets and almost no novelists have so assiduously tried to "see" once more their early work.

It is important also to recognize that the revisions made for the New York Edition were not a sudden venture but the culmination of a professional habit. Two works of 1871 have been studied in this regard. *Watch and Ward*, first published in the *Atlantic Monthly*, appeared in book form in 1878. The prefatory note that the short novel "has now been minutely revised" is supported by some eight hundred verbal changes. Most of these show tightening of style, cropping of wordiness, and excision of hackneyed expressions familiar to every professional writer. The revised text is more direct, even more colloquial. The same kind of improvement came in the three successive revisions of "A Passionate Pilgrim," which also appeared first in the *Atlantic Monthly*. It was revised when published as the title story of James's collection in 1875; again for inclusion in *Stories Revived* (1885); and once more for the New York Edition.[17]

In the chapter on James's plays, his drastic revision of "Daisy Miller" and *The American* for the stage has already been discussed. A somewhat similar case is the "cut" version of *What Maisie Knew*.[18] Apparently at the request of the English magazine editor, several thousand words, chiefly of interpretive comment, were cut from the latter part of the novel. Similarly, James cut long passages from *The Ambassadors* for serial publication, but restored them when the book appeared in 1903. Many other revisions prior to those made for the New York Edition remain to be studied.

Final revisions of three early novels have received much attention: *Roderick Hudson* (1875); *The American* (1876-77); and *The Portrait of a Lady* (1880-81). An early study of *Roderick Hudson* exaggerated the extent of James's revisions for the New York Edition by simply overlooking James's revision for book publication in 1875 and also for the first English book publication in 1879. The proof sheet of *The American* reproduced in Lubbock's edition of James's *Letters*, with seventeen additions on a single page, seems to support Professor Gettman's characterization of the 1907 edition as almost another book. Professor Gettman, however, concludes that there are no essential changes in character; moreover, "alterations in diction move in the direction of the specific, the concrete, and the explicit." Successive revisions of *The Portrait of a Lady* show the same characteristics, and lead Professor Krause to suggest that there was "a fundamental continuity in James's development which becomes obscured by the tendency to group his work in periods." An important factor in this continued development was James's tireless search for figurative language that would be fresh, rich in meaning, consistent in tone.[19]

James's habit of dictating his later fiction has some bearing on his style, but it is hard to say how much. He began to dictate perhaps as early as 1896, as a means of reducing the drudgery of writing. Whether dictation actually proved easier is doubtful. In 1914 James refused a request for sample pages of manuscript on the ground that his work was done over and over until an immaculate typescript emerged, whereupon the early drafts were burned. This implies that the labor of penning the original draft was merely turned into the labor of repeated revision. It is doubtful whether the practice of dictation added materially to James's prolixity; for age must have had something to do with the occasional garrulity of the autobiographical volumes. On the other hand, dictation may have increased the colloquial tone which some have found more prominent in the later work.[20]

III *James in Perspective*

In the development of realism in America, three names are linked: Mark Twain, William Dean Howells, and Henry James. Born within eight years of each other, all three lived into the twentieth century. They left a literary world far different from the one dominated by the New Englanders in America and by Dickens, Thackeray, and Tennyson in England in the 1850's. It is a curious fact that although Howells was the intimate friend and the editor of both Twain and James, the man from Missouri and the New Yorker had almost no contact. Howells seems to have realized that he must enjoy the two friendships separately. Twain and James represented the opposite ends of the literary spectrum for their generation. One could, as Twain did, rely on homespun subjects and feelings, and build a style out of native idiom. One could, as James did, learn from French and Russian writers, and use European experience to enrich native feeling. It is a measure of Howells' breadth of mind that he could sympathize with both attempts.

Twain had enormous success in his own time, despite the fact that his writing was in subject and in style a challenge to existing standards of the mid-nineteenth century. There has never been a Twain revival for the simple reason that his popularity has been continuous. The serious study of Twain may be considered as beginning with Van Wyck Brooks's *The Ordeal of Mark Twain* (1920), and thus it precedes by a few years the James revival. In the main, the study of Twain has been biographical, bibliographical, and broadly cultural rather than literary or critical. The causes of Twain's pessimism, the identification of his journalistic pieces, his antecedents in earlier American humor, and his social and political ideas have attracted much attention. Study of his literary quality has not led far beyond what is obvious. It is possible that there is something ominous in the "survival" of Twain. *Huckleberry Finn* is his one great book, and a substantial part of its appeal is nostalgic. Twain's failure to deal with the adult world in adult terms, his virtual omission of the relations between men and women—these are limitations which will increasingly be felt.

There has been a moderate revival of Howells in recent years, but chiefly on the scholarly level. Howells' stout defense of Realism, his friendly encouragement of writers so diverse as Twain, James, Stephen Crane, and Hamlin Garland far outweigh his prejudice against Dreiser. The long row of Howells' novels, written with such professional competence over fifty years, commands respect. Yet Howells is diffuse. He could not concentrate in a few novels an intense expression of his humor and insight. His style is always fluent and intelligent; it is rarely rich. It is easy to share the admiration expressed for his books by both Twain and James; it is difficult to share their superlatives. In his letters James makes many comments recognizing that Howells had a limited talent, a certain naïveté, an insufficient concern with form and style.[21]

Like Twain and Howells, James himself had limitations. Several years ago they were conveniently summarized, with some refutation, by Clifton Fadiman: "1. He, and hence his work, is rootless. . . . 2. His snobbery imposed on him a pathetically limited subject matter. . . . 3. Even within this world his emotional range is narrow. . . . 4. He sacrificed content to form. . . . 5. His style is esoteric to the point of unreadability."[22] There is some truth in all these charges, but, as has been shown in this book, there is a development, a consistency in James's career that makes of these objections substantial critical problems instead of mere peevish complaints.

James's alleged rootlessness derives from his struggle to combine native Americanism with European culture, a struggle most relevant to Americans—and to Europeans—of the present. James's supposed snobbery did nevertheless permit him to consider fundamental questions about human relations bound to become more and more central in an affluent society. The narrowness of emotion in James's work is usually associated with the absence of sexual detail in his fiction. Yet the patterns of sexual relationship—the struggle to purify love of its possessiveness, the stern law that every choice is a renunciation—are developed with insight. In this regard, James's very reticence is sometimes an advantage to a generation now flooded with a virtually uninhibited journalism and fiction. As to form and style, readers who have confronted the experimental literature of the twentieth century—Joyce, Eliot, Pound, Faulkner—no longer feel that form and style can be separated from content. And they do not find James as difficult as did readers of the early 1900's.

A more important limitation, perhaps, is James's failure to deal with the subconscious, the instinctive, the primitive, as psychologists since his day have taught writers and readers to do. James believed in the conscious mind. He believed in civilization as an accretion of conscious effort, and he thought the absence of civilization "vulgar," a favorite epithet of his. James's rich use of imagery is a partial expression of the intuitive, but the intuitions are disciplined by taste and reflection. It is possible that this limitation, too, has some advantage. To a generation in which technological discipline is omnipresent, but discipline in general ideas nearly absent, James offers an imposing example of human potential.

It is doubtful whether any other nineteenth-century figure has more successfully made the transition to the twentieth. Even in the decade of greatest neglect, the voices of Eliot and Pound were raised in James's defense. Hemingway, in *The Green Hills of Africa,* has the narrator say: "The good writers are Henry James, Stephen Crane, and Mark Twain. That's not the order they're good in. There is no order for good writers."[23] In 1936 Stephen Spender was using James as a key to the destructive element in our society. In 1943 W. H. Auden wrote his moving poem, "At the Grave of Henry James." Meanwhile influential magazines underlined the significance of James in special issues: *The Egoist* (January, 1918); *The Little Review* (August, 1918); *Hound and Horn* (April-June, 1934); *The New Republic* (February 15, 1943; devoted to William and Henry James); *The Kenyon Review* (1943); *Modern Fiction Studies* (Spring, 1957); *Nineteenth Century Fiction* (June, 1957). The James revival has been "in" for thirty years. James is no longer an intellectual fad. He is established as a vital part of American literary achievement. His work is the best cultural bridge yet built between Western Europe and America.

Notes and References

Chapter One

1. In a review, *Time* referred to James as "the Winston Spencer Churchill of fiction": May 3, 1948, p. 100. Leon Edel, *Henry James: The Conquest of London: 1870-1881* (New York, 1962), p. 282, refers to James's comments on Britain as being "almost in Churchillian cadences."

2. E. V. Lucas, *Edwin Austin Abbey, Royal Academician*, 2 vols. (London and New York, 1921), I, 268.

3. In a letter to Howells, *The Letters of Henry James*, selected and edited by Percy Lubbock, 2 vols. (New York, 1920), I, 135.

4. *Ibid.*, II, 389.

5. This comment, made in the essay "On Henry James," was first published in the Henry James number of *The Egoist* (January, 1918), and reprinted in the *Little Review* (August, 1918). Accessible in *The Question of Henry James: A Collection of Critical Essays*, ed. F. W. Dupee (New York, 1945), p. 110.

6. *Henry James: Autobiography*, ed. F. W. Dupee (New York, 1956), p. 278. This volume combines *A Small Boy and Others* (1913); *Notes of a Son and Brother* (1914); and *The Middle Years* (1917). See *Notes*, Ch. 4.

7. *Autobiography*, pp. 147, 120, 30, 142, 129, 136.

8. *The Notebooks of Henry James*, ed. F. O. Matthiessen and Kenneth B. Murdock (New York, 1947), pp. 40-41.

9. Young Emerson's observations are quoted in F. O. Matthiessen, *The James Family* (New York, 1948), p. 99. Leon Edel, *Henry James: The Untried Years: 1843-1870* (New York, 1953), p. 43, quotes Perry's account.

10. *Autobiography*, pp. 414-15 (*Notes*, Ch. IX); Edel, *The Untried Years*, pp. 173-83.

11. Ralph Barton Perry, *The Thought and Character of William James*, 2 vols. (Boston, 1935), I, 203. Perry says, I, 203, that Robertson enlisted February, 1864. Edel, *The Untried Years*, p. 184, says Robertson followed Wilkinson "a few months later."

12. *Essays in London and Elsewhere* (London, 1893), p. 48.

13. Leon Edel first identified and reprinted this story in " 'A Tragedy of Error': James's First Story," *New England Quarterly*, XXIX (September, 1956), 291-317. Also available in *Henry James: The Complete Tales*, ed. Leon Edel (Philadelphia, 1962), I.

14. For information on first appearance of James's stories, see the chronological list of his fiction in the Bibliography.

15. *Letters*, I, 24. Letter to William James, Perry, I, 311-15. See Robert L. Gale, "Henry James and Italy," *Nineteenth Century Fiction*, XIV (September, 1959), 157-70.

16. *James Family*, p. 263. *The Untried Years*, pp. 323-33.

Notes and References

17. *Letters*, I, 31. *Notebooks*, 23-24. "Occasional Paris," *Portraits of Places* (London, 1883), p. 75.

18. *Henry James: Letters to A. C. Benson and Auguste Monod* (London and New York, 1930), pp. 97-98.

19. Mary Ellen Chase, *Thomas Hardy from Serial to Novel* (University of Minnesota Press, 1927), p. 86, gives an amusing example of editorial delicacy. In the book version of *Tess of the Durbervilles* (1891) Angel Clare picks up Tess in his arms to carry her over a small stream. In the serial he was equipped with a wheelbarrow so that she could be carried without physical contact. Howells' novel *The Shadow of a Dream* (1890) is an extreme example of guilt feeling between two lovers because they were aware of their mutual feelings before the death of the woman's husband.

20. *Henry James: Parisian Sketches*, ed. Leon Edel and Ilse Dusoir Lind (New York, 1957), p. 219.

21. Letters to William James, Perry, I, 372-73. To his mother, *Letters*, I, 23.

Chapter Two

1. *Watch and Ward* (New York, 1960), p. 18.

2. *Roderick Hudson* (Boston, 1876), p. 129. Chapter five in later editions.

3. Leon Edel, *Henry James: The Conquest of London: 1870-1881* (Philadelphia and New York, 1962), p. 112.

4. 1876: p. 46.

5. *Henry James: Letters to A. C. Benson and Auguste Monod* (London and New York, 1930), pp. 19-20. *Art of the Novel*, pp. 18-19.

6. In the original version Newman is described as thirty-six; in the 1907 version, forty-two.

7. *Art of the Novel,* pp. 35, 37.

8. *Conquest of London*, p. 272; *Letters*, I, 52-53; Charles Morgan, *The House of Macmillan* (New York, 1944), p. 115; *Letters*, I, 69.

9. *The Novels and Tales of Henry James* (New York, 1907-09), XVIII, 92, 93. The "New York Edition"; hereafter referred to as NY, with volume number. For description of this basic edition, see Bibliography.

10. The friend was Mrs. Lynn Linton, a minor literary figure in London. The correspondence is reprinted in my article, "The 'Shy Incongruous Charm' of Daisy Miller," *Nineteenth Century Fiction*, X (September, 1955), 162-65.

11. *The American Novels and Stories of Henry James*, ed. F. O. Matthiessen (New York, 1947), pp. 58, 75 (Chapters III and IV).

12. *Confidence* (London, 1921), pp. 126, 192. This is Vol. IV of the so-called "London Edition"; see Bibliography.

13. To his brother, James wrote: "The young man in *Washington Square* is not a portrait—he is sketched from the outside merely, not *fouillé*. The only good thing in the story is the girl." Perry, I, 381.

14. *American Novels and Stories*, pp. 287, 291, 294, 295.

Chapter Three

1. *The James Family*, pp. 132-33.
2. Edel, *The Middle Years: 1882-1885* (New York, 1962), p. 63.
3. *Alice James: Her Brothers—Her Journal*, ed. Anna Robeson Burr (New York, 1934), p. 150.
4. *The Middle Years*, pp. 356-86.
5. *Ibid.*, pp. 384-85.
6. *The Portrait of a Lady* (Boston, 1882), p. 94.
7. *Ibid.*, pp. 518-19. NY IV, 437.
8. 1882: pp. 428, 471.
9. *Notebooks*, p. 18.
10. *French Poets and Novelists* (London, 1878), p. 261.
11. 1882: p. 111.
12. *American Novels and Stories*, pp. 434, 746.
13. *Ibid.*, pp. 434-35. On the point of Lesbianism, Oscar Cargill cites three critics, without accepting their views, in *The Novels of Henry James* (New York, 1961), p. 140, fn. 21. The three critics are C. Hartley Grattan, Osborne Andreas, and Michael Swan. See also Irving Howe's "Introduction" to the Modern Library edition (New York, 1956), p. xxiii.
14. *Ibid.*, pp. 465, 499, 540, 669, 744. Chapters 8, 14, 19, 34, 42.
15. *Ibid.*, pp. 556, 557, 559, 571, 597, 659. Chapters 21, 22, 25, 33.
16. *Ibid.*, pp. 436, 440. Chapters 3, 4.
17. *Ibid.*, pp. 440, 441, 442. Chapter 4.
18. *Ibid.*, pp. 576, 577, 707. Chapters 23 and 38.
19. *The American Scene*, ed. W. H. Auden (New York, 1946), p. 264.
20. Daniel Lerner, "The Influence of Turgenev on Henry James," *Slavonic and Eastern European Review*, XX (December, 1941), 46-51. In 1877 James had reviewed *Virgin Soil;* from this novel he took plot and character patterns. Subsequently, Sylvia E. Bowman has shown that *The Portrait of a Lady* is indebted to "On the Eve"; see "Les Héroines d'Henry James dans *The Portrait of a Lady* et d'Yvan Tourguéniev dans *A la Veille*," *Etudes Anglaises*, XI (Avril-Juin, 1958), 136-49.
21. NY V, 169. Chapter XI.
22. NY V, 200; VI, 49. Chapters XII and XXIV.
23. NY VI, 145-46. Chapter XXX.
24. Virginia Harlow, *Thomas Sergeant Perry: A Biography* (Durham, N.C., 1950), p. 319.
25. Lionel Trilling published an "Introduction" to a new edition of the novel (New York, 1948). This essay is included in his collection, *The Liberal Imagination* (New York, 1950), pp. 65-96. He says, p. 65, that *The Bostonians* and *The Princess Casamassima* are the two novels by James "which are most likely to make an immediate appeal to the reader of today."
26. *Complete Tales*, IV, 243, 254, 272.
27. *Lady Barberina and Other Tales*, ed. Herbert Ruhm (New York, 1961), p. 94. Quotation is from the 1884 text; variants in the New York edition seem to blur the passage.

28. *American Novels and Stories,* pp. 357, 374, 373.
29. *Complete Tales,* IV, 503, 512, 515, 516.
30. *Complete Tales,* IV, 443, 448.
31. "Occasional Paris," *Portraits of Places* (London, 1883), p. 95.
32. NY X, 308, 291, 411.
33. NY XVI, 71, 42, 43, 46.
34. Perry, I, 407-8.
35. NY XIII, 62, 106, 154.
36. Leon Edel discusses James's use of these terms, *Complete Tales,* I, 8-10.

Chapter Four

1. *The Complete Plays of Henry James,* ed. Leon Edel (Philadelphia and New York, 1949), p. 179. This edition, hereafter referred to as *Plays,* includes all of James's dramatic efforts, with elaborate introductions to each piece and to the volume as a whole.
2. *Henry James: The Tragic Muse,* Introduction by Leon Edel (New York, 1960), pp. 122, 141, 597. This edition gives the 1890 text. Nash's remark on Spain derives from James's acquaintance, Herbert Platt; see *Notebooks,* p. 31.
3. *Ibid.,* 610. James's views of the stage, especially in England, may be sampled in his letters to Elizabeth Robins, an actress who played Claire in *The American* and later appeared in Ibsen's *Master Builder.* See her *Theatre and Friendship: Some Henry James Letters* (New York, 1932), pp. 39, 48, 111, 112, 139, 167.
4. Edel, *The Untried Years,* 199.
5. *Henry James: The Scenic Art,* ed. Allan Wade (New York, 1957; first published 1948), pp. 25, 36, 134, 179, 189. *Letters,* I, 60.
6. *Plays,* pp. 73-113. "Pyramus and Thisbe" appeared first in the *Galaxy,* April, 1869; "Still Waters" in the *Balloon Post* (six numbers published as a benefit for French sufferers in the siege of Paris), April 12, 1871; "A Change of Heart" in the *Atlantic Monthly,* January, 1872.
7. *Plays,* pp. 117-19.
8. *Plays,* pp. 254-452. James's prefatory note is given p. 255.
9. *Plays,* pp. 473-83.
10. *Notebooks,* p. 348.
11. *Plays,* pp. 519-23, 549-53.
12. *Plays,* pp. 607-37.
13. *Plays,* pp. 641-74. The letters between Shaw and James, given in full in the introduction, are of great interest.
14. *Plays,* pp. 761-807.
15. *Plays,* pp. 811-16.
16. "The Wings of Henry James," *New Yorker,* XXXV (November 7, 1959), 184-97. Jed Harris, *Watchman, What of the Night* (New York, 1963), gives an informal account of his production of *The Heiress;* see especially pp. 13-58.

Chapter Five

1. Clare Benedict, *The Benedicts Abroad* (London, 1930), p. 93. Clare Benedict was the niece of Constance Fenimore Woolson.

2. *Notebooks*, pp. 136-37. Cargill in *The Novels of Henry James* (New York, 1961), pp. 218-19, draws attention to the parallel between James's story and Maupassant's "En Famille," which James commented on in his article on Maupassant, *Fortnightly Review*, March, 1888 (included in *Partial Portraits*).

3. *Notebooks*, pp. 126-27, dated November 12, 1892.

4. NY XI, 155. The second paragraph of Chapter I indicates that Maisie was six at the time her parents were divorced; she was ten or twelve at the end of the story.

5. Chapters 19 and 21. Cargill, in his study of the novels (p. 259, note 13) says that in 1950 a television version was canceled on grounds of taste.

6. *The Ghostly Tales of Henry James* (New Brunswick, N.J., 1948). Besides the tales discussed in this section, Professor Edel includes in his volume: "The Romance of Certain Old Clothes" (1868); "De Grey" (1868); "The Last of the Valerii" (1874); "Ghostly Rental" (1876); "Nona Vincent" (1892); "The Private Life" (1892); "Sir Dominick Ferrand" (1892); "The Real Right Thing" (1899); "The Great Good Place" (1900); "The Beast in the Jungle" (1903); and "The Jolly Corner" (1908).

7. *Art of the Novel*, pp. 169, 254. (In discussions of "The Turn of the Screw" and "The Altar of the Dead.")

8. To *In After Days* (New York and London, 1910) James contributed an essay, "Is There a Life After Death?" He expressed hope rather than conviction.

9. Gerald Willen, *A Casebook on Henry James's The Turn of the Screw* (New York, 1960), has conveniently brought together with the text of the story, James's preface, and fifteen critical essays. Of these the second is Mr. Wilson's, "The Ambiguity of Henry James," which first appeared in the Henry James issue of *Hound and Horn*, 1934. Revised for inclusion in Wilson's *The Triple Thinkers* (New York, 1938), it was again revised for the second edition of that work, with an eight-page supplementary note dated 1948. For Mr. Willen's *Casebook*, a brief paragraph dated 1959 was added. Mr. Wilson's essay treats the story in the perspective of James's whole career.

10. John Silver, "A Note on the Freudian Reading of 'The Turn of the Screw,'" *American Literature*, XXIX (May, 1957), 207-11, suggested that the governess may have learned about Quint, perhaps in the village. Silver's suggestion, included in the *Casebook*, is accepted by Mr. Wilson in his 1959 note. Oscar Cargill's "Henry James as Freudian Pioneer," included in the *Casebook*, has been repudiated by Cargill in a subsequent article: "*The Turn of the Screw* and Alice James," *PMLA*, LXXVIII (June, 1963), 238-49. The second article, however, preserves the contention that, in characterizing the governess, James drew upon his observation of his sister's nervous disorders, and probably upon an

early case study by Freud, known to have been familiar to F. W. H. Myers, a friend of Henry James. As early as 1896 William James favorably mentioned Freud's studies.

11. Dorothea Krook, *The Ordeal of Consciousness in Henry James* (Cambridge University Press, 1962), devotes a chapter to the story, pp. 106-34, and an appendix, pp. 370-89. She rejects most of Wilson's argument, and makes little use of articles by Cargill and Silver. In keeping with the general aim of her book, she sees the actual corruption of the children as the central theme; the story is "a fable about the redemptive power of human love: the power of love—here the governess's love for the children—to redeem the corrupt element in a human soul, and so to ensure the final triumph of good over evil; though (as so often in tragedy) at the cost of the redeemed soul" (122).

12. NY XVI, 90, 82, 105.

13. NY XVI, 238, 252, 259, 263.

Chapter Six

1. *The American Scene,* with an Introduction by W. H. Auden (New York, 1946), p. 237. *The American Essays of Henry James,* ed. Leon Edel (New York, 1956).

2. *The Sacred Fount,* Introductory Essay by Leon Edel (New York, 1953), p. 29. Other allusions to "the sacred fount" are found, pp. 38, 47.

3. Roger Burlingame, *Of Making Many Books* (New York, 1946), pp. 36-37.

4. In 1913 James wrote a friend, enclosing for Stark Young's guidance, two lists of five novels each. The first list is *Roderick Hudson, The Portrait of a Lady, The Princess Casamassima, The Wings of the Dove, The Golden Bowl.* The second, "more advanced" list is: *The American, The Tragic Muse, The Wings of the Dove, The Ambassadors, The Golden Bowl.* See *Letters,* II, 332-33. It is interesting that *The Wings of the Dove* and *The Golden Bowl* appear on both lists.

5. NY XXII, 323, 326.

6. The "Project" for *The Ambassadors* was published in part in the Henry James number of *Hound and Horn* (1934). It is given complete in the *Notebooks,* pp. 370-415; there are other comments on the story, especially pp. 225-29.

7. Discovery of the reversed chapters was made by Robert E. Young, "An Error in 'The Ambassadors,'" *American Literature,* XXII (November, 1950), 245-53. Leon Edel, "The Text of *The Ambassadors,*" *Harvard Library Bulletin,* XIV (1960), 453-60, traces the confusion and other problems.

8. Letter to William, March 29, 1870, *The James Family,* p. 263.

9. NY XIX, 115, Chapter V. NY XX, 341, Chapter XXXIV. NY XIX, 162, Chapter VII.

10. Dorothea Krook, *The Ordeal of Consciousness in Henry James* (Cambridge University Press, 1962), pp. 232-324, devotes two chapters to *The Golden Bowl.* Miss Krook sees Maggie Verver as fighting the

devil "in a shape more subtle and insidious than any that even Shakespeare had any knowledge of—for the reason, perhaps, that it had not yet fully emerged in the consciousness of man at the time Shakespeare wrote" (267). Maggie's love for the Prince is both selfish and selfless. The novel represents James's total vision: "the sense of the grimness and bitterness of human life is inseparably fused with the sense of its beauty and blessedness . . . neither cancels out the other . . . the ambiguity is intended to express precisely this experience of their permanent, inseparable fusion" (p. 324).

11. *The Whole Family* (New York and London, 1908), p. 144. Twelve authors contributed chapters in this sequence: William Dean Howells, Mary E. Wilkins Freeman, Mary Heaton Vorse, Mary Stewart Cutting, Elizabeth Jordan (editor of *Harper's Bazar* and planner of the project), John Kendrick Bangs, Henry James, Elizabeth Stuart Phelps, Edith Wyatt, Mary Raymond Shipman Andrews, Alice Brown, Henry Van Dyke. For correspondence and background of this odd venture, see my article, "Henry James and *The Whole Family*," *Pacific Spectator*, IV (Summer, 1950), 352-60; also Leon Edel, "Henry James and the *Bazar* Letters," *Bulletin of the New York Public Library*, LXII (February, 1958), 75-103.

12. Shane Leslie, "A Note on Henry James," *Horizon*, VII (June, 1943), 412-13. The letter was to Jocelyn Persse.

13. *Henry James and H. G. Wells: A Record of their Friendship, their Debate on the Art of Fiction, and their Quarrel*, ed. with an Introduction by Leon Edel and Gordon Ray (Urbana, Ill., 1958), pp. 245, 249, 262, 264, 267.

14. Virginia Harlow, *Thomas Sergeant Perry* (Durham, N.C., 1950), pp. 349-50.

Chapter Seven

1. *The Antic Muse: American Writers in Parody*, ed. Robert P. Falk (New York, 1955), pp. 127-45, brings together these and other parodies of James. Edith Wharton recorded the anecdote about James in *A Backward Glance* (New York, 1934), p. 243. It is also given, with much other anecdotal material, by Simon Nowell-Smith in *The Legend of the Master* (New York, 1948), pp. 45-47.

2. *The Letters of Henry James to Walter Berry* (Paris, 1928), letter #14.

3. See *The Untried Years:* for Henry James, Sr., pp. 50-51, 137-38 (second reference notes suppression of the 1858-59 sojourn in Newport from *A Small Boy and Others*); for Mary James, the mother, pp. 46-48; and for William, pp. 58-63, 240-52. The facts stated by Professor Edel do change somewhat the image of the James family as an extremely "happy" one. My objections are merely of degree.

4. *Autobiography*, p. 331.

5. *Ibid.*, p. 246. Letters to Walter Berry, to Holmes, and to John La Farge in 1910 express sentiments similar to those in the better known letter to Perry.

6. *The James Family*, pp. 315-45. See especially pp. 317, 323, 338-40. The last quotation is from *Letters*, II, 43.

7. *The James Family*, pp. 338, 344.

8. Quentin Anderson, *The American Henry James* (New Brunswick, N.J., 1957), p. 230. A chapter from *Moralism and Christianity* is given in *The James Family*, pp. 49-58. It is worth noting that there is no clear allusion to Blake in the writings of James. The title *The Golden Bowl* may be drawn from Poe's well-known phrase (though James did not care for Poe); or it may come from Blake's motto to "The Book of Thel," as Professor Anderson assumes (p. 224).

9. These well-known passages are in Chapter 2, Book Five; in Chapter 2, Book Twelve.

10. R. W. Short, "The Sentence Structure of Henry James," *American Literature*, XVIII (May, 1946), 71-88.

11. The underlined words, of course, are not "equally" abstract. "Tone" is not considered abstract here since it is used figuratively. The degree of abstraction in James's figurative language would seem to defy analysis.

12. The foregoing analysis profits from Walter J. Slatoff's methods in analyzing Faulkner's style. See his *Quest for Failure* (Ithaca, N.Y., 1960), pp. 7-132 especially.

13. Robert L. Gale, *The Caught Image: Figurative Language in the Fiction of Henry James* (Chapel Hill, N.C., 1964), focuses and consolidates the findings previously published in several special studies. Gale has tabulated nearly 17,000 images in the 135 fictional works. He defines an image as "a single figurative expression—a simile or a metaphor, including any passage containing imaginative or extended personification—in which neither the literal nor the figurative half of the similarity or identity changes appreciably in content."

Alexander Holder-Barrell in *The Development of Imagery and its Functional Significance in Henry James's Novels* (Bern, 1959), emphasizes the importance of imagery in James's successive revisions of his work. There was, he believes, "a continuous development in his use of imagery and its significance" (p. 16). These captions suggest the approach of this study: "The Expanding Image," "The Characterizing Image," "Images Expressing the Abstract in Terms of the Concrete," "The Constructive Image," "The Transition from Metaphor to Symbol."

14. Kathleen Tillotson, in the London *Times Literary Supplement*, July 23, 1954, commented that there are almost no edited texts of Victorian novels. Mary Ellen Chase's study of Hardy, already cited, emphasizes the changes from magazine serial to book publication.

15. Theodora Bosanquet, "Henry James," *Fortnightly*, CI (June, 1917), 1003. The passage is compressed in her *Henry James at Work* (London, 1924), p. 12.

16. Leon Edel, *Henry James: The Middle Years: 1882-1895* (Philadelphia and New York, 1962), p. 90.

17. See my article, "Henry James's Revisions of *Watch and Ward*," *Modern Language Notes*, LXVII (November, 1952), 457-61; and Albert

F. Gegenheimer, "Early and Late Revisions in Henry James's 'A Passionate Pilgrim,'" *American Literature*, XXIII (May, 1951), 233-42.

18. Ward S. Worden, "A Cut Version of *What Maisie Knew*," *American Literature*, XXIV (January, 1953), 493-504.

19. Helene Harvitt, "How Henry James Revised *Roderick Hudson*: A Study in Style," *PMLA*, XXXIX (March, 1924), 203-27. Raymond D. Havens, "The Revision of Roderick Hudson," *PMLA*, XL (June, 1925), 433-34 pointed out that many of the supposed late revisions had been made by 1882. Leon Edel's edition of the novel (New York, 1960) traces the process of revision. See *Letters*, II, 70, for a facsimile of a proofsheet of *The American*. Edel's statement is in *The Conquest of London*, p. 257. See Royal A. Gettman, "Henry James's Revision of *The American*," *American Literature*, XVI (January, 1945), 279-95; and Sydney J. Krause, "James's Revisions of the Style of *The Portrait of a Lady*," *American Literature*, XXX (March, 1958), 67-88. Isadore Traschen, "Henry James and the Art of Revision," *Philological Quarterly*, XXXV (January, 1956), 39-47, concludes that revision was "a single and continuous act of James's imagination."

20. F. O. Matthiessen, *Henry James: The Major Phase* (New York, 1944), p. 109, says he was dictating by 1896. Lubbock, *Letters*, I, 273, says 1898. The letter describing the burning of work sheets was to Hamlin Garland; see *The Selected Letters of Henry James*, ed. Leon Edel (New York, 1955), p. 173.

21. Letters to T. S. Perry in 1909, 1912, and 1913 make such comments. James speaks of Howells' critical opinions, which "grow more beautifully ingenuous, or less and less sophisticated as he grows older." He speaks of Howells' odd lack of social tradition. He says "dear W. D. H. is marvelous for youth and hilarity and innocence and an optimism that is not of this world and that is fed on such *voulues* ignorances." See *Thomas Sergeant Perry*, 329-30, 339-40, and 341-42. These opinions, however, do not convict James of hypocrisy in his letters to Howells. His affection and respect for Howells were genuine. Howells' service to James has been emphasized in *Discovery of a Genius: William Dean Howells and Henry James*, Compiled and edited by Albert Mordell, with Introduction by Sylvia E. Bowman (New York, 1961). This volume collects some seventeen essays on James by Howells between 1875 and 1903.

22. *The Short Stories of Henry James*, ed. Clifton Fadiman (New York, 1945), pp. xi-xii. Similar objections are vigorously advanced by Maxwell Geismar, *Henry James and the Jacobites* (Boston, 1963).

23. Ernest Hemingway, *The Green Hills of Africa* (New York, 1935), p. 19 (Chapter One). Hemingway's better-known comment that "All modern literature comes from one book by Mark Twain called *Huckleberry Finn*" occurs two lines below. A chapter from Spender's volume and the poem by Auden are reprinted in *The Question of Henry James*, pp. 236-50.

Selected Bibliography

This Bibliography includes a separate and complete chronological list of the 135 works of fiction published between 1864 and 1917, the principal collections of his novels, stories, and plays, and the chief bibliographical aids for the study of Henry James. The principal secondary works appear in footnotes to the text, and are not repeated here. For the principal volumes published by James himself, see the Chronological Table, following the Table of Contents.

The following numbered list gives all novels, "short novels" (as defined by Edel), and tales in the chronological order of their first publication. If this was in a periodical, as it usually was, the periodical is specified, with date. If first publication was in book form, the name of the volume is specified. Inclusion in the New York Edition is indicated by NY, with volume number. For works not so included, James's first book publication or a recent reprint is cited.

A. *Chronological List of Works*

1. "A Tragedy of Error," *Continental Monthly*, February, 1864. Identified by Leon Edel and reprinted in the *New England Quarterly*, September, 1956. See also Edel's *Complete Tales of Henry James* (eight of the projected twelve volumes have appeared).

2. "The Story of a Year," *Atlantic Monthly*, March, 1865. *Complete Tales*. Not reprinted by James.

3. "A Landscape Painter," *Atlantic Monthly*, February, 1866. *Stories Revived*, 1885. *Complete Tales*.

4. "A Day of Days," *Galaxy*, June 15, 1866. *Stories Revived*, 1885. *Complete Tales*.

5. "My Friend Bingham," *Atlantic Monthly*, March, 1867. *Stories Revived*, 1885. *Complete Tales*. Not reprinted by James.

6. "Poor Richard," *Atlantic Monthly*, June-August, 1867. *Stories Revived*, 1885. *Complete Tales*.

7. "The Story of a Masterpiece," *Galaxy*, January-February, 1868. *Complete Tales*. Not reprinted by James.

8. "The Romance of Certain Old Clothes," *Atlantic Monthly*, February, 1868. *A Passionate Pilgrim*, 1875. *Complete Tales*.

9. "A Most Extraordinary Case," *Atlantic Monthly*, April, 1868. *Stories Revived*, 1885. *Complete Tales*.

10. "A Problem," *Galaxy*, June, 1868. *Complete Tales*. Not reprinted by James.

11. "De Grey: A Romance," *Atlantic Monthly*, July, 1868. *Complete Tales*. Not reprinted by James.

12. "Osborne's Revenge," *Galaxy*, July, 1868. *Complete Tales*. Not reprinted by James.

HENRY JAMES

13. "A Light Man," *Galaxy*, July, 1869. *Complete Tales.*
14. "Gabrielle de Bergerac," *Atlantic Monthly*, July-September, 1869. *Complete Tales.* Not reprinted by James.
15. "Travelling Companions," *Atlantic Monthly*, November-December, 1870. *Complete Tales.* Not reprinted by James.
16. "A Passionate Pilgrim," *Atlantic Monthly*, March-April, 1871. NY XIII.
17. "At Isella," *Galaxy*, August, 1871. *Complete Tales.* Not reprinted by James.
18. *Watch and Ward* (short novel), *Atlantic Monthly*, August-December, 1871. Boston, 1878. London ed., 1921-23, XXIV.
19. "Master Eustace," *Galaxy*, November, 1871. *Stories Revived*, 1885. *Complete Tales.*
20. "Guest's Confession," *Atlantic Monthly*, October-November, 1872. *Complete Tales.* Not reprinted by James.
21. "The Madonna of the Future," *Atlantic Monthly*, March, 1873. NY XIII.
22. "The Sweetheart of M. Briseux," *Galaxy*, June, 1873. *Complete Tales.* Not reprinted by James.
23. "The Last of the Valerii," *Atlantic Monthly*, January, 1874. *A Passionate Pilgrim*, 1875. *Complete Tales.*
24. "Madame de Mauves," *Galaxy*, February-March, 1874. NY XIII.
25. "Adina," *Scribner's Monthly*, May-June, 1874. *Complete Tales.* Not reprinted by James.
26. "Professor Fargo," *Galaxy*, August, 1874. *Complete Tales.* Not reprinted by James.
27. "Eugene Pickering," *Atlantic Monthly*, October-November, 1874. *A Passionate Pilgrim*, 1875. *Complete Tales.*
28. *Roderick Hudson*, novel, *Atlantic Monthly*, January-December, 1875. Boston, 1875. NY I.
29. "Benvolio," *Galaxy*, August, 1875. *The Madonna of the Future*, 1879. *Complete Tales.*
30. *The American*, novel, *Atlantic Monthly*, June, 1876-May, 1877. Boston, 1877. NY II.
31. "Crawford's Consistency," *Scribner's Monthly*, August, 1876. *Complete Tales.* Not reprinted by James.
32. "The Ghostly Rental," *Scribner's Monthly*, September, 1876. *Complete Tales.* Not reprinted by James.
33. "Four Meetings," *Scribner's Monthly*, November, 1877. NY XVI.
34. "Rose Agathe," originally "Théodolinde," *Atlantic Monthly*, May, 1878. *Stories Revived*, 1885. *Complete Tales.*
35. "Daisy Miller," *Cornhill Magazine*, June-July, 1878. NY XVIII.
36. *The Europeans*, short novel, *Atlantic Monthly*, July-October, 1878. London, 2 vols., 1878. London Edition, 1921-23, III.
37. "Longstaff's Marriage," *Scribner's Monthly*, August, 1878. *The Madonna of the Future*, 1879. *Complete Tales.*

38. "An International Episode," *Cornhill Magazine,* December, 1878. NY XIV.
39. "The Pension Beaurepas," *Atlantic Monthly,* April, 1879. NY XIV.
40. "The Diary of a Man of Fifty," *Harper's New Monthly Magazine* and *Macmillan's Magazine,* July, 1879. *The Madonna of the Future,* 1879. *Complete Tales.*
41. *Confidence,* short novel, *Scribner's Monthly,* August-October, 1879. London, 1879. London Edition, 1921-23, IV.
42. "A Bundle of Letters," *Parisian* (Paris), December 18, 1879. In *The Diary of a Man of Fifty,* 1880. *Complete Tales.*
43. *Washington Square,* short novel, *Cornhill Magazine* and *Harper's New Monthly Magazine,* July-November, 1880. Boston, 1880. London Edition, 1921-23, V.
44. *The Portrait of a Lady,* novel, *Macmillan's Magazine,* October, 1880-November, 1881; also *Atlantic Monthly,* November, 1880-December, 1881. NY III, IV.
45. "The Point of View," *Century Magazine,* December, 1882. NY XIV.
46. "The Siege of London," *Cornhill Magazine,* January-February, 1883. NY XIV.
47. "The Impressions of a Cousin," *Century Magazine,* November-December, 1883. *Tales of Three Cities,* 1884. London Edition, 1921-23, XXIV. *Complete Tales.*
48. "Lady Barbarina," originally Barberina, *Century Magazine,* May-July, 1884. NY XIV.
49. "Pandora," New York *Sun,* June 1 and 8, 1884. NY XVIII.
50. "The Author of Beltraffio," *English Illustrated Magazine,* June-July, 1884. NY XVI.
51. "Georgina's Reasons," New York *Sun,* July 20, 27, August 3, 1884. *Stories Revived,* 1885. London Edition, 1921-23, XXV. *Complete Tales.*
52. "A New England Winter," *Century Magazine,* August-September, 1884. *Tales of Three Cities,* 1884. London Edition, 1921-23, XXV. *Complete Tales.*
53. "The Path of Duty," *English Illustrated Magazine,* December, 1884. *Author of Beltraffio* and *Stories Revived,* 1885. London Edition, 1921-23, XXV. *Complete Tales.*
54. *The Bostonians,* novel, *Century Magazine,* February, 1885-February, 1886. London, 1886. London Edition, 1921-23, VIII, IX.
55. *The Princess Casamassima,* novel, *Atlantic Monthly,* September, 1885-October, 1886. NY V, VI.
56. "Mrs. Temperly," originally "Cousin Maria," *Harper's Weekly,* August 6-20, 1887. *A London Life,* 1889. London Edition, 1921-23, XXVI. *Complete Tales.*
57. "Louisa Pallant," *Harper's New Monthly Magazine,* February, 1888. NY XIII.

58. *The Reverberator*, short novel, *Macmillan's Magazine*, February-April, 1888. NY XIII.

59. "The Aspern Papers," *Atlantic Monthly*, March-May, 1888. NY XII.

60. "The Liar," *Century Magazine*, May-June, 1888. NY XII.

61. "The Modern Warning," originally "Two Countries," *Harper's New Monthly Magazine*, June, 1888. In *The Aspern Papers*, 1888. London Edition, 1921-23, XXVI.

62. "A London Life," *Scribner's Magazine*, June-September, 1888. NY X.

63. "The Lesson of the Master," *Universal Review*, July 16, August 15, 1888. NY XV.

64. "The Patagonia," *English Illustrated Magazine*, August-September, 1888. NY XVIII.

65. *The Tragic Muse*, novel, *Atlantic Monthly*, January-December, 1889. Boston, 1890. NY VII, VIII.

66. "The Solution," *New Review*, December, 1889. *The Lesson of the Master*, 1892. London Edition, 1921-23, XXVI.

67. "The Pupil," *Longman's Magazine*, March-April, 1891. NY XI.

68. "Brooksmith," *Harper's Weekly*, May 2, 1891. NY XVIII.

69. "The Marriages," *Atlantic Monthly*, August, 1891. NY XVIII.

70. "The Chaperon," *Atlantic Monthly*, November-December, 1891. NY X.

71. "Sir Edmund Orme," *Black and White*, November, 1891. NY XVII.

72. "Nona Vincent," *English Illustrated Magazine*, February-March, 1892. *The Real Thing*, 1893. London Edition, 1921-23, XXVI.

73. "The Private Life," *Atlantic Monthly*, April, 1892. NY XVII.

74. "The Real Thing," *Black and White*, April 16, 1892. NY XVIII.

75. "Lord Beaupré," originally Beauprey, *Macmillan's Magazine*, April, 1892. *The Private Life*, 1893. London Edition, 1921-23, XXVII.

76. "The Visits," originally "The Visit," *Black and White*, May 28, 1892. *The Private Life*, 1893. London Edition, 1921-23, XXVII.

77. "Sir Dominick Ferrand," originally "Jersey Villas," *Cosmopolitan Magazine*, July-August, 1892. *The Real Thing*, 1893. London Edition, 1921-23, XXVI.

78. "Collaboration," *English Illustrated Magazine*, September, 1892. *The Wheel of Time*, 1893. London Edition, 1921-23, XXVII.

79. "Greville Fane," *Illustrated London News*, September 17, 24, 1892. NY XVI.

80. "Owen Wingrave," *Graphic*, Christmas number, 1892. NY XVII.

81. "The Wheel of Time," *Cosmopolitan Magazine*, December, 1892-January, 1893. *The Wheel of Time* and *The Private Life*, 1893. London Edition, 1921-23, XXVII.

82. "The Middle Years," *Scribner's Magazine*, May, 1893. NY XVI.

83. "The Death of the Lion," *Yellow Book*, April, 1894. NY XV.

84. "The Coxon Fund," *Yellow Book*, July, 1894. NY XV.

85. "The Altar of the Dead," *Terminations*, 1895. NY XVII. No periodical publication.
86. "The Next Time," *Yellow Book*, July, 1895. NY XV.
87. "The Figure in the Carpet," *Cosmopolis*, January-February, 1896. NY XV.
88. "Glasses," *Atlantic Monthly*, February, 1896. *Embarrassments*, 1896. London Edition, 1921-23, XXVII.
89. *The Spoils of Poynton*, originally "The Old Things," short novel, *Atlantic Monthly*, April-October, 1896. London, 1897. NY X.
90. "The Friends of the Friends," originally "The Way it Came," *Chap Book*, May 1 and *Chapman's Magazine of Fiction*, May, 1896. NY XVII.
91. *The Other House*, short novel first written as a play, *Illustrated London News*, July 4-September 26, 1896. London, 1896. Not in London Edition, 1921-23. Ed. Leon Edel (New York, 1947).
92. *What Maisie Knew*, short novel, *Chap Book*, January-August, 1897; also *New Review*, February-September, 1897. London, 1897. NY XI.
93. "John Delavoy," *Cosmopolis*, January-February, 1898. *The Soft Side*, 1900. London Edition, 1921-23, XXVII.
94. "The Turn of the Screw," *Collier's Weekly*, January 27-April 2, 1898. NY XII.
95. "Covering End," story based on the play *Summersoft*. With "The Turn of the Screw" in *The Two Magics*, 1898. No periodical publication.
96. "In the Cage," first appeared in book form, 1898. NY XI.
97. *The Awkward Age*, novel, *Harper's Weekly*, October 1, 1898-January 7, 1899. London, 1899. NY IX.
98. "The Given Case," *Collier's Weekly*, Dec. 31, 1898-January 7, 1899. *The Soft Side*, 1900. London Edition, 1921-23, XXVII.
99. "Europe," *Scribner's Magazine*, June, 1899. NY XVI.
100. "The Great Condition," *Anglo-Saxon Review*, June, 1899. *The Soft Side*, 1900. London Edition, 1921-23, XXVII.
101. "Paste," *Frank Leslie's Popular Monthly*, December, 1899. NY XVI.
102. "The Real Right Thing," *Collier's Weekly*, December 16, 1899. NY XVII.
103. "The Great Good Place," *Scribner's Magazine*, January, 1900. NY XVI.
104. "Maud-Evelyn," *Atlantic Monthly*, April, 1900. *The Soft Side*, 1900. London Edition, 1921-23, XXVIII.
105. "Miss Gunton of Poughkeepsie," *Cornhill Magazine* and *Truth*, May, 1900. NY XVI.
106. "The Special Type," *Collier's Weekly*, June 16, 1900. *The Better Sort*, 1903. London Edition, 1921-23, XXVIII.
107. "The Abasement of the Northmores," *The Soft Side*, 1900. NY XVI. No periodical publication.

108. "The Third Person," *The Soft Side*, 1900. London Edition, 1921-23, XXVII. No periodical publication.
109. "The Tree of Knowledge," *The Soft Side*, 1900. NY XVI. No periodical publication.
110. "The Tone of Time," *Scribner's Magazine*, November, 1900. *The Better Sort*, 1903. London Edition, 1921-23, XXVII.
111. "Broken Wings," *Century Magazine*, December, 1900. NY XVI.
112. "The Two Faces," originally "The Faces," *Harper's Bazar*, December 15, 1900. NY XII.
113. *The Sacred Fount*, novel, London, 1901. London Edition, 1921-23, XXIX. Ed. Leon Edel (New York, 1953). No serialization.
114. "Mrs. Medwin," *Punch*, August 28-September 18, 1901. NY XVIII.
115. "The Beldonald Holbein," *Harper's New Monthly Magazine*, October, 1901. NY XVIII.
116. "The Story in It," *Anglo-American Magazine*, January, 1902. NY XVIII.
117. "Flickerbridge," *Scribner's Magazine*, February, 1902. NY XVIII.
118. *The Wings of the Dove*, novel, New York, 1902. NY XIX, XX. No serialization.
119. *The Ambassadors*, novel, *North American Review*, January-December, 1903. London, 1903. NY XXI, XXII.
120. "The Beast in the Jungle," *The Better Sort*, 1903. NY XVII. No periodical publication.
121. "The Birthplace," *The Better Sort*, 1903. NY XVII. No periodical publication.
122. "The Papers," *The Better Sort*, 1903. London Edition, 1921-23, XXVIII. No periodical publication.
123. *The Golden Bowl*, novel, 1904. NY XXIII, XXIV. No serialization.
124. "Fordham Castle," *Harper's Magazine*, December, 1904. NY XVI.
125. "Julia Bride," *Harper's Magazine*, March-April, 1908. NY XVII.
126. "The Married Son," one of twelve chapters in the collaborative novel, *The Whole Family* (New York, 1908); this chapter first appeared in *Harper's Bazar*, June, 1908. Never reprinted by James.
127. "The Jolly Corner," *English Review*, December, 1908. NY XVII.
128. "The Velvet Glove," *English Review*, March, 1909. *The Finer Grain*, 1910. London Edition, 1921-23, XXVIII.
129. "Mora Montravers," *English Review*, August-September, 1909. *The Finer Grain*, 1910. London Edition, 1921-23, XXVIII.
130. "Crapy Cornelia," *Harper's Magazine*, October, 1909. *The Finer Grain*, 1910. London Edition, 1921-23, XXVIII.
131. "The Bench of Desolation," *Putnam's Magazine*, October-December, 1909, January, 1910. *The Finer Grain*, 1910. London Edition, 1921-23, XXVIII.
132. "A Round of Visits," *English Review*, April-May, 1910. *The Finer Grain*, 1910. London Edition, 1921-23, XXVIII.

Selected Bibliography

133. *The Outcry*, short novel based on play of same title, 1911. No prior serialization. Not included in London Edition, 1921-23.
134. *The Ivory Tower*, incomplete novel, 1917.
135. *The Sense of the Past*, incomplete novel, 1917.

B. *Collected Editions of Fiction, Plays, Letters*

The Novels and Tales of Henry James. 24 vols. New York: Charles Scribner's Sons, 1907-09. Titles are indicated in the "Complete List" of James's fiction, preceding this section. Notable omissions are *The Bostonians* and *Washington Square*. For this "New York Edition" James revised the texts with care, and he provided eighteen prefaces giving origins, aims, and evaluations of works included. These prefaces were collected and published with an introductory essay by R. P. Blackmur as *The Art of the Novel* (New York: Charles Scribner's Sons, 1934). In 1917 the posthumously published incomplete novels *The Ivory Tower* and *The Sense of the Past* were issued uniformly with the original New York Edition. The edition does not include the novelized plays, *The Other House* (1896) and *The Outcry* (1911). The New York Edition is now being reissued by the publisher.

The Novels and Stories of Henry James. 35 vols. London: The Macmillan Company, 1921-23. The so-called "London Edition." Includes all works in the New York Edition (except the two posthumously added incomplete novels); several novels not in the New York Edition (*Watch and Ward, The Europeans, Confidence, Washington Square, The Bostonians, The Sacred Fount*); and forty additional tales (vols. XXIV through XXVIII). The London Edition does not include the two novelized plays: *The Other House* and *The Outcry*.

The American Novels and Stories of Henry James, ed. F. O. Matthiessen. New York: Alfred A. Knopf, 1947. Includes *The Europeans, Washington Square, The Bostonians*, the posthumous *The Ivory Tower*, and eight stories. "Notes" for *The Ivory Tower* were by error omitted from some early copies of this edition.

The Complete Tales of Henry James, ed. Leon Edel. Philadelphia: J. B. Lippincott Company, 1962-. The projected twelve volumes will include all 112 tales. Published so far: Vol. I, 1864-68; Vol. II, 1868-72; Vol. III, 1873-75; Vol. IV, 1876-82; Vol. V, 1883-84; Vol. VI, 1884-88; Vol. VII, 1888-91; Vol. VIII, 1891-92.

The Complete Plays of Henry James, ed. Leon Edel. Philadelphia: J. B. Lippincott Company, 1949. Includes texts for all of James's dramatic works, including adaptations of "Daisy Miller" and *The American*. Full general introduction, supplemented by introduction and notes for each separate work.

The Letters of Henry James, ed. Percy Lubbock. 2 vols. New York: Charles Scribner's Sons, 1920. Includes 403 letters from about one hundred correspondents, with brief biographical comment by Lubbock, a close friend of James. Professor Edel is now at work on a new and more comprehensive edition of James's letters, of which he estimates there are more than ten thousand extant. The Edel-Laurence *Bibliography* lists (Section C) 174 books and articles in which published letters may be found. For about a hundred of these sources, my article, "The Published Letters of Henry James: A Survey," *Bulletin of Bibliography*, XX (January-April, 1952), 165-71, XX (May-August), 187, supplies range of dates, brief indication of content, particularly literary allusions.

C. *Bibliographies*

EDEL, LEON and DAN H. LAURENCE. *A Bibliography of Henry James*. (London: Rupert Hart-Davis, 1957). Second ed., rev., 1961. Lists all book and periodical publications, letters (scattered in 172 separate works), translations, and miscellaneous items. Gives precise dates of publication, details of English and American issues, original prices, and much other information. Supersedes Le Roy Phillips' *Bibliography* (1906; rev. 1930). To the original edition, the 1961 revision adds to section A (Original Works) four recent collections: *Parisian Sketches, The House of Fiction, Literary Reviews and Essays*, and *French Writers and American Women;* to section B (Contributions to Books), *Henry James and H. G. Wells*; and to C (Published Letters), two further sources, bringing the list to 174. The absence of a prefatory note indicates that other revision was minor.

BEEBE, MAURICE and WILLIAM T. STAFFORD. "Criticism of Henry James: A Selected Checklist with an Index to Studies of Separate Works," *Modern Fiction Studies*, Henry James Special Number, III (Spring, 1957), 73-96. The most valuable single list of commentary. It should be supplemented by Modern Language Association annual bibliographies and by current issues of *American Literature*.

Eight American Authors: A Review of Research and Criticism (New York: Modern Language Association, 1956). The chapter on James (pp. 364-418), by Robert E. Spiller, treats bibliography and biography; organizes criticism under "Contemporary," "Alienation" (1916-34), and "The James Revival" (1934-54). A new edition, with supplementary references by J. Chesley Mathews, was published by W. W. Norton and Company, 1963.

Literary History of the United States, ed. by Spiller, Thorpe, Johnson, and Canby (New York: The Macmillan Company, 1948), III, 584-90. *Id., Bibliography Supplement*, ed. Richard M. Ludwig (New York, 1959), pp. 213-15.

RICHARDSON, LYON. N. *Henry James: Representative Selections* (New York: American Book Company, 1941). Annotated bibliography, pp. xci-cxi, is an excellent selection as of 1941.

WOODRESS, JAMES. *Dissertations in American Literature, 1891-1955, with Supplement, 1956-1961* (Durham, N.C.: Duke University Press, 1962). Lists 103 dissertations on James, more than for any other American author.

Index